A TREASURY OF

SUNDAY MISCELLANY

A TREASURY OF SUNDAY MISCELLANY

Edited by MARIE HEANEY

RTÉ

A TREASURY OF SUNDAY MISCELLANY
First published 2009
by New Island
2 Brookside
Dundrum Road
Dublin 14

www.newisland.ie

ISBN 978-1-84840-050-4

British Library Cataloguing Data. A CIP catalogue record for
this book is available from the British Library.

Printed in the UK by CPI Mackays, Chatham ME5 8TD

New Island received financial assistance from
The Arts Council (An Comhairle Ealaíon), Dublin, Ireland

10 9 8 7 6 5 4 3 2 1

CONTENTS

A Sense of Place

A Sense of Humour

A Sense of Poignancy

A Sense of Poetry

A Sense of the Past

ACKNOWLEDGMENTS

Poem 'Original Sin on the Sussex Coast' from *Collected Poems* by John Betjeman © 1995, 1958, 1962, 1964, 1968, 1970, 1979, 1981, 2001. Reproduced by permission of John Murray (Publishers).

The quotations from the poetry of Patrick Kavanagh are reprinted from *Collected Poems*, edited by Antoinette Quinn (Allen Lane, 2004) by kind permission of the Estate of the late Katherine B. Kavanagh, through the Jonathan Williams Literary Agency.

The quotations from W.H. Auden are reprinted from *Collected Auden*, edited by Edward Mendelson, by permission of Faber & Faber Ltd.

The quotations from Louis MacNiece are reprinted from *Collected Poems*, published by Faber & Faber Ltd., by permission of David Higham Associates.

Extract from 'In Memoriam Francis Ledgwidge' by Seamus Heaney, from *Field Work* (Faber & Faber, 1979) is reproduced by permission of the poet.

The publishers have made every effort to contact all copyright holders. If notified, the publishers will be pleased to rectify any errors or omissions at the earliest opportunity.

INTRODUCTION

Sunday Miscellany, one of the most beloved progammes on RTÉ Radio I, is now in its fortieth year and has been heard over four decades by millions of listeners. Just as Michael O'Hehir's voice recalls Sunday afternoons for a generation of Irish people, so the leisure and pleasure of Sunday mornings is evoked by Samuel Scheidt's *Galliard Battaglia*, the signature tune of *Sunday Miscellany*.

In an Ireland that has changed greatly, the programme has been a comforting, if not always comfortable, transmission. It remains still the familiar mixture of 'music and musings' envisaged by the earliest producers in 1969, an eclectic mix of reflection, recollection, information, humour and reportage interspersed with music attuned to the spoken material.

But the programme has not remained static. Over the years, successive producers have put their individual stamp on the series, discovering new voices and bringing different perspectives to bear on the material, the presentation and the choice of music.

Sunday Miscellany has also mirrored the changes in Irish society. The contributors have addressed these changes – cultural, religious, economic, ethnic – in subtle ways through reportage, historical parallels and reflective pieces, but they have also given expression to the shared values and common experiences that bind our society together.

Over the years the hallmark of *Sunday Miscellany* has been the 'musings'; those reflective pieces, often emotionally charged, recounting moments of 'epiphany' – 'spots of time' as Wordsworth called them – apparently insignificant moments that impress themselves on our memory forever. It is worth noticing that none of these pieces is fictional; they are intimate and often moving revelations.

Compiling a book of material written for radio has built-in drawbacks, the fundamental one being the loss of the accent, cadences and colloquialisms of the contributor. This can constitute a serious loss in cases where delivery may be the most memorable part of the contribution. In his introduction to *Sunday Miscellany 2*, published in 1976, Ronnie Walsh deals with this issue:

> There are those among our contributors who feel, with some justification, that to present in print a broadcaster's script is akin to putting a magician on stage without his tall hat, wide cuffs, silk scarves, and with neither box nor saw nor beautiful lady.

He goes on:

> So I offer this selection in the belief that it makes entertaining reading. If it happens that as you read you can also hear the accents, burrs, inflections and pronunciations of the authors, then so much the better.

Alas, there are few left who can remember those voices that Ronnie Walsh refers to. Most of them have been silenced forever, though some may live on in the archives. Others – like the Northern cadences of Benedict Kiely or Hilary Boyle's cut-glass accent – still echo in the memory, but almost all the rest have faded.

Yet there is more to a memorable broadcast than just the delivery – the author has something to *say*. This is where the written word has the advantage over the spoken one; it can give permanence to what was essentially transitory. And that is the *raison d'être* of the six collections of *Sunday Miscellany* scripts that have been published so far.

The first *Sunday Miscellany* programme was broadcast in 1969, but it was not till 1975 that a written collection, also called *Sunday Miscellany*, was published by RTÉ. Ronnie Walsh was the editor, and in 1976 he edited a second volume, *Sunday Miscellany 2*.

Then there was a gap of nearly twenty years before *Sunday Miscellany: A selection from 1995–2000* was published by TownHouse in association with RTÉ. I was the editor of that volume and a subsequent one published in 2002. Clíodhna Ní Anluain, the current producer of the progamme, has edited two further collections: *Sunday Miscellany: a selection from 2004–2006* and *Sunday Miscellany: a selection from 2006–2008*, both published by New Island in association with RTÉ. The present volume, a celebration of the fortieth anniversary of the radio programme, is a selection from those six previous volumes.

In compiling the collection I have tried to make it as representative as possible by including as many contributors as possible. I have limited my choice to just one script from each author and even then, have had to leave out many pieces that I would have liked to include. In the case of some of the writers from the two earliest volumes – household names who continued to contribute to the programme for many years – I have made an exception and included more than one item.

In the case of later contributions, if there was a choice I settled for a piece that related to work already included in order to give thematic coherence to the book. To this end, too, I devised chapter headings and placed the material where it seemed most appropriate. It is interesting to observe the same themes and preoccupations appearing again and again over the years.

In the course of the programme's history the gender balance has changed. There were only four women contributors in the two collections published in the 1970s, but in later volumes, as in this one, women and men are more or less equally represented. Some of those authors are professional, full-time writers; for others writing is a part-time activity fitted in around their many diverse occupations.

Though the contributors have been the lifeblood of *Sunday Miscellany*, administrators, technicians and, in particular, producers have played a crucial role in keeping the programme relevant, cherished, and on air throughout four decades. I can think of no better way to salute them all than by echoing Ronnie Walsh's valedictory remarks in *his* introduction to *Sunday Miscellany 2*:

> This occasion should not pass without my thanking all who have contributed to the success of the programme over the years and whose loyalty to its standards has been invaluable.

> To them my thanks.

> To you good listening, and good reading.

Marie Heaney
Dublin, August 2009

A SENSE OF A PRESENCE

FROM MONTAIGNE TO ALISTAIR COOKE: THE SPOKEN ESSAY

Anthony Cronin

Whether or not Francis Bacon wrote the plays of Shakespeare, and I think it highly unlikely that he did, he and Shakespeare had at least one thing in common. They were both influenced by a French writer called Michel de Montaigne who had invented, in the year 1580, a new literary form which he called the essay. The name suggests a great deal about it. The French word *essai* means simply an experiment and it goes back to the Latin *exigium*, a weighing, which comes from *exigere*, to examine.

Montaigne's essays were exactly what he said they were: experiments. They approached their theme tentatively and often obliquely, rather than in the manner of propositional argument and final exposition; they were an exploration of a subject; a raid on it, as somebody said, rather than a conquest; they could and often did deal with philosophical, political and other weighty matters, but they were not formal philosophical or political statements; they often contained stories or started with a story, but they were not simply anecdotes; and in fact the form has one great virtue which lots of writers spotted straight away: you could put anything, literally anything at all into it, from the price of onions and the joys of friendship to corruption in high places and the assassination of tyrants.

In adopting this form, Montaigne was taking a chance, for his essays were dependent for their interest really on one thing only: the interest of the personality revealed, and therefore the interest of the experiences which had made it what it was. Well, anybody from William Shakespeare to the present company who ever fell under the spell of that wise, gentle, sceptical, experienced and, not least, humorous man knows that Montaigne's chance came off; but of course in taking it, Montaigne was, in a sense, assuming no more than we all do every day in conversation with our friends, for almost every time we open our mouths, even to say for example, 'two fourpennies please', we are to some extent assuming an interest on the part of our audience in the personality we are about to reveal and the experiences, or lack of them, which have made it what it is.

What lots of writers, from Francis Bacon on, spotted was, as I say, the fact that you could put anything at all into this form. All writers dream of a rag-bag into which anything or almost anything that has ever bothered or disturbed or amused or enlightened or revivified them will go; and all writers are, to some extent, furious with the necessary artificialities of art. Why should I, they say, who am a real man with real interests, with a real, perhaps bleeding heart and a personality which, however tattered and torn in the wars it may be, is indubitably my own, have to tell you a highly artificial story about merely invented people in order to get across what I have to say, and what about the price of onions? It will be damned hard to work that into my new verse drama about that Scotch fellow who murdered a king, not to mention the hole in my doublet and the leak in the roof or that latest dark lady of mine who won't even go into a sonnet, or into anything else either for the matter of that.

Well, as we all know, in art at least, if nowhere else, it is indubitably true that the longest way round is the shortest way home. It is by means of a fiction that the truth gets told and even in conversation we use a lot of artifice if we are sensible and/or wise and sober. The hole in the author's doublet gets into a lot of verse plays, obliquely or otherwise, and the truth he is after may be better off for the obliquity.

Yet, all the same, there is the attraction of the form that reveals the real man. We know Michel Eyquem, the Seigneur de Montaigne. We even know Francis Bacon, the dodgy statesman and lawyer. And we most certainly know William Hazlitt, who wrote about the want of money, prizefighting, acting and other interesting matters better than anybody else ever did, he that never fought or acted in his life. But how well do we know William Shakespeare? It was this that made Herman Melville impatient. He said that it was a terrible waste to have written all those plays and he declared he would rather have had 'the still, rich utterances of a great soul in repose than any of them.'

Well, be that as it may, in our own time the old form that Michel Eyquem, the Seigneur de Montaigne, invented, took on, as if it could ever need one, a new lease of life under the guise of what was called the radio talk. In fact of course the spoken essay. Those who ever heard Sir Max Beerbohm or our own late great James Stephens, or indeed (and happily we can all still hear him), that master, our contemporary, Alistair Cooke, not to mention some of my friends here in this volume whom it would be invidious to single out, luxuriating in the old essay and bringing a few new tricks to it, will know what I mean. The interest of the personality revealed, I said. Well, anyway, the price of onions, the hole in my doublet, the leak in the roof,

> The insolence of office and the spurns
> That patient merit of the unworthy takes.

A. J. ALAN

Maurice Craig

I wonder how many people now remember the name of A. J. Alan? Certainly those who habitually listen to this Sunday morning programme should remember him, and remember him with gratitude. For A. J. Alan – whose real name was Leslie Harrison Lambert (he was a civil servant in real life) – A . J. Alan was the man who invented the art of talking on the wireless, as we used to call it in those days, as though he was talking to somebody in front of him and not to a microphone. He invented what has been called the 'fireside manner'. As practised by us on Sunday morning it should, I dare say, be more properly called the 'bedside manner'. Anyway, he invented it.

He began broadcasting from London way back in the 1920s. In those days, the technique of broadcasting was still a kind of translation of public speaking. The broadcaster squared himself up to the microphone (which was, and still was in my early broadcasting days in Radio Éireann, a great apparatus like a heavy-lift crane, dangling its burden in front of the speaker). He took a stance in front of this rather intimidating apparatus. He straightened his tie as though he were in front of a mirror, and he commenced to address it as though it were some kind of public meeting.

In those days, and for long afterwards, all the BBC announcers were required by the terms of their contracts to wear a dinner-jacket and a black tie to read the news. No spotted bow-ties were allowed in those days. Oh, no: no indeed! Not at all like the telly. Those were the days of that terrifying autocrat, Sir John Reith.

Well, with every artform there comes a moment when it suddenly comes of age: when some genius says, for example, 'Away with the horse-less carriage: let us have the motor-car.' It seems quite easy to us, with hindsight. How ridiculous, we think, to go on behaving as though we were driving a team of horses. Or, in radio terms, how ridiculous to think that radio is simply a medium for reading leading articles to people who are too lazy to read them for themselves. How obvious, we think, to take the hearer into our confidence: to talk to him as though he were a friend with a drink in his hand, sitting a few feet away on the other side of a comfortable fire.

How easy. But it wasn't easy at all. It was a new invention.

A few years ago I bought for two shillings the collected volume of A. J. Alan's broadcasts. It's called *Good Evening, Everyone*, and it has a fore-word by Sir John Reith himself. The cover has a wonderful period flavour (it came out in 1928) and so have the contents. Perhaps I should explain that, in form at least, all of A. J. Alan's broadcasts were stories, or even anecdotes, often with very little substance to them. Nearly everything lay in the manner of the telling. And of course that manner has dated: the props are the props of the twenties, and so are the turns of phrase. The colloquialisms, and still more the slang, of our parents' generation are so embarrassing to us that we cannot bring our tongues to pronounce them – at least I can't. In spite of this, it is impossible not to admire the air of impromptu which was, as I have said, his original contribution.

There are discs of at least some of A. J. Alan's pieces – of course he lived long before the days of tape-recording – and once in a while his voice can still be heard. I am not nearly old enough to have listened to him at the time, but it does sound a very convincing rendering of the way some grown-ups used to talk when I was a child. Incidentally, he says in his own preface to his book (and I quote):

> Everything I say over the microphone is taken down in shorthand and transcribed afterwards, and when the idea of publishing my experiences was mooted I began to try to turn them into something like English. However, after a glance at my first efforts in this direction the publishers called loudly for the transcript of the shorthand notes, and

insisted on using it instead. You must, therefore, blame them and not me if any of the expressions in this book seem to verge upon the colloquial.

The first thing to be said about this is that not a word of it is to be believed. In fact, A. J. Alan took the greatest care with every syllable, every little bit of timing, and all the apparently artless hestiations. He had it all written up on large placards which were held up in front of him as he spoke — just like the teleprompter of today, in fact.

The other thing which rings oddly today is his obvious anxiety to apologise for sounding colloquial. After taking endless trouble to sound natural, he is afraid, however mildly, of looking too natural in print. It is, or was, not the done thing to appear in public in one's shirt-sleeves, so to speak.

If, as the old Roman poet said, the essence of art is to conceal art, then A. J. Alan was indeed an artist, even if a very minor one. I think it may be worth recalling that he spoke his first words over the air on 30 October 1924 — just over fifty years ago. The essence of his charm can only be conveyed in his own voice, and at some length, to establish his leisurely manner. Since we cannot manage that, I will end with a phrase in which, though pretending to be a typical Englishman muddling through, he is really unloading on his hearer an aphorism of an almost mathematical symmetry.

'It's no use,' he says, 'crying over the stable door after the horse has spilt the milk.'

LAURENCE STERNE

John Jordan

For years, or it seemed like years, Mr Harold Hobson, senior drama critic of *The Sunday Times*, was wont when comparing the current conditions of the theatre in London and Paris to comment, 'They order this matter better in France.' The cultivated readers of *The Sunday Times*, among whom I once counted myself, would have recognised this pronouncement as the opening statement by Mr Yorick, the narrator of Laurence Sterne's unfinished travelogue *A Sentimental Journey*, published in the year of his death, 1768.

Now it happens that Sterne was born 261 years ago today and, quite fortuitously, in Clonmel. Sterne's father Roger was an ensign in a regiment which fought with the Duke of Marlborough's army, and fought in the War of the Spanish Succession until the Peace of Utrecht in 1713, the year of Laurence Sterne's birth. For the next six years the Sterne family was bandied back and forward across the Irish Sea according as the father was re-posted. 1719 found them at the barracks in Wicklow, but several months were spent at the parsonage of Annamoe, seven miles from Wicklow, where a relative of Mrs Sterne's was rector. There, possibly, Sterne added to Wicklow folklore, for he fell into a moving mill race and escaped unhurt. Forty years later he recorded: 'The story is incredible, but known for truth in all that part of Ireland where hundreds of the common people flocked to see me.' After about 1724 Sterne lost contact with Ireland; he was sent to school at Halifax, Yorkshire, and from thence to Jesus College, Cambridge. He took his degree and in 1738 was ordained a priest of the Church of England. He married, not altogether unhappily, and became a minor clerical pluralist. There was no reason why he should not have continued along the even highway of a country parson.

But he was at best a clergyman by convenience, though he appears to have been zealous in his duties. The fly, some would say the viper, in the ointment was his Cambridge friend, John Hall-Stevenson, who lived in a Gothic pile which he called Crazy Castle: there, certain cultured bucks were alleged to indulge in monstrous orgies, and a club known as 'the Demoniacs' was formed – the whole set-up was after the model of the famous Hell Fire clubs of the eighteenth century. But there, too, was a vast and exotic library and in it browsed for many hours the Rev. Laurence Sterne. There, he stored up reams of quaint learning which he was to unwind in one of the world's comic masterpieces; a book that surely influenced Joyce, Beckett and Flann O'Brien; a book that demolished all preconceived notions of the novel – *Tristram Shandy*, the first two volumes of which took London by storm in 1760.

Seven more volumes were to follow – making nine in all. It purports to be the autobiography of a gentleman Tristram Shandy – but never before or since has an autobiography begun in the womb, and never before or since has it taken nearly four volumes to get the hero born. And not perhaps until we get to Flann O'Brien's novels, especially the neglected second one, *The Hard Life*, do we find such extraordinary, obsessive fantasies in otherwise commonplace people. You remember how in that lovely little book the hero's half uncle, his guardian Mr Collopy, is dominated in all his days and nights by the question of providing public toilets for the ladies. He ends up, disastrously, presenting a petition to the Pope on the question. Mr Collopy is the true fictional descendant both of Tristram Shandy's father, Walter, and his adorable Uncle Toby. Uncle Toby had been wounded in the groin in the Spanish Succession wars and during his long convalescence he has become obsessed with the conduct of those wars. On his bowling green and into his kitchen garden, with his servant Corporal Trim, he has laid out fortifications, benches, sentinel boxes and all the paraphernalia of a mock war. But his obsession goes with the kindest of hearts, the tenderest of dispositions. Irritated beyond a normal man's patience by a fly which buzzed about his nose all dinner time: 'Go, go, poor devil, quoth he, why should I hunt thee? This world is surely wide enough to hold both thee and me.'

But Tristram's father's hobby horses are even more curious: they are Names and Noses. He has, says his son, 'an extensive view of things' and he holds that a man's destiny may be shaped by the name given him at baptism. So also with the structure of a man's nose. Mr Shandy has 'a system of noses'. His researches have been peculiar and thorough. He has finally found his northern star in a German philosopher called Hafen Slawkenbergius, a name which innate modesty, a delicacy of feeling towards old women of both sexes, precludes me interpreting. I'll say only that *Hafen*, the scholars tell us, is German slang for that article of household ware which Austin Clarke noticed under James Joyce's bed and called Miss White. While I am on the topic of Clarke, it was he who led me unknowingly to read *Tristram Shandy* for the first time five years ago. There is a reference to Slawkenbergius in his poem 'From a Diary of Dreams'; I will never forget the faint, ever so faint, shadow of displeasure on his face when he had to tell me, petrified in my ignorance, that Slawkenbergius was from *Tristram Shandy*.

At any rate this apocryphal Slawkenbergius was, for Mr Shandy, 'an institute of all that was necessary to be known of noses and everything else'. And Slawkenbergius is all for large noses. Sterne attained enormous popularity on the continent. Did Rostand know the tale of a great nose which Sterne attributes to Slawkenbergius and draw from it for *Cyrano de Bergerac*?

But today I am thinking not alone of Sterne and Slawkenbergius, but of a certain dear, high-questing nose which, when in exile in 1967, I so much looked forward to seeing again – for Patrick Kavanagh died seven years ago next Saturday 3 November 1967. And this afternoon, as is the practice for the last Sunday of November, many will be making to Patrick's grave at Iniskeen in County Monaghan something rather more than a sentimental journey.

ROBERT LLOYD PRAEGER

Des MacHale

We are continually reminded that we are living in an age of scientific specialisation. The word 'science' no longer refers to a single subject, but to a strange collection of ill-assorted bedfellows under the blanket of what used to be called the scientific method. Maybe we have not yet reached the position of the American nose specialist who was an expert on diseases of the left nostril and admitted to knowing little or nothing about the right. But if science continues to develop as at present, the day cannot be far away. Paradoxically, scientists are beginning to feel the need for closer contact between the sciences and, to meet the demand, a whole series of new subjects has been spawned. Today we have Cybernetics, Biomathematics, Chemical Engineering, Biochemistry, Ecology, Geophysics and a whole host of others which make it impossible for a single individual to claim that he is familiar with one of the broader divisions of science, let alone the whole of science.

In the history of science, however, there have been, even in our own country, a number of extremely gifted individuals whose scientific interests and knowledge covered vast areas. An example extraordinary of the class was Robert Lloyd Praeger who was born in County Down in 1865 and who spent a large portion of his life in Dublin. Praeger's major contribution to science was in the field of botany. But he wrote with equal authority on geology, archaeology, history, zoology, ornithology, travel and even linguistics in a way that would certainly delight present-day scientist and poet alike. Here was a man with a totally integrated love of nature and creation – a man of visions and breadth in whose writings scientific facts are elevated and imbued with a poetic magic which present-day science, for all its progress and precision, definitely lacks.

Praeger's major work, *The Way That I Went*, in which he describes his scientific rambles throughout the whole of Ireland, is surely one of the finest guidebooks ever written. The book has many memorable passages, from a description of the sunset over Clew Bay as seen from Croagh Patrick, to an exciting account of a trip to the tiny island of Rockall. But the part that stands out in my memory is the extraordinary incident of the Limavady Golf Ornaments Trial, in which Praeger played an important part. The circumstances are as follows.

A man, ploughing a field situated on flat ground near the tidal estuary of the River Roe close to Limavady, uncovered a number of beautiful gold ornaments. He sold them to his employer for a few pounds, but his employer sold them to a collector, Mr Robert Day of Cork. Day finally disposed of them to the British Museum for £600. At this stage, the Royal Irish Academy heard of the discovery and through the State Solicitor claimed the gold ornaments for Ireland as treasure trove. Roughly speaking, the law of treasure trove amounts to this: if precious objects are found under circumstances which point to their having been lost or abandoned, then it is a case of 'finders keepers'. But if there is evidence that they were concealed or deposited with the intention of ultimate recovery, then the Crown claims them on behalf of the unknown next-of-kin as treasure trove.

The trustees of the British Museum refused to deliver up the objects on the grounds that they were not treasure trove. They claimed that, around the time of the deposition of the articles, the waters of Lough Foyle flowed over the lands in question so that the gold ornaments could not have been deposited with a view to recovery. And they furthermore suggested that they had been cast overboard from a ship as a votive offering to the sea god and had therefore been abandoned.

At this stage, Praeger, who had done a considerable amount of work on the geology of raised beaches and their associated flint implements, was called in by the Royal Irish Academy. He had no doubt that the field in question, which was about four feet above high-water level, clearly formed part of the uplift in Neolithic times and was therefore dry land when the gold ornaments were deposited. Praeger actually unearthed conclusive geological evidence at Portstewart, thirteen miles away, that in Neolithic times the level of the beach had been the same as in modern times and that the area had not been submerged in the intervening period.

But scientific evidence is one thing, courts of law another. The case was brought before the Royal Courts of Justice in June 1903, before Justice Farwell. Counsel for the Irish side included Sir Edward Carson, later Lord Carson. The case is possibly unique in that the majority of the witnesses were scientific experts of one kind or another.

J. L. Myres, lecturer in Classical Mythology at Oxford University, gave evidence on the practices of votive offerings and there was a detailed discussion of Manannán MacLir, the Irish sea god, and many references to Frazer's *Golden Bough*. The judge became restive over the wealth of folklore and legend and protested once or twice. Praeger, together with Professor Cole and J. R. Kilroe of the Irish Geological Survey, gave evidence on the geological background to the case.

After a lengthy trial, the judge summed up as follows: 'It is really little short of extravagant to ask the court to assume the existence of a votive offering of a sort hitherto unknown, in a land where such offerings were hitherto unknown, in a sea not known for 2,000 years, and possibly for 4,000 years, to a sea god by a chieftain both equally unknown, and to prefer this to the commonplace but natural inference that these articles were a hoard hidden for safety in a land disturbed by frequent raids, and forgotten by reason of the death or slavery of the depositor. I find that the gold ornaments are treasure trove and should therefore be returned to Ireland.

They now form part of the glittering collection of prehistoric gold ornaments in the Gold Room of our National Museum. The exact date of their burial has never been determined, nor has the origin of the gold used in their manufacture. Some geologists suspect that the gold may have come from the granite of the Wicklow Mountains, where in 1795, a schoolmaster picked up a gold nugget, thereby causing a gold rush from Dublin. But the mother quartz vein containing the gold, presumably known to prehistoric man, still remains hidden despite the progress and technical expertise of Modern Science.

THE TAILOR

Eric Cross

Twenty-five years ago, the Tailor of Garrynapeaka, in the parish of Inchigeela, in the barony of Muskerry, in the county of Cork, died. Died physically at least, for when does a man such as the Tailor die in a total sense? Had the book about him never been written; had there never been the absurd controversy concerning its banning, I feel sure that still seldom a day would pass in Iveleary that, by a fireside, at the bar of a public house, someone would not still quote one of the Tailor's sayings or retell one of his stories.

In local memory, through the book and recently through Eamonn Kelly's magnificent recreation of him on the stage, something of the Tailor remains and is not dead. And that something which remains was that quality which drew so many to the circle of his friendship when he lived. It was that quality of being just a little larger than life: of using life and not merely being used by it: of living from the inside out and not from the outside in.

Yet there was always every reason why it should have been just otherwise, and that he should have been cowed by life. All his life he had suffered the very considerable handicap of a withered leg. His economic and social position held more of disadvantage than advantage. Yet he treated all these aspects which made his life with cavalier disdain. He ignored them. He laughed at them.

But he did this not alone with the personal aspects of his life: he did the same with words and ideas. He played with them. He had fun with them.

'The world is only a blue bag. Knock a squeeze out of it when you can.'

He did that with enormous gusto, interest and curiosity, and always with sympathy. With an all-embracing sympathy with his neighbours and his friends and with the animals about him; even, one might say, with the birds and the flowers and the trees. It was not that nothing human was alien to him, it was that nothing living was alien to him.

He was very obviously richly endowed with that great gift of the human being: imagination. But it is a gift which we can use in two ways; either to make worse of the world and experience, or to make the best of it. The Tailor used it always in its positive way, to enhance. By contact with him, by the knowing of him, you caught the contagion, and left him, feeling better and with a better point of view.

And perhaps, in the last analysis, it is for this reason that he was attacked. He, with all his handicaps, should not have done this. In doing it he was showing up all those who, with much greater material and physical assets than he had, denigrated experience. In his airy and inno-cent way he was, unconsciously, severely critical of all those who, fear-fully and with mean spirit, belittled every aspect of human life. 'Come day, go day. God send another day' is not the prayer of the unco' good. It was the prayer, in all the details of his living, of the Tailor. He was all of a piece. He was an integrated man. He was a civilised man.

I read and re-read the essays of Montaigne, the first great humanist writer. Sometimes I wonder if my interest in them may not be a shared interest between Montaigne and the Tailor, for on page after page I come across expressions of the essential spirit of the Tailor of Garrynapeaka, written so long ago. For instance:

> I cheerfully and thankfully and with good heart accept what nature hath created for me; and I am therewith well pleased, and am proud of it. Great wrong is offered unto that great and all-puissant Giver, to refuse His gift which is so absolutely good; and disannul or disfigure the same, since He made it perfectly good... All things that are according to nature are worthy to be esteemed.

Of such kin was the Tailor.

LONGFORD

John Jordan

On 4 February 1961, Edward Arthur Pakenham, Sixth Earl of Longford, died. And with him died a tradition in the Irish theatre which has not been rekindled. He was the last private patron.

Before I say a few words about his massive individual contribution to the Irish theatre, let us recall that over forty years ago it was he who came to the financial rescue of Hilton Edwards and Micheál Mac Liammóir, and though their ways parted in 1936, in a sense the connection has not been broken, since Edward Longford's widow, Christine, Countess of Longford, is now a co-director with Edwards and Mac Liammóir of the Gate Theatre (now temporarily closed) and surely when it re-opens Londford's buoyant and portly shade will once again, for many of us, be present in the vestibule, button-hole and all.

Edward Longford was, in the horticultural sense, a 'sport', as indeed is his brother Frank, the present Earl, Labour peer and biographer of President de Valera. By birth and education he was of the ascendancy class. (One of his first plays, produced at the Gate in 1934, *Ascendancy*, was about his grandfather, a very different kind of Earl.) But like some of the women, and not so many of the men of that class, he became in youth a passionate – often a comically passionate – nationalist. There is a story that he once rammed a man's hat down over his eyes when he failed to stand for the National Anthem at the Dublin Horse Show, though he had done so for 'God Save the King'. His nationalism was heartfelt enough to make him learn Irish, and as well as a translation of *The Midnight Court* he published three volumes of verse from the Irish. He was of course something of a scholar in many languages: he translated Calderón from the Spanish, Molière and Beaumarchais from the French, Aeschylus (with his wife), Euripides and Sophocles from the Greek. His version of *Oedipus Rex* was the one which Anew McMaster played both in Dublin and up and down the country.

And mention of the country reminds that for over twenty years, Longford Productions spend about half a year touring with the current Dublin repertory. I defy anyone to produce a comparably rich touring repertory in these islands during the period in question. Between June 1945 and June 1947 I saw Longford Productions at the Gate with: George Coleman's eighteenth-century comedy *The Jealous Wife*; Shaw's *Arms and the Man*; Pinero's *The Magsitrate*; Ibsen's *The Lady from the Sea*; Shaw's *The Doctor's Dilemma*; Shakespeare's *A Midsummer Night's Dream*; William Saroyan's *The Time of Your Life*; Shaw's *You Never Can Tell* and *Heartbreak House*; Beaumarchais's *Marriage of Figaro*; Thornton Wilder's *Our Town* (in which by the way our genial chief newscaster Charles Mitchell made his début over twenty-five years ago); Shakespeare's *Twelfth Night*; Chekhov's *The Seagull*; Molière's *The School for Wives* and Ibsen's *Hedda Gabler*, to name only the more important offerings.

And the young and poor could see the masterpieces of the world for as little as a shilling; Patrick Kavanagh used to say, 'Longford's is the best bob's worth in town.'

In later years when I mixed a great deal with actors and ersatz actors, I grew accustomed to hearing snide remarks and little stories about Edwards and the way he ran his company, about who got into it and who didn't. At this point of time, it is possible to look back twenty-five years and note how many of our most distinguished players either cut their teeth or polished their histrionic invories in Longford-land, as it was known in the profession: Milo O'Shea, Aiden Grennell, Godfrey Quigley, Iris Lawlor, Eve Watkinson. And less familiar to the day's Dublin audiences, Dermot Walsh who graduated to the West End and British movies, John 'Sandy' Welsh who went to British TV, and Edward Mulhare who followed Rex Harrison in *My Fair Lady* on Broadway. If I am not mistaken, Donal Donnelly began as an ASM (Assistant Stage Manager) with Longford. And of course for years there reigned in Longford-land one of the most underrated of Irish actors, Maurice O'Brien, whose performance as Arnolphe in Edward's own version of *A School for Wives* was a comedic masterpiece.

Edward was, I suppose, a rich man. But his theatrical company was not a toy: it was a solid contribution to the life of the country, if not of the city he loved, and to use Lady Gregory's pet phrase, he worked after his fashion for 'the dignity of Ireland'.

SEÁN Ó TUAMA (1926–2006)

Eoghan Ó hAnluain

It is natural, I suppose, how, on hearing of the death of an admired and cherished writer, we turn to the written word – partly out of nostalgia, partly out of homage, but partly also out of the need for reassurance in the face of loss.

I have in front of me a copy of an old journal, somewhat tattered now from much handling over the years by myself and by students. It was an instinctive response to reach for it when word came from Cork of the recent death of Seán Ó Tuama. It is an edition of *An Síol*, a journal published by An Chuallacht Ghaelach, the Irish Language Society of University College Cork. Its date is 1950, over half a hundred years ago. It has been a treasured possession for many years and all the more so now since Seán Ó Tuama's death.

In this edition of the journal are included two remarkable essays in literary criticism: one by Seán Ó Tuama and one by his former Professor of English, Daniel Corkery, whom Ó Tuama regarded as the finest teacher of literature he had ever met. Corkery's essay is an incisive analysis of a sixteenth-century poem by the poet Tadhg Dall Ó hUiginn, while Seán Ó Tuama writes a remarkable seminal introduction to the little known but emerging poet from West Cork, Seán Ó Ríordáin.

What is remarkable about these two essays is that one can trace the influence of Corkery on Ó Tuama quite clearly. Corkery's essay is a close and intimate reading of the poem and concerns itself not, as was the accepted approach, with examining the external forms of syllable count and correct rhyming, but rather that inner dynamic which gives a worthwhile poem its distinctive artistic quality and human appeal.

This same approach to literature was to be the hallmark of Seán Ó Tuama's own criticism, whether of a traditional folk love song or a medieval literary love lyric, or of contemporary writing in prose or poetry.

Born in 1926 in Cork City, Seán Ó Tuama attended the North Monastery Christian Brothers' School and University College Cork, where he later became Professor of Modern Irish Literature. He was a visiting professor at Harvard and at Oxford. His anthology *Nuabhéarsaíocht 1939–1949* first focused critical attention on the achievement of poetry in Irish from contemporary poets of that period. Since then Seán Ó Tuama's influence as a writer, dramatist, critic, teacher and mentor has been pervasive. He also played hurling with the famous Cork Hurling club Glen Rovers. How right that a *camán* should be central to his funeral rites.

An early recollection of mine of Ó Tuama was his challenging lecture, *Fáistine na Litríochta*, on the prophetic nature of literature, delivered at the Oireachtas, the Irish Language Festival in 1961. The lecture was attended by President Éamon de Valera and Sinéad de Valera in the Old Hibernian Hotel in Dawson Street, Dublin.

Apart from the superb lecture, which can be read in his collected essays, *Tuath agus Bruachbhaile*, what remains most vividly in my memory of that night in the Hibernian is the haunting image of the late John Jordan, critic and lecturer in English at University College Dublin and an esteemed poet and regular contributor to *Sunday Miscellany*, along with the distinguished portraitist Seán Ó Súilleabháin RHA, as they made their unsteady way to the front of the crowded room and sat themselves in close proximity to His Excellency, Uachtarán na hÉireann. They were both well on.

But their presence that night was an indication of the high regard in which they both held Seán Ó Tuama as a critic and literary commentator. Throughout the brilliant lecture, from highlight to highlight, and from the appropriate time, they unobtrusively growled their inebriated approval. A fitting contribution indeed. It was a memorable night. For Ó Tuama and for his audience it was, as so often with him, 'something to perfection brought'.

Those of us who were trying to find an appropriate form of language in which to discuss literature in Irish were offered a critical voice by him, and not only in concise and adequate vocabulary but in articulation. Some time ago, I saw and heard on television the selfsame voice and rhythms and precisely shaped sounds in the remarkable tones of the late Bab Feiritéar, the renowned West Kerry storyteller.

I had never heard or seen her in person before that but I could hear and see then the precision of language and articulation which Ó Tuama had made his own and then transformed to an imaginatively intellectual medium for his own original readings of life and literature and for his distinctive voice in poetry and plays.

That remarkable, individual, yet rooted voice is to be heard in all his great scholarly works – *An Grá in Amhráin na nUaisle* and probably most memorably in his masterly introduction to his edition of *Caoineadh Airt Uí Laoghaire*. His voice lies gently but insistently on the ear and askes persuasively to be heard. That same voice had a particularly vital realisation in his many plays which must now await new and re-imagined productions.

It was a phrase of Mícheál Ó Guithín, *an file*, son of Peig Sayers, which inspired one of Seán Ó Tuama's most moving short poems. It evokes with great tenderness the vulnerable world of an adolescent girl who has been chastised by her elders. He called it, so very appropriately, 'Rousseau na Gaeltachta'.

Lig di a dúirt a file,
Is ná smachtaigh í,
Níl inti seo ach gearrchaile
Is is breoiteachta é an t-eagla
A chrapann an nádúr.

Lig di a dúirt an file,
Is ná smachtaigh í,
Lig di fás gan bac ar bith
Go dtína hairde cheapaithe:
Tá an t-aer fós bog os a coinn.

THE LAST DAY
NOT AT SCHOOL

Benedict Kiely

When the editor of a magazine asked me recently if I could write down for him my memories of those days of wrath, those dreadful days, on which so long ago myself and the other gurriers went back to school after the summer holidays, I sat down in a dark corner and gave the matter serious thought. And I found that although I have a fair memory when I try, I couldn't remember a damned one of those days. Damned is exactly the word I was searching for.

Psychiatrists tell us that we are inclined to forget things that we find it unpleasant to remember; and the great jockey, Lester Piggott, came up with one of the wise remarks of all time when he said that the only thing he ever learned at school was that you had to go there. What little Lester wanted to learn could not be taught in a classroom. Nowadays I can never see a chiseller creeping like a snail, not so much unwillingly as uncomprehendingly, to school without thinking of Lester Piggott.

Yet if I've found now that I can't remember a day on which I was supposed to go back to school, I find also that I do remember a day when I went back to school by accident and was supposed to be going to work for the first time.

Incidentally, a lovely lady who went to college with me has, in relation to the use of the word 'supposed', a theory that our beloved Ireland is one vast supposition and may not, in truth, exist at all. Everyone in

Ireland is 'supposed' to be doing something or being somewhere, and not infrequently 'supposed' to be doing something else or being somewhere else. Just listen hard this day and count how often you hear the word 'supposed' used and even how often you use it yourself.

The day, though, that I went back to school when I was supposed to go to work is so tied up with the personality of a man long-dead, a great teacher, that any talk about the day becomes nothing more or less than a memoir of that man. He was a Clareman by birth, from Kilkee. He was a graduate of one of the great English universities, I forget which. He taught, or tried to teach, Latin and English to myself and a lot of other young gentlemen whose hearts may not really have been in literature, ancient or modern.

He was one of those teachers, and they're not all that common, who became a legend to the generations. He taught men who are now seventy years of age, and who remember him vividly. He died suddenly in 1939. His initials were M. J. and his wife, I know, called him Michael but we knew him simply and respectfully, as Joe. He wasn't the sort of man who'd acquire a more elaborate, or caricaturing, nickname because he had, first and before all things, an awe-inspiring presence. Not that he was violent or severe. He was just so unmistakeably *there*: six feet and a little more in height, broad-shouldered; he had been an amateur boxer in one of the heavier weights, and one arm, cracked in conflict, was always slightly bent.

He dressed always in dark suits with a pinstripe and wore strong, expensive, well-polished boots. He wore rimless spectacles with a golden chain hooked over his right ear. He had gone more or less bald but what hair he had he combed forward and kept continually combing it with his right hand as he walked the classroom, never raising his voice immoderately but talking firmly, persuading us that not only was a little learning not a dangerous thing but that it might even be of benefit to us in the life that lay ahead.

'It'll all be the same in a hundred years,' he'd say, 'but in the meantime you might for a while like to read a book, or make a little money, or even eat and have a house to live in.'

He loved literature even to the point of loaning us his own books in the hope that we would read them and return them. That's always a hazardous confidence to place in students, yet I don't think any of us ever let him down, and he had his own humorous way of reminding us if the end of term approached and the books were still unaccounted for.

He'd look at the class silently for a few minutes, twisting his lips wryly, the light glinting off his glasses. He was the great master of the pregnant silence. Then he'd say solemnly: 'Let down the windows and bring me back my books.'

One particularly bad borrower did bring back a book on the very last day of term, walked up the classroom, left the book on the master's desk, walked back again to his seat. Nobody made a sound. Outside the window the sun shone on the convent field, and the pet brown donkey that the nuns kept in honour of Bethlehem grazed in content. Then he said: 'John, a mission in your parish? Is it the Redemptorists?'

In those days the boys who came in by bicycle, train and bus from rural corners and country towns used to bear their parcels of bread with them to eat at lunchtime in a restaurant where they could get a cup of real tea for a penny. The simple life – and no mistake. But it often happened that hunger would overtake some poor devil in mid-morning and he'd begin to munch, with what secrecy he could muster, in the classroom. Once, a decent boy from Fintona had his mouth as full as it could hold when that same silence, awesome but never evil, because humour was always there, descended on the room. Then came the question: 'Colm, what are you chewing?'

There was a sudden agonised swallow: 'My lunch, sir.'

'Continue, Colm, just for one awful moment I thought it was the cud.'

Then he had the most wonderful way of catching with a silly question a half-sleeping student and waking him up to laughter but not to recrimination. He'd read out, say: 'For often in O'Connor's van/To triumph dashed each Connacht clan.'

A silence. Then: 'Tell me, James, what were they doing always racing about in that old van?'

Or reading from William Morris how Svend and his brethren built great roads that over their smooth surfaces the wains might go, he'd stop suddenly to ask a slumberer if the weans then had nowhere to play except on the streets.

Or on the highest level of all he might read from *Richard II* Bolingbroke's complaint of how his enemies had maltreated him:

From out my windows torn my household coat,
Razed out my impress, leaving me no sign,
Save men's opinion and my living blood
To show the world I am a gentleman.

The silence, and then the question: 'Tell me Michael, were the Bolingbrokes so badly off that they had to keep an old coat stuffed in the window?'

One day he sent me out to the cloakroom to get from his overcoat a copy of Chesterton's *The Flying Inn*, which he had promised against his judgment to loan me. 'In the right pocket,' he said, 'the cigarette butts. Leave them be. In the left pocket, your friend, Mr Chesterton.'

The Chestertonian paradox, oddly enough, did not appeal to him – perhaps it was too close to the comic part of himself – and he practically despised Belloc for those articles during World War I, in *Land and Water*, in which Belloc kept forecasting, from day to day, the fall of Prussia: and that fall kept obstinately postponing itself. Yet in days when Bernard Shaw and others were making monumental fools, or worse, of themselves on such subjects as the efficiency of Hitler, this Clareman, teaching school in an Ulster town, spoke in and out of season against Hitler and Mussolini. One of the more notable diversions in class was his gentle but firm argufying with a friend of mine who was pro-Mussolini for the odd, or perhaps not so odd, reason that his elder brother was in the Irish college in Rome.

The last letter I had from Joe a week before he dropped dead in the High Street in Omagh, was a dire and accurate prophesy of the disasters to come in the Hitler war.

The day that I set off to work in the local post office and went, instead, absent-mindedly to school, he was out smoking and sunning himself between classes, and we laughed uproariously at my mistake. Then he brought out the great brown suitcase he carried his gear in, took out a book and gave it to me. He said: 'Oddly enough I felt you might be here today so I brought this along.'

And as I walked away (to be late on my very first day as a wage-labourer) he called after me, 'Stick with Shakespeare and you'll go far.'

Years afterwards when I was on the far side of an ocean and a continent and the high Cascade mountains teaching in the University of Oregon I'd pause in the middle of a class and see him, the pinstripe suit, the glint on his glasses, the wry smile on his lips. And I could hear him say: 'I told you so, didn't I? Go any further and you'll be round the world and on the road home.'

IMPRESSIONS OF COLOUR

Vincent McDonnell

When I was growing up in the 1960s, the colour of my world could have been described as drab grey. A revolution might have been taking place among the young of London and New York, but it was far removed from the wilds of rural Mayo. The only illumination in my grey world came from books, music and Fr John, my English teacher, who first brought colour into my life.

Such was his influence on me that when I found myself, a teenager, in London in 1970, I didn't head for the Irish haunts of the Gresham Ballroom or the Galtymore. Instead I made my way up Trafalgat Square to the National Gallery. I wanted to see the Impressionist paintings Fr John had introduced me and my fellow students to over the previous five years.

He was a big, gentle man who never raised his voice, yet commanded absolute respect. I still picture him in his black suit, smudged with chalk dust, and with his reading glasses perched on the end of his nose. He was never without a bundle of books clutched to his chest or carried precariously beneath an arm. In time, those books were to become a window into another world where light and colour were celebrated.

He was an ideal teacher because he believed in what might be described as a holistic approach to education. He tolerated the prescribed English texts and, like me, would have much preferred to proscribe most of them. He covered enough of the course to ensure that his students were prepared for their exams and spent the reminder of the time on education.

It was during this time that he introduced us to his bundle of beloved books. Here was the poetry of Dylan Thomas, Robert Frost and Emily Dickinson, and the paintings, in glorious colour and light and movement, of a group of artists I'd never heard of – the French Impressionists.

Until then, art for me was Millet's depiction of the Angelus, the ubiquitous Sacred Heart and the dark brooding images of Christ and His saints. They gazed down threateningly, mournfully or accusingly from every wall throughout my home. They hung in the schools and the churches and there seemed to be no escaping them, until the advent of Fr John.

The first painting he ever showed us was Renoir's *Les Parapluies*. As he spoke about the colours, the use of light and the harmony of the composition – the circular umbrellas and child's hoop – I could not mistake his passion. Here was a painting which had no religious significance. It might simply be a photograph of people sheltering from the rain, yet instinctively I knew it was more than that.

Over our years together, Fr John told us of the other Impressionists and showed us colour plates of their paintings. He introduced us to Van Gogh, my own favourite, and to Monet, whose use of light and colour simply dazzled. And we all fell in love with Degas's dancing girls in their white diaphanous dresses.

So it was that at nineteen I found myself face to face with paintings I had only ever seen in books. Here was the original *Les Parapluies*, here were Monet's lilies and Degas's dancers. And here too was Van Gogh's *Cypresses*, not a smooth surface at all but with the paint layered on as Fr John had once explained to us.

Signs forbade touching the pictures but I couldn't resist. Leaning in over the rope barrier I traced the layers of paint with my finger, following the stroke of Van Gogh's palette knife. In that moment, I heard the echo of Fr John's voice and I knew that we who had known him had been blessed.

He was long gone to rest, but his legacy remains. And whenever I find myself in London, I visit the National Gallery. I make my way to the Impressionists' gallery and sit there quietly and let the colours wash over me. And as I sit there, I fondly remember the first time I saw Fr John and his bundle of books, and how I never imagined the colour and pleasure they would bring into my life.

INTRODUCING OLYMPIA

Nuala Ní Chonchúir

At the Paris Salon of 1865, Édouard Manet's painting *Olympia* caused a scandal. This luminous nude was referred to as, among other things, 'a female gorilla' and 'a deformity'. Parisians swarmed to the Salon hoping to be outraged. Finally, the painting had to be cordoned off to protect it from the angry hordes. Today, Olympia hangs in the Musée d'Orsay and the painting is acknowledged as Manet's great masterpiece.

I'm not sure when I first thought to myself that *Olympia* was the most beautiful painting in the world. By the first time I saw her in the flesh, so to speak, my stomach flip-flopped and I stood in awe for a long time.

Manet, who was an academic painter, painted *Olympia* as a homage to Titian's *Venus*. But Parisians were horrified because the model he used was considered altogether too brazen. How dare she gaze from the painting with such sensuality, her only clothing a black ribbon around her neck and a dusky blossom pinned to her hair? And why was her hand placed across her leg in such a suggestive way? Who *was* this woman who appeared to be little more than a streetwalker?

The model that caused this uproar was Victorine Meurent, a slender, working-class Parisienne with alabaster skin, who has been portrayed by art historians as a prostitute and a drunkard. Even though she is a central figure in nine of Manet's greatest works, including *Le Dejeuner sur l'Herbe*, like most artists' models she has been written out of the picture. She is seen as a body rather than as a person in her own right.

But Victorine, as it happens, was very much her own person. Although little of the facts of her life remain, it is known that she used to live at 191 Rue du Faubourg-Poissonnière.

This street lies on the edge of Montmartre, just a skipping distance from the shining domes of the Sacré-Coeur. By happy coincidence, the hotel I booked for a winter weekend in Paris was situated on that very street. These days, the ground floor of number 191 is a *boulangerie* and *pâtisserie*, its window a carnival of crusty breads and pastry treats. A large wooden doorway opens to the yard that leads to the apartments overhead.

I stood outside the building on a biting January morning and imagined Victorine tripping out through that very door, to spend a few *sous* on hot bread on her way to model for Manet. Or indeed, on her way to buy materials for her own paintings. Because, as it turns out, Victorine Meurent was an artist as well as a model. And what's more, like Manet, she exhibited at the prestigious Paris Salon. Her painting *Bourgeoise de Nuremberg* was exhibited there in 1879 along with two paintings by the man for whom she had previously been a favourite model.

Manet's biographers seem to have been filled with a peculiar distaste for Victorine. They record her as a pathetic figure, poor and dying from alcohol addiction by the 1890s. However, Victorine lived until March 1927. She actually died at the age of 83 in the Parisian suburb of Colombes, where she lived with a female companion.

But what of Victorine's pictures? Although she was a member of the French Society of Artists and she exhibited at least up until 1903, sadly no trace remains of Victorine's paintings. What we *do* have to remember her by is a painting of an assured young woman, who commands attention with her fearless gaze: Manet's magnificent *Olympia*.

LOLA MONTEZ – THE MOST BEAUTIFUL WOMAN IN EUROPE

John MacConville

Away back in the early years of the last century, a young ensign in the English Army, Edward Gilbert, who was stationed in Limerick, married a Miss Oliver of Castle Oliver near Kilmallock. And a year later this union was blessed with a baby daughter who was christened Maria Dolores Eliza Rosanna Gilbert – and who grew up to be the most beautiful woman of her generation, maybe of any generation. What surprises me, though, is how few people have ever even heard of this Limerick girl whose beauty, it is said, drove men mad with desire, and at whose shrine half the crowned heads of Europe paid tribute.

When she was nineteen, in order to avoid a marriage to a very rich but distinctly elderly retired judge who her mother had decided would make an ideal husband for her, Maria Dolores ran away with a dashing young officer, Captain Thomas James. She married him and followed the drum to India, but the marriage never really took and four years later he divorced her for adultery. Divorce in those days being a social sin as well as a religious one, Maria no longer was accepted in the circles she had always moved in and returned to London where she made up her mind to become a dancer.

She took lessons from Miss Fanny Kelly, the leading dancing mistress of the time, and then went to Spain to study Spanish dancing, after which she came back again to London. And under the name of Lola Montez she made her début as a Spanish dancer at Her Majesty's Theatre in the Haymarket, but was hissed off the stage at her very first performance, her dancing was so atrocious. This didn't worry her in the least, though, and she blamed her failure on the fact that she had been recognised as Mrs James by some members of the audience who, she claimed, were simply jealous of her great talent. She now left London and travelled to Germany where she was completely unknown. And when she opened in Dresden the young men about town there were so overcome with her beauty that they didn't give a damn how she danced.

And this was the beginning of a truly triumphant tour – Berlin, where she was fêted by every high-ranking officer in the city; Warsaw, where she was invited, with some passion, to become the mistress of Prince Ivan Pashewich who, at sixty-nine, was reckoned the greatest roué and the best judge of a woman in all Poland; St Petersburg, where she received two proposals of marriage, one from Prince Shulkoski and the other from Count Alexander Owinski, and where the emperor himself showered presents on her. And then Paris.

Paris, where she danced at the Porte Sainte Martin Theatre, entrancing the men but rousing the women to fury because, as she said herself, 'she was spoiling their trade'. And when at a performance one night she was hissed by every woman present, she walked slowly to the front of the stage, lifted up a long and shapely leg, then, taking off her garter, threw it into the middle of the audience. And when the lucky man who caught it held it up in triumph, the cheers of his friends rang through the theatre while the ladies sat in silent disgust.

It was in Paris that Lola, as she was now known everywhere, first became a great and notorious lover, and the men in her life were as famous as they were numerous: Joseph Méry, Victor Hugo, Alexander Dumas, Franz Liszt, to name but a few. And finally, Alexandre Henri Dujarier, literary critic and half-owner of a well-known Paris newspaper. But Dujarier was different from the others, for he was the only man she gave her heart to as well as her body. She would undoubtedly have married him, only he was killed in a duel, leaving Lola in such a state of grief that for months after his death she went nowhere and became practically a recluse. When at last she began to pick up the threads of her life again, she found that she could no longer go on living in Paris, every stone and every street of which was full of tender memories for her. And so she moved to Bavaria.

Here she tried to get an engagement as a dancer at the Court Theatre, but when the director saw her dancing he wouldn't touch her at any price. So she sought an audience with the King of Bavaria, Ludwig I, who was patron of the theatre and a noted connoisseur of beautiful women. When, after a lot of trouble, she eventually got to see him, His Majesty stared with such obvious delight at her magnificent bosom that she seized a pair of scissors which was lying on his desk and cut her bodice right open, telling him as she did so to have a right look while he was about it. He must have liked what he saw, too, because she got her engagement and in no time at all had been installed in a huge mansion where the king sent her a poem every morning to be read to her the second she awoke – that is, of course, on the mornings when he wasn't there to read it himself.

She was created La Baronne Rosenthal and Contesse de Landsfield, with a royal pension of twenty thousand florins a year, and in no time at all was Queen of Bavaria in all but name. And you could say king also, for Ludwig rarely made a decision of any kind without first of all consulting her. She pretty well ruled the country until 1848 when he was dethroned.

Having no use for a king without a kingdom, Lola very sensibly left Ludwig now and returned to London. But the good days were over and after two more marriages and a period of lecturing on beauty to the women of America, she gave up all wordly things and, like so many other nineteenth-century beauties, ended her days by doing good works. She died in New York on 17 January 1861 and was buried in the Greenwood Cemetery there.

Poor Lola. She was only forty-three when she died – worn out from love, I suppose.

WHERE BAGGOT STREET MEETS PEMBROKE STREET

Phyl Herbert

Mapping time and place comes easily to me now. Mapping a person's life is not so easy. I'm walking down Lower Baggot Street, past Doheny & Nesbitt's along the road from O'Donoghue's pub then Toner's and I stop at 132 Baggot Street where Gaj's restaurant used to be. I allow myself to walk back a few decades. I stop at the early 1970s and I walk up the stairs, open the door into a Georgian dining room, where I first encounter the smiling face of the owner, Margaret Gaj. She is talking with her friend Lady Longford. It is a cold day and the red coal fire offers a warm welcome. It is lunchtime and all the solid mahogany tables are occupied. Mairead, the friendly waitress from Donegal, calls me over to a table by the window. There is one empty chair. Goulash is the special of the day. My first ever introduction to beef goulash. The menu is the cheapest in town, the customers the most exotic.

I sit beside a well-known poet from Northern Ireland; he is talking to a theatre critic. I am included in the chat. I listen to the music of different accents from the four corners of Ireland. There are freshly cut flowers on each table. I light my cigarette after my first course and order freshly ground coffee. I listen to the debate at the table and watch the smoke curlicue towards the high ceiling along with the high-minded words. The aftertaste of the meal and the conversation revive and exhilarate me. On my way out, I notice posters announcing more than one protest meeting in the area.

I come down the stairs and face Dublin of 2007. I turn into Pembroke Street, where time has stood still and walk by an unbroken line of Georgian houses and up to the Focus Theatre in Pembroke Place. This tiny theatre is forty years old. The small cottages that surrounded it forty years ago have been knocked down and have now become fancy apartments. Again, I allow myself to travel back to the late 1960s, early 1970s. I enter the theatre and meet Deirdre O'Connell, her blue eyes sparkling beneath a crown of reddish-blonde hair draped on her head in a chignon.

The play is *Huis Clos* by Jean Paul Sartre and I remember Mary Wilson and Sabina Coyne's brilliant performances. The audience is transported, the atmosphere electric. At the interval, the little coffee room backstage is decked with flowers and the walls are covered with black and white photos of scenes from plays by Ibsen, Strindberg, Chekhov, Tennessee Williams, Doris Lessing. Photos of actors like Mary Elizabeth Burke-Kennedy, Tom Hickey, Joan Bergin and, of course, Deirdre herself. The big portrait of Deirdre by Brian Bourke takes pride of place.

I'm back to reality again. Deirdre is no more. She is sadly missed. In June 2001, she made her final exit. But her Focus lives on. It was Deirdre's vision and dedication in the early years that made it possible for the Focus to survive. The building itself was bought with Deirdre's personal savings and the help of her husband, the late Luke Kelly. She introduced the Stanislavski method of acting to Ireland and taught aspiring and experienced actors on Saturdays and Sundays for a ridiculously low fee. There were many years when she struggled to survive but always put the theatre first. When the theatre was in danger of closing its doors, she would go to work in New York. The money she earned was sunk back into the Focus. Deirdre provided a rare theatre experience in Dublin back then. She not only acted, but directed and taught and mapped the route to the skills needed to provide good theatre.

I make contact with Margaret Gaj, now eighty-eight years of age and as passionate as ever. She had just heard news on RTÉ Radio I's *Liveline* about the condemning of the six most dangerous species of dogs. She showed me photos of her two sons when they were around four and six years of age playing with the family pet, a Doberman pinscher. She said they are very affectionate animals and the fault always lies with the owner and the environment.

She showed me a book called *Mondays at Gaj's: The Story of the Irish Women's Liberation Movement* by Anne Stopper, published in 2006. In it, I learned for the first time that Margaret Gaj was one of the founder members of the movement. The group met in the room over her restaurant from 1970. The first chapter in the book entitled 'Not Just a Restaurant' covers the story of her life during those days. It pays tribute to the enormous generosity and compassion of the woman in whose restaurant customers were invited to eat without payment, the waitresses knowing not to give them a bill. Her most defining characteristic was her sense of equality and social justice. She had many political affiliations. She was a great friend of Dr Noël Browne. She was instrumental in the creation of the Prisoners Rights Organisation in 1973 along with Joe Costello. Deirdre O'Connell was a regular visitor to Gaj's restaurant; after all, she had only to walk up Pembroke Street from her beloved theatre in Pembroke Place.

These two women had a lot in common. Both had Irish ancestry. They came to Ireland as young women where they embraced a vision of excellence, established a setting and opened their doors to those seeking the best food and art for mind and body.

REMEMBERING
BETTY FRIEDAN

Ailbhe Smyth

Growing up in Ireland in the late 1960s and 70s, I was a very confused
young woman. Ah well, you might say, weren't we all? But every generation has its own confusions and problems, and of course, just to
complicate things, they're not the same for different social groups and
classes – and genders. For a young woman like myself, a daughter of the
white Dublin bourgeoisie with a university education, the confusion was
acute, all the more so since the underlying problem had no name.

There I was, there we were, growing numbers of young women
freshly released from our convent schools, flocking or being herded into
universities around the country with very little equipment for life except
our Leaving Cert results, polite manners and a pair of white gloves. The
whole world lay before us, they said, and we innocently believed them.
We didn't know then – how could we? – that we'd need to ditch the
manners and the gloves and reinvent it. For we had an impossible
mission: to be educated 'new' women, achieving and succeeding out
there in a world which believed we should all be at home all of the time
servicing husbands and children and households and what have you.
And with hardly a role model in sight. But that's all in retrospect.

I got a degree, got a job, got married and set up house in double-quick
time. That it all fell apart just as quickly was a blessing, although it didn't
seem so at the time. The difficulty was that without being able to say quite
how or why, I knew I was caught in a contradiction I couldn't climb out

of on my own. I was getting two messages about who and what and how I should be, so bewilderingly at odds as to make me – literally – ill.

The penny dropped slowly, and for me, reading was a crucial part of the process. Some time in the early 1970s, I read Simone de Beauvoir's *The Second Sex*, then Betty Friedan's *The Feminine Mystique*, among other amazing feminist books. They were a revelation and my excitement was immense. I saw that I wasn't mad or bad, or stupid or alone.

'A woman,' Friedan said, 'has got to be able to say, and not feel guilty, "Who am I, and what do I want out of life?" She mustn't feel selfish and neurotic if she wants goals of her own, outside of husband and children.'

She named the 'problem that has no name' for women of my generation and milieu, putting her finger on the pulse of those living contradictions, revolutionising how women thought about ourselves and our lives. Above all, Betty Friedan urged us to take the gloves off, to take action to change the world, to stand up and fight for our right as women to independence, equality, justice and human fulfilment.

So, another marker gone, I thought to myself when I heard of her death at eighty-five last week. The twentieth century is indeed over. I didn't agree with all her views – not with the watered-down reformism of her later years, and certainly not when she called lesbians like myself the 'lavender menace'. The phrase makes me laugh now (I love lavender), and she did most apologetically recant.

But caveats are mean-spirited. I thought about Friedan's legacy, about the extraordinary debt I owe her and her generation of brave, visionary feminists who taught me, confused and privileged young woman that I was, to think more clearly, to challenge more firmly and to inhabit the world with courage and a passion for justice. Betty Friedan believed in women's right to live fully, creatively and freely. Way back in 1963 when *The Feminine Mystique* appeared, she asked, 'Who knows what women can be when they are finally free to become themselves?'

To be sure, hers was not the only voice, the whole world or the whole story. There was more to come, more work to be done, and there still is, in scads, but she fought the good fight for women with fire and vigour, and I honour her and mourn her passing. May she rest in peace.

And in this twenty-first century, with its myriad new challenges and dilemmas, may feminists have the vision and the strength to go on fighting for women's freedom: for ourselves, for our daughters, for all women everywhere.

SEAMUS MURPHY

Eric Cross

I met Seamus Murphy for the first time soon after he had returned from Paris and established his workshop-studio in the yard of Sonny Murphy's pub, the Northern Star, in Blackpool. I saw him for the last time, after a lapse of many years, for two nights a fortnight before he died. More than anyone I have known, more than my own relations, Seamus entered into my life. He became a part of it despite long periods when I did not see him. Physical presence was not necessary for my constant awareness of him.

Before the war, when I was romantically traipsing round Ireland with a horse-drawn caravan, Seamus would join me for the odd weekend, or week, and enliven the day's journey, the night's drinking, with his intimate knowledge of places and people. When I lived in Gougane he would come frequently for a weekend and, as frequently, stay for weeks – as long as the money lasted.

When I was living in Cork it was seldom a day passed that I did not push open the wicket gate into the yard behind the pub and, as likely as not, spend the better part of the day there. His studio in Blackpool was the salon of Cork, but a strictly masculine salon. It was a gathering place for all sorts and conditions of men. It was a focus point for a score of aspects of the vivid, zestful life of Cork in those days. The news, more particularly the unwritten news, the news between the print, was discussed, enlarged on, disputed. Personalities and motives were ruthlessly examined. Old history was revealed. Old and new scandals were given an airing.

You never knew who would turn up or who you would find there. Billy Dwyer, the then Maecenas of Cork and a staunch supporter of Seamus, spent a lot of his time there. Almost everyone visiting Cork – actors, artists, writers, politicians, hurling heroes, greyhound breeders, old stonies, Munster Fusilier pensioners – focused on the studio. Seamus was very seldom alone. In the midst of whatever was going on, Seamus was the centre of the group of idlers, whistling and riding, tapping and hammering. Nothing passed him by. Often, with a twinkle in his eye, he would pause for a moment to drop in a wry comment, to ask a provocative question, to keep the pot boiling. Someone would brew tea or someone was in funds and we might repair to the conveniently adjacent pub – surely the most stark, comfortless establishment in the whole of Ireland, but where, nevertheless, there was so often the sport of Cork.

Seamus and I were, by background training, temperament and interest, poles apart. But it was Seamus who, unconsciously – yet, sometimes with a direct challenge of an example – taught me, influenced me. He taught me how little I knew about human beings and how intolerant I was towards them. To Seamus all human beings were, one way or another, of interest to him. All, no matter who they were, in that yard in Blackpool were on level terms and all were under the influence, themselves and real. For Seamus, working away, was always himself, so completely real – warm, tender, open, compassionate, understanding and zestful. He was also wilful and stubborn at times, for he was human.

Of course I was interested in his craft and in this direction he taught me much. He conveyed, communicated, initiated me into the craftsman's attitude towards his way of living. I still see raw stone, worked stone or a finished building with the added vision which Seamus gave me. Others have written and spoken about his work and his achievement. The work remains in the most durable form of all materials as a memento to the artist and the craftsman. But it was the man behind the work which always interested me, which still interests me and which will interest me while I have a memory.

As a result of knowing Seamus I measure a man much more in the terms of what would be Seamus's appraisal than those of my original self. I wonder what Seamus might think of him. Would he pass his shrewd scrutiny or would he be assessed and dismissed for his pretentiousness and unreality? Seamus gave me a sure measure. No man is an island. We are all affected and influenced by those whom we meet. To lesser or greater extent we weave others into the fabric of our lives. While I live, some part of Seamus Murphy continues to live in me – and that is the better part.

A LARK IN A HOUSE OF OWLS

Orla Murphy

In a house of owls, my father, Seamus, was a lark. Dawn on summer mornings would see him in the kitchen, looking up above the white-washed wall of the back garden to the eyelet of sky beyond the sycamore tree. He could hear the reveille of the army bugler in the barracks that topped one of the hills out of which the terraces of Cork's northside are carved. He made the breakfast, squeezing oranges, stirring in boiling water and sugar, making toast. It took the ashen-faced intervention of an American visitor, a specialist on Michael Collins and, it seems, on unnecessary risk, to end Seamus's habit of wangling slices of Mother's Pride out of the toaster with the bread knife. While the eggs boiled, he brought marmalade, butter and cereal from the red-painted cupboard in the corner. There was no fridge: houses built into the cliff face had pantries where no sun ever entered, and tiled floors ensured permanent chill. The single window leaked grey light from the yard where meat kept fresh in the safe, a wood-and-mesh box on four tall legs beyond the reach of cats whose unsanctified surplus was donated to the Distillery in Blackpool. Donated, not sold, as Seamus, thinking of Myles na gCopaleen's cautionary tale about the woman who sold kittens, would not risk prosecution by the Vice Squad for living off the immoral earnings of a cat.

After breakfast, he left the house, manoeuvring his bicycle along the hall out across the terrace and, balanced on one pedal, freewheeled down the hill onto Wellington Road, past the schools, across Patrick's Hill and down the steep drop to the Watercourse Road where ten minutes brisk cycling brought him to the big wooden gate that led to his studio.

At that point, Bebhínn, my sister, and I could hear already the sound of chisel on stone from the corrugated-iron shed where Seamus carved statues and inscriptions in daylight, in the open air. On the other side of the yard was the studio proper, where he worked in winter and where he made many portrait-heads in clay to be later cast in bronze, or carved in stone. There, in the veiled light that angled in from the north, it was the silence of that assembly of heads looking at us from various heights, that I remember. And the clean smell of plaster and clay. The Scullery was the name given to the studio by Seamus's friend, the poet Seán Ó Ríordáin. Visitors would spend hours looking, and listening to Seamus, but we preferred to watch as he sharpened chisels, heating a coke fire in a barrel, dipping the reddened chisel into water then plunging it back into the fire.

The heat, the hissing of the water as it boiled at the touch of the chisel, the anvil's profile like a knight's helmet: all these were magic. And then the little chisel, in his hand, gliding through stone, leaving only white dust in its wake. Oh it looked so easy, the taming of one element by another, where the chink chink of the chisel sounded the refrain in a game of merry craft over solid mass.

Clay was easier: warm, smooth and malleable. He put an apple-sized lump on the wooden table in the studio and patiently watched as we tinkered. He offered us spatulas or scrapers, and encouragement. We could remember how it was done: we had seen it at home during those long summer evenings; it must have been summer, as the attic where he shaped our skulls, or recreated us, was unheated. There was talk but there must also have been silence because we could hear the army band, this time practising marches in the barrack square. Seamus stood about four feet away with his back to the light, and held a lump of clay in his left hand, asking questions about school, or music, or anything he knew to be of interest, as he worked. It was a time of sensations: the inter-mittent sounds of the band, the flitting of swallows across the skylight, and the cool touch of the calipers ear to ear, forehead to chin, as he checked dimensions.

The surface was built up with tiny pieces of clay, which he rolled between finger and thumb and pressed on with the most elegant of all the tools, a wooden spatula, double-ended, slender and light, polished with age and use. He concentrated all of his effort on the head itself but took care over detail: a bow in Bebhínn's hair, a Cork brooch below the collar for me, saying that the Cork brooch was like the Tara brooch but that the pin was placed vertically.

At last, when the light started to wane, the clay head was wrapped in wet towels. He washed his hands and went down four flights of stairs to the living room to work on a drawing or, at last, to read.

History, biography and poetry filled the shelves of the bookcases. The radiogram played concerts by the symphony orchestra. The sky dimmed beyond the uncurtained windows and seagulls flew downriver to their night roosts. As our parents read their books, they could hear, far below in the tunnel of sandstone and limestone, the late train, making its way through North Cork to Dublin and to the world beyond.

MY PART IN THE CREATION OF A GIANT

Tony Brehony

In the autumn of 1953, the *Cork Examiner* reported that its Christmas edition, the *Cork Hollybough*, would feature short stories by 'Ireland's leading writers, Tony Brehony and John B. Keane.'

I had never heard of John B. Keane and I'm sure he had never heard of me, but by happy chance, some months later we met in a pub of Doneraile, the Cork village where John was then working. Over a few pints, it didn't take long to establish that we had much more in common than just our literary aspirations. We were both engaged to be married, he to a girl in Listowel and I to a local Doneraile girl. We were also fully agreed on the fact that, on the amount of money we were earning, there was no way we could ever afford such a step. John was getting £2.10s a week as an assistant in a local chemist's shop and I had just been demobbed from the Royal Navy with a war pension which barely topped £3 a week. And despite the *Examiner*'s optimistic suggestion that we were Ireland's leading writers, our literary earnings weren't impressive either – John's first novel had just been rejected and I was suffering from early writer's block.

That's when I told him that I was sick and tired of the poverty-level income that writing short stories was providing and I was going to make a fresh start – I had secured a real job with a company in Dublin paying £12 a week plus a company car, and my already short writing career was going to be put on a very long finger.

'Twelve quid a week!' John B.'s eyes were alight with his envy. 'And a motor car? Jaysus, boy, you're home and dry! God help me, if I could get something like that I'd be out of this bloody kip in the morning.'

So after much more liquid deliberation on the vagaries of life and of literature, I promised John with boozy confidence that I'd get him a job in the same company in Dublin – I had, I assured him, the right connections. He agreed to hold himself on a twenty-four-hour stand-by for my call and he gave me addresses in Doneraile and Listowel where I could contact him urgently by telegram. We celebrated our new positive approach to life with some more drink and then we went our separate ways.

I never met John B. Keane again but, for the next thirty years, I watched him climb the dizzy heights to the very top of the literary ladder. Over the same thirty years, I struggled up my own rickety ladder in the murky world of industry and never once put a creative pen to paper until I retired.

Looking back now at my own meagre contribution to Irish literature since those heady days long ago when the *Examiner* nominated me alongside John B. Keane as one of Ireland's leading writers, I can only plead that, unlike John, I peaked too early. On the positive side, however, there is the fact that, by failing to get John B. Keane a job in 1953, I didn't deprive the world of literature of his genius. For that, surely I deserve some acclaim. We who are not giants must content ourselves with lesser things.

SATISFACTION

Hugo Hamilton

In 1972, there were said to be thirty-five pubs in Listowel. That was the figure we were given, at least, when we got here. We tried counting them all. Tried to go into each one of them, but then lost count soon enough. And there was one we couldn't get into, where the door was always locked. We had to knock. Somebody came out, took one look at us and told us to go away each time.

We probably didn't have the right dress code. A small group of musicians and singers, all around nineteen or twenty years of age, gathered together along the way, from Dublin, Newbridge, Kilkenny. Bearded. Long hair. Deliberately shabby. One of us with an inspired Lazarus look, wearing a torn fur coat and a pair of canvas tennis shoes that were falling apart as he stood. Bits of us were being left behind everywhere we went.

We were just out of school, full of rebellion and an almighty thirst. The idea was to play a few tunes in each pub, make a collection, then move on. The money would finance our journey around the West. It would take us to Miltown Malbay and Lahinch and Lisdoonvarna. Then, on to a folk festival somewhere near Ballyvaughan.

We sang a song or two. Played a few requests, usually a slow air called 'The Cualann' which brought silence to any bar. We ended with a masterful version of 'Finnegan's Wake' and occasionally, on demand, did 'Satisfaction' or 'Stairway to Heaven' as an encore, but then we were already out the door, on to the next bar.

Funny, that word 'Satisfaction'. It had never been expressed with such feeling before, as if the concept itself had only just been discovered. Up to then, the pursuit of pleasure was seen as a vulgarity. The word had no relevance in our lives, employed mostly at school with the slap of authority.

'I can get no satisfaction out of him,' you heard Christian Brothers say. Your exam results were always unsatisfactory. Nobody was ever satisfied. Except for those who drank pints of stout or bought brands of ready-rubbed pipe tobacco. They had satisfaction guaranteed. Or did they?

Now, the word had real meaning. It was out, so to speak, like an untethered ram. A naked word, revealing everything. Examined and elongated in the mouth in order to extract everything out of life that had been denied up till then.

Sa-tis-fac-tion.

We trawled through the pubs of Listowel looking for it. And if there were thirty-five pubs in a town, then we didn't see why we could not have a pint in each one of them.

The pub we wanted to get into belonged to the well-known writer John B. Keane. And because we were turned away so often, we kept coming back. We drew up a plan. We narrowed it down to one person, the most respectable one among us, hoping that he would get past the door and then secretly let the rest of us inside.

This Trojan Horse principle had worked a million times before – at parties, in dance halls, late-night bar extensions, rock festivals – but, unfortunately, not in John B. Keane's pub. It was a literary fortress.

But then the man himself came to the door and I can remember the humour in his eyes as he told us to go away and choose any one of the other thirty-four pubs in Listowel apart from his.

'You'll get no satisfaction here,' he might as well have said.

At one point, he stood back, almost inviting us in, just to see how packed the place was. A heavy cloud of smoke and sweat and perfume blew towards us. You couldn't move in or out, he indicated. An entire bar full of men and women slow dancing with pints in their hands.

'There's all of Croke Park in there,' he said, as though he had fought his way to the door himself to get out of the place.

We agreed with him and moved on. It was no place for us. Lazarus – in his fur coat and tennis shoes – said he wouldn't be seen dead in there.

LISTOWEL CALLING LONDON

Joseph O'Connor

In the winter of 1989, I was living in South-East London, in the not entirely lovely suburb of Lewisham. It was a tough district that had escaped bombing in the Second World War, mainly (so it was said by some of the locals) because the Luftwaffe had looked down from their passing-by airplanes and assumed it had been bombed already.

For some years, I had been trying to write, but it was not going well. Writing was like trying to juggle with mud. I would send out short stories to the literary magazines. They would come back in an unstoppable stream.

I had entered a short-story competition in the *Irish Post* newspaper to win a trip to Listowel for its world-famous Writers' Week. I had not won the competition – nor had I deserved to – but to lose seemed typical enough for any young Irish person of the era. You felt you had emigrated from a country that had failed, and that the last one to leave should turn out the lights.

One evening, I came home to my cheerless bedsit to find there was a message on the answering machine. The voice was familiar, as it would have been to any Irish person. It was the voice of John B. Keane.

Would I come to Listowel for the festival, he was saying. 'What matter you didn't win. We'd love to have you anyway. I hope London is good to you. Kerry's full of O'Connors. You probably own Carrigafoyle.'

John B. Keane had rung my flat. John B. Keane had dialled my number. To me, it was the equivalent of winning the Booker Prize. In all the great city of London that night, there was no happier soul than mine.

His *Letters of an Irish Parish Priest* and his *Letters of a Matchmaker* were books my grandparents loved. As a young teenager, I had read them, been amazed by their contents. In the parish priest book, the narrator tells a story about two lovers overheard on a Kerry beach. The man utters to his sweetheart, about to plunge into the waves, perhaps the most romantic line in the whole corpus of Irish literature. 'Your buttocks have me intoxicated.' There were clearly other Kerrys than the one to be found in the pages of Peig Sayers' autobiography.

But there was loneliness in the books too; there was brokenness and loss. There were people who had taken wrong turnings. Everything about his work was based on one profound insight: that a small place, in a small country, could be the whole round world and all its adventures, if only you had the eyes to see.

For some reason I cannot remember, I didn't go to Listowel. But some years later, after my first book was published, I did go, and I met that genius of storymaking. To say he was kindly would be like saying it sometimes rains in Kerry. The weather in his eyes was always warm. Like many of the greatest writers, he was modest about his work. Not falsely – it was a modesty that came from self-assurance, I always felt – but he never seemed to want to discuss it. He would talk of other matters, with laughter and delight, and a kind of casual wisdom he didn't seem to know he had. He would remember the names of your children, despite never having met them. He would ask to see their photographs. He would tell you they were beautiful. And what were you writing? And would you not give up the smoking?

'Always remember, your family is everything.'

I was privileged to meet him a few times, always in the town of Listowel, a place I can never visit – and never will in my life – without thinking of his kindness and grace. But I never got the chance to say to him what I wanted. That I had seen the Bull McCabe in Lewisham High Street, shaking his stick at the traffic. That I had seen the ghost of Sive in New Cross Gate and the Hiker Lacey in Deptford. That his people walked Piccadilly and the Tottenham Court Road and Archway and Camden and Kentish Town High Street, in those distant days, those unhappier times, when to be Irish in London was to be suspect or a joke, and to be poor was no laughing matter.

Who wrote about them? Few but John B. Keane. Who told their stories? Who saw behind their tears? The quarrels over land, the secrets of families, the wants of young lovers, the memories of old men, the hurts done to these outsiders and the hurts they did themselves. That he had taken all of these and made of them stories that would speak to people all over the world.

A writer's life is punctuated with moments of remembered blessing. One of mine happened on a cold, wintry day, when life was not good and I felt very far from home. On an answering machine in London came the message like sunshine: 'It's John B. Won't you come to Listowel?'

REMEMBERING JOHN MCGAHERN

Denis Sampson

When I arrived at John McGahern's house for the first time, almost thirty years ago, I found John turning the hay. There was an old tractor in the shed, but he was doing the job by hand. In the warm August afternoon, we worked together round the small field that runs down towards Lake Laura. We walked the field and paused to look out over the lake. Some cows had waded in to cool off.

Constable might have painted the scene, Hardy might have described us or Heaney put us in a poem. I think John would have been pleased with such immortality, if he had not already accomplished it for himself. In his first years as a writer, a painter friend introduced him to Constable, to the letters and the life as much as the work. He liked the Romantic painter and spent a lifetime searching in words for the sources of light in a dark landscape, for intimations of heaven in the hell he had been given.

I have to admit, however, that on that day I did not really belong. I was young. Leitrim and heaven were not really my landscapes. I had grown up on a farm a hundred miles down the Shannon valley, but I had been brought up to go away, into education and wherever that might lead. My older brother was the farmer, and even when I saved the hay years before, my head was already in books. I had sweated over many fields, and put methylated spirit on my welts, but I knew I would never return from far-off places to root myself, as John had done.

Far from the land, in Canada, I discovered his first books. Some years went by, and, then, I had the good fortune to meet him in Montreal. Now, in the summer of 1979, I had driven up to the farm. I had spent a long time searching for it, as all I had was the postal address. It didn't even mention the nearest village. Of course, he and Madeline had no phone then. They had indeed withdrawn to their own lake district.

But perhaps 'withdrawn' conveys the wrong impression. He had distanced himself from the cultural traffic of cities, and from the kind of daily wonders that newspapers record, so that he could more fully create his own heaven. It was more than escaping from distractions, or freeing himself from gossip and intrigues. As a historian of the human heart, he did find gossip useful, but, for him, the talk of his old neighbours across the lake, or in Earley's pub in Mohill, was more useful than the gossip of Grafton Street. More useful because the art he wished to create had to be grounded in the work and the suffering and the wild humour of local life.

John's formal conversation was often pointed by a favourite expression from memory: a couplet from Yeats, a phrase from Beckett, an epigram from Proust, a definition from Auden. As he quoted the words of those he admired, a reverent stillness entered the room and a silence followed. It was as if there was no more to say on that subject. So sure was his reading, and his rereading, that he created his own company.

I had the feeling that he had come not only into his own place, but that he had also found his own time. It was the time of my childhood, of his childhood, of Constable and Wordsworth, of the timelessness of memory and art. In the company of Yeats and Beckett and Proust, he would refine his own style in this place. His writing room was not cork-lined, but it was in that room that he won his immortality. His kind of philosophical contemplation brought to light a supreme reality in the hayfield and the lake. He wanted to bring the history of his own deepest feelings and the history of his community and time into relation with such a sublime reality.

I could never become a farmer, but in John's work I found images of my humanity and my nature. When I visited the farm, I came to stay, for it was in his novels and stories that I discovered my sublime home.

THE SIR EDMUND HILLARY BIRTHDAY CLUB

Joe O'Toole

So Sir Edmund Hillary has left us. It was a year ago this month that, arriving in New Zealand, he gazed out at me from the Auckland newspapers' front pages. Sir Edmund Hillary at eighty-seven years of age, returning from what was expected to be his last trip to the Antarctic ice.

That evocative photo image transported me back half a century.

I was almost seven years old when my father read from the *Sunday Press* the story of Edmund Hillary becoming the first man to conquer mighty Mount Everest, to stand proudly on what they called 'the top of the world'. He told me that Mount Everest was five miles high. Five miles. My child's mind struggled. That's from Dingle to Lispole straight up in the air. As he read the story, a new world of crampons, pitons, ice axes and more emerged. Well, we climbed every foot of that ice mountain with Edmund Hillary hammering home every spike, tying every safety rope and sucking the rarefied air until, frostbitten and weary, we reached the barren icy summit with himself and Sherpa Tenzing.

He was an instant hero but we like our heroes local so there was an immediate natural affinity between the ice man Edmund Hillary and Abha-na-Scail man, Tom Crean. In that way, Edmund Hillary took his place among the pantheon of West Kerry greats. Somewhere along the way, I had made the interesting discovery that Tom Crean and Edmund Hillary shared the same 20 July birthday. More importantly, though, it was also my very own birthday. We three were linked inseparably and forever in my fantasy youthful birthday club.

Now, in New Zealand, 2007, with these memories flashing and flooding through my mind, I pondered the chances of meeting with the great man. The Irish consul enthusiastically agreed to help and, within a few days, confirmed the stunning and unexpected news. Sir Edmund would be delighted to meet and, better again, Lady Hillary had generously invited us to afternoon tea at their home.

Their Auckland home nestled in sumptuous bougainvilleas. The front door was welcomingly ajar when we arrived and a cheery 'Come on down' was the response to our speculative knock. Lady Hillary, a friendly, attractive and sophisticated woman without airs or graces, greeted us.

'I was just baking us some scones,' she said, 'Ed is in the lounge,' and she handed me the tray.

He was erect, large-framed and taller than I had expected as, with a twinkle in his eye and a welcoming smile, he put us at our ease, explaining that his hearing was not as good as it used to be. Gentle, charismatic, understated and softly spoken, his presence filled that room. As we enjoyed Lady Hillary's home-made scones, Sir Ed explained that it was the two Irishmen Crean and Shackleton who were his great heroes and role models. It turned out that his grandfather and Lady Hillary's grandparents were Irish and he had been to Abha–na-Scail in the Dingle Peninsula and paid homage to Crean, the one he most admired. He laughed heartily at some local West Kerry stories about Tom Crean. He had never realised and was delighted when I pointed out that he shared the same birthday with Tom Crean and he smiled indulgently when I told him that it was also my own.

'You and Ed must exchange birthday cards this year,' Lady Hillary suggested. We did.

Later, he recalled vividly his extraordinarily surreal experience when, years previously, he had first walked into the century-old huts constructed by Scott, Shackleton, Crean and others, and which are still there to this day, undisturbed on the ice.

'I was on my own,' he told us. 'When I walked into those huts for the first time, I might have emerged from a time machine. Things lay exactly as the exploration teams had left them nearly a century earlier. It was as if they had walked out the door just a few minutes previously. Cutlery and delph on the table, basic tools on the floor, the men's trousers and other clothes on the shelves and canned food, especially tins of beans, ready to be opened. It was eerie. I could feel their presence around me and with me and then I saw a figure come towards me with his arms out; I knew it was Shackleton and he smiled before he faded away. In all my life,' he continued, 'I never had a similar experience. I'm neither mystic nor overly spiritual and you may make what you will of it, but, for me, it was real.'

There was a quiet moment after he had finished speaking. His last words to us were a question.

'Would you ask the Irish government to support the preservation of the Antarctic huts in memory of those great Irishmen?'

We did, and Ireland responded generously. And that was how I came to meet my hero, this previously remote global icon, Sir Edmund Hillary, New Zealand by birth, Irish by blood, one of our own.

I'll be sorry not to be sending him a birthday card this year.

MOLLY

Aodhan Madden

This is a ghost story. There can be no other way to describe it. It all began on a late summer's day in a busy suburban street. I had just got off the bus in Phibsboro when I thought I saw her. She was standing in the porch of St Peter's Church. She seemed to be staring at me. There was a lot of traffic between me and her, yet that stare sought me out and held me. Then the bus passed between us and she was gone.

That couldn't be Molly, I thought. She was dead ten years at least. Yet I found myself walking across the road and into the church – just to confirm that I had made a mistake. The church was empty.

I decided it was merely some trick of the imagination and so I went off about my business. I was still a little troubled though; that strange, intense stare followed me all afternoon.

After a few days I had almost forgotten the incident, but then late that Sunday evening the phone rang. At first I heard nothing. I was about to put the phone down when I heard a low sobbing sound coming, as if from a great distance. It was an old woman crying. My blood turned cold. I thought of Molly. I slammed down the phone.

Was this some nasty hoax?

Molly and I had no particularly strong bond – she was hardly even a friend, just an elderly neighbour whose lawn I sometimes cut in the summer. I went to her funeral out of sense of duty really, she being the last of an old and respected family. There was no obvious personal context here for a hoaxer to exploit.

The two events had to be coincidental.

I had never given much thought to Molly before. Even in life she was a shadowy figure; in death, she disappeared all together. She had no living relatives, no close friends. The few people at her funeral were all neighbours.

Some time later there was a knock on the front door. It was a solitary rap and at first I thought it was the wind. I looked through the spyhole; there was nobody there. Yet I had this funny sensation that someone had been there; a vague trace lingered.

I ran upstairs to look out the window. She was standing at the garden gate. I couldn't see her face. All I saw was an old woman beating her sides in a slow, rhythmic movement that suggested great distress. But as soon as I saw her the movement of her hands merged into the swaying of the myrtle bush in the garden and her image seemed to melt into the shadows.

It had to be the wind; the rap on the door, those indistinct movements at the garden gate. People just don't come back from the dead.

I still could not get Molly out of my mind. I began to remember her toiling away in her garden, grimly pulling out weeds.

'Rain coming,' she would say, pointing to the sky, even in the sunniest weather.

There was another detail which I saw now and never noticed when she was alive. She never actually looked at me in all the years I passed her in her garden. Her head was always tilted to one side, her eyes avoiding contact with the world.

She was always sweeping leaves outside her front gate and even late at night I sometimes saw her bent over her broom, already ghostly, I now thought.

I decided to call to her house recently. It is still derelict and the front garden overgrown with weeds. I sat in the morning sun thinking about her near the end, sitting on her own window ledge with a heavy coat draped over her shoulders as she watched me mowing her lawn.

Was it possible, I thought, that the key to all this lay in the very private reality of Molly's own life? Was it possible that she was reaching out from some forgotten and anonymous place, claiming the right to be remembered?

I sat for ages in her garden. On summer evenings she sometimes sat in that drawing-room window looking out at the world passing by. Did

I ever wave back to her then? I wondered. Or did her very familiarity invite indifference? I'm sure I must have passed her in her window right through my childhood and nothing ever registered, nothing save the vaguest impression of her being there.

'Rain coming, Molly,' I heard myself saying out loud. Of course she cannot hear me now. But sometimes I like to think that the odd word, the odd remembrance cast into the great silence of eternity might calm her troubled progress. I would remember Molly and place some humble marker on the forgotten space she once occupied.

MALCOLM

Richard Craig

Far from Skibbereen, Paddy and I were in Fort William. The war had just ended and we were enjoying the new freedom of travel abroad. This was the beginning of our first walking tour of the Scottish Highlands.

We decided to head as far north as possible before seeking a place to shelter for the night. Our rucksacks and boots were new and we were disappointed that nobody observed our good looks and how fast we walked. As it grew dark the surrounding mountain seemed to become larger and more mysterious. Being inexperienced, we had overloaded our rucksacks and we were not accustomed to the weight or the newness of our boots. As a result our walking pace slackened due to painful feet. The wind rose to gale force and the rain poured down, battering against our faces and sapping our youthful enthusiasm. We decided to seek shelter.

We were both relieved and somewhat apprehensive as we approached a farmhouse where lights were still burning. A stout, pleasant-faced middle-aged lady opened the door and I let Paddy do the talking.

'I am Paddy Mulroy from Skibbereen, and my friend and I wonder if we could sleep in your barn?'

'I am Mary MacDonald and you certainly can sleep in the barn.'

Soon we were in the barn happy to be lying in warm hay. It was the first time I had lain in hay and been covered by it. I fell asleep listening to the snores of the collie dog also sharing the barn but concealed by the almost total darkness.

Paddy, already washed and dressed, wakened me in the morning. Using the freezing water from the trough at the side of the barn, I washed, shivered and rubbed my skin hard with the towel. Suddenly I caught sight of a young man. He wore a khaki uniform and the beret and footwear of a commando. He smiled at me as though in welcome. I was about to call a greeting to him when he completely disappeared.

Back in the barn Paddy looked at me and asked, 'What's happened to you? You look as if you've just seen a ghost.'

'Perhaps I have,' I answered.

Seeing us approach the farmhouse, Mrs MacDonald opened the door and called on us to enter.

'Come in and have some breakfast,' she said.

We sat in silence enjoying the boiled eggs, toast and mugs of sweet, steaming tea. Observing Paddy with a wistful look, Mrs MacDonald said:

'You boys remind me of my son, Malcolm. He was your age when he went to the war.'

I had just been examining a framed photograph near me. It consisted of a group of young commandos looking bright and happy. My attention was drawn to a tall young soldier; he was wearing sergeant stripes and looked both handsome and fearless.

'Do you know those boys in that photograph Mrs MacDonald?' I asked. 'Somehow I get the feeling I have seen one of them somewhere.'

'Which one?' she asked and I pointed to the sergeant.

'Yes!' she said. 'That was Malcolm, my son. He was a very brave boy and took part in many raids on the French coast. He was killed in Normandy on D-Day 1944.'

A SENSE OF OCCASION

LUNCH WITH DE GAULLE

Claude Cockburn

I was sitting in a squalid little café in a back street in Algiers. I was in a squalid little café in that back street because I was on the run. I had been expelled from Algiers by both the American and the British Military authorities. This was in the 1940s, just after the Germans had been driven out of Algeria – out of North Africa – and I, on the other hand, had been expelled by them and didn't intend to leave.

And I was waiting to be taken out to lunch. But I was very nervous because I was afraid that on my way to lunch I should be picked up by the British or the American Military Police.

But suddenly into this strange little alleyway came three enormous limousines, all flying the French tricolour, and I was taken into one of them and we shot up the hill to the residence of the President at the top of the hill, and I went to lunch. The man I was going to lunch with was General de Gaulle.

General de Gaulle, who was theoretically and constitutionally and of his own right the chief man in Algiers, would certainly have been outraged, was outraged, by the thought of the Americans and the British expelling somebody from his territory without consultation with him. This was one of the reasons why I was asked to lunch.

We sat down to lunch at a long, narrow refectory table, myself and the General at one side, and opposite us two rather stout colonels covered with medals. They, to my surprise, seemed to be eating only with their left hands. I didn't have very much opportunity to observe them to begin with, because conversation with de Gaulle is a fascinating business; he is a fascinating man, erudite, humorous, exciting in every possible way. A man, one could say, who corresponds to everything one means by a civilised man, meaning particularly in this case a man who understands that life can be both serious and funny. We talked about, among other things, Ireland; he told me about his Irish ancestry. We talked about the relations of Western Europe with the Soviet Union and about Marxism and Catholicism and many other subjects.

And all the time the two fat guards were sawing away at their steaks with their forks. I did notice a curious expression on the face of the General every time he looked across the table at them. Later I discovered that the reason was that the General, who hates and hates pompous people and has an enormous veneration, we may say, for gallantry, considered that these two colonels ought in fact to be fighting with the Resistance in France rather than eating fatly in Algiers. He had therefore seen fit to tell them that he was entertaining to lunch an extremely dangerous Red terrorist who at any moment might make an assault upon his person.

'Remember Trotsky,' he told them, 'how he was suddenly slain with an ice-pick.' And he instructed them that throughout lunch they must not for a moment relax their hold upon their pistols with their right hand. Throughout lunch therefore, de Gaulle's rather malign and profound sense of humour was titillated by the sight of these two fat men trying to eat steak with their forks.

And this was very characteristic of the General. It was in one sense, I suppose, an ordinary sort, if you like, of almost schoolboy practical joke. On the other hand it was intended to be, and was, a political lesson to those chaps. And I think that if the world in general and particularly perhaps the British had ever understood this tremendous element of the joker in de Gaulle's character, they would have understood him better and probably have made less mistakes with regard to him.

And the same is true of the French. Many French politicians became prisoners of their own propaganda about de Gaulle, considering him an austere, humourless sort of character, and thus always laid themselves open to the joker, the clown in de Gaulle, and always followed the banana skin to be placed straight under their feet.

And even today I think that de Gaulle's sudden withdrawal to Sneem is regarded by many of them as a kind of practical joke in the sense that so many of them expected to be able to go to Colombey-les-deux-Églises and at least pretend to have gained the endorsement of the General for whatever they were trying to do. Whereupon he suddenly, without a word to any of them, disappears to Sneem. And if anybody thinks that on wet days in Sneem — I hope there will be few of them — the General is going to be bored, let us not forget that he has one more tremendous opportunity to exercise his capacity for the explosive joke.

In writing his last volume of memoirs, for which, having all those secret documents in his possession, he certainly has enough material to blow out of the water half the politicians in France.

THE COUNTESS VON SPEE

Mervyn Wall

In 1936 I was holidaying in Germany, and in Bonn I called to see the Dean of the Minster Church. I had lived alongside that ancient cathedral for two years as a boy and had known the Dean well. He had grown older, but was the same courtly man I had known years before. He welcomed me and invited me to lunch, but before he let me into the dining room, he drew me aside to explain the identity of one of the other guests who were to lunch with him, the Countess von Spee.

She was, he said, the last of a noble, seagoing, Baltic family, of which all the male members had perished in the Battle of the Falkland Islands in the First World War. I have since read an account of that battle, and I don't think that what he told me was quite correct, but was rather the popular German story. But I'll repeat what he said.

The German South Seas Fleet, when war broke out, was cruising in the South Atlantic thousands of miles from home and with no chance of getting there because of the British and French fleets blocking the way. It was commanded by the Admiral Count von Spee, and his two sons were captains of two of the other warships. A mixed British and New Zealand force cornered them off the Falkland Islands and defeated them. Rather than let their damaged ships fall into enemy hands, the Count von Spee and his two sons scuttled their vessels and went down with them. Only two members of the family now survived — the Count's widow and a small daughter. Grief brought about the early death of the

Countess and the small daughter was left as the only representative of that distinguished family. The Kaiser, by imperial decree, conferred on the daughter her mother's title of Countess, and it was that girl, now grown-up, that I was to meet at lunch. The Dean said that she was a convert to Catholicism and had devoted her life to charitable work all over Germany.

I was introduced some minutes later to a pleasant, lively woman of about thirty, dressed entirely in black, relieved only by a small gold cross hanging from a chain about her neck. I was seated beside her, and she told me that she was lodged in the Dean's house, acting as secretary to him in organising and furthering charitable work in the town of Bonn.

She was a lively young woman and taunted me jokingly with my lack of interest in ships and the sea, although I lived in Dublin on the sea's edge. When she chatted with gay pride about the three pocket battle-ships which she had launched, I realised that she must be quite a public heroine throughout Germany, and I remember becoming silent as the irony of the situation impressed itself on me. As she spoke with satis-faction of the launching of those three battleships, I became increas-ingly conscious of that small gold cross, the symbol of Christianity, hanging from the neck of this obviously good and humane woman and winking at me in the midday sunlight.

After lunch she invited me to her room to show me three inscribed oaken shields, on which were mounted with silver clasps the broken necks of the three champagne bottles with which she had launched those three battleships, among them the one named after her father, the *Graf Spee*. When I left and walked past the great cathedral doorway, there was a sudden blare of martial music, and round the corner came a detachment of Nazi Storm Troopers, arms swinging and in perfect step. I thought of the winking of that little gold cross. Winking at what? Perhaps human blindness and folly.

In 1941, the pocket battleship named after her father, the *Graf Spee*, was cornered off the River Plate and bettered by three British cruisers of far inferior gunpower. The captain phoned Berlin for instructions – should he come out of the neutral harbour where he had sought refuge and go down honourably with all his guns firing, or should he surrender his ship to Uruguay to be impounded for the rest of the war? His instructions came back from Hitler himself. He was to scuttle his ship in the channel so as to block the neutral port of Montevideo which had succoured his vessel, effected repairs and given him provisions. The captain obeyed orders, set his crew ashore, scuttled his ship, and, lying down on a flag of the Imperial German Navy, not the Nazi flag, he shot himself.

I followed avidly the newspaper and radio accounts of those events, remembering every detail of that luncheon party in the Dean's house five years before.

THREE CHEERS
FOR DEMOCRACY

Norman Freeman

Whenever I hear someone say that they're not going to vote, or they give out about the flaws in our democratic system, I'm reminded of a voyage I made many years ago. I was the radio officer on a ship which went to South America to load beef for the British market.

Our first loading port was Buenos Aires, capital of Argentina. On our arrival, the shipping agent came on board. Like many Argentinians, he was a man of Italian background. He had an important warning to impart to us all.

'We gotta the military rule here in Argentina. In a bar or some kind of dive, don't get into a fight, OK? Otherwise police come, everybody gets arrested. Who knows what happens!' He shrugged his shoulders to indicate menace.

With these warnings in our ears we strolled about the streets of this great city, a vibrant place full of life and energy, resounding with the rhythm of the tango. But we were careful. We saw the bullet marks on the front of the Casa Rosada, the presidential palace that had been stormed by the army in its successful coup.

We then set off for Brazil, passing almost within sight of Uruguay, which was also under military rule at that time. We arrived at Porto Alegre, in the southern part of Brazil. We had hardly tied up alongside when a blond man, representing the agents, came on board. Like many in that part of Brazil, he was German. Almost the very first words he uttered were a warning.

'We now have in control the colonels. A *putsch*, you understand. The President is ousted. Military rule. Better for nobody to get into trouble in bars and…other places.'

So here we were, going about with some caution in one of the largest and most populous countries in the world, a country of endless diversity, of great wealth and poverty, of colour, of the smell of coffee and exotic tobacco, of the sound of the samba and Brazilian-accented Portuguese.

We eventually set sail for Europe. Brazil is so vast that it took us five days to clear the coast of this country where the military ruled. After another five days we were abreast of Africa. In the radio room I began hearing signals of the marine radio stations in the Canary Islands. They and the Spanish mainland were then under the repressive dictatorship of General Franco. At much the same time, the stations in Madeira and Lisbon could be heard. At that time Portugal had been under the dictatorship of one Dr Salazar for decades. The jails of the Iberian Peninsula were full of political detainees.

At long last, after three weeks sailing in the shadow of military rulers and dictators of one kind or another, our ship reached the Bay of Biscay. That evening I switched the main transmission aerial into the receiver. With earphones on head, I managed to tune in and amplify the sound of Radio Éireann on the medium wave.

There was a report of that day's proceedings in Dáil Éireann. Some deputies complained that they could not get in or out of the Dáil without running the gauntlet of groups or individuals, some with placards, protesting about a variety of matters. One TD, whose name I cannot recall, was reported as saying: 'I can't go outside the Dáil without some fellow giving me dog's abuse about the price of a pint.'

Now, while I could never condone our elected representatives being subjected to 'dog's abuse', at the same time I found myself saying, 'Three cheers for democracy.'

THE ENAMEL JUG

Peter Jankowsky

In winter, the playground of the kindergarten was reduced to a few grassy square metres rising, just about, over low-lying ground which, from autumn onwards, turned into a morass, the remnant of a number of allotments, now devastated by war action. All around the mud loomed the typical four-storey houses of Berlin, many of them now in ruins. A group of children were playing on the little patch of green, five-, six-year olds, a single boy and half a dozen girls. It wasn't peaceful play: it consisted of chases and scuffles, the girls nagging the boy, he making them scream by pulling their sleeves and their hair – all bitterly enjoyable in the dim November light of the first winter after the end of the war.

Unnoticed by the playing children, another boy had appeared on the scene; like an emanation of their grim surroundings, a tall, scraggy lad of maybe fourteen years, poorly dressed in something uniform-like that hung down from his shoulders, as did his long arms. His right hand clutched the handle of an enamel jug, the kind you would take to a field-kitchen for a ladle-full of soup. He stood there motionless, watching, his pale face without expression.

The little boy had just burst into a wild dervish dance, making the girls scatter and scream, when the din was cut as if by a knife, by the tall boy's voice.

'Look away!' he ordered the girls calmly. The children all froze and looked at him. The small boy stood in front of the tall one, looking up at him. He saw him raise his right arm slowly, the handle of the chipped enamel jug clenched in his fist, he saw him swing his arm back as far as he could. And then the stranger, with all his might, brought the pot down on the little boy's head, hitting it just above his right eyebrow and cutting down to the bone.

They all could hear the short, hard knock, as if on wood; the little boy heard it from within. Blood spurted out promptly, then after a moment of silent shock came a howl, more of horror than of pain. Fingers covering the violated face were flooded with blood and tears and saliva. He stumbled forward, calling for the kindergarten nurse, the girls fluttering all around him, now screaming with genuine terror. They completely forgot about the tall boy who had vanished, unseen, back from where he had first appeared, the ruined city. The bleeding boy was brought to a first-aid station in the neighbourhood. The wound needed a few stitches and with a big bandage, like a turban, he was delivered home into the arms of mother and grandmother.

And that's where that day ended for me — in a nest of warmth and nourishment and care. Where did the tall boy go? Where had he come from? For half a century now, his darkly looming figure, his right arm swung back, has been a regular visitor to my sleepless hours. Why had he wanted to erase me from his world? For that had been his intention, no doubt about that; had he had an axe instead of that enamel jug, he would have used it, such was his ferocity. Over the years I have brooded over every one of the few details I can remember. Those uniform bits, for instance. Had he perhaps been one of the unfortunate teenage boys the Nazis had drafted in at the very end of the war, had taught to kill, to be heroes, to defend their mothers and sisters? Had he, in his confused mind, wanted to rescue those little girls from their tormentor? Even then I had felt that jealousy had been a motif, not so much of me being with girls, but of me not being alone.

And that pitiful enamel jug — had he no one to feed him? Were his parents dead, maybe still buried under the rubble? Was he just roaming around, homeless, gone feral, after all he had seen, all he had lost? Was he, when we met, as impregnated with death and killing as I was as yet untouched by it? I will never get the answers to these questions, but over a lifetime they have brought him ever closer to me, my would-be executioner, my older brother Cain.

GO BACK TO YOUR MOTHER

Paul Andrews

When a bishop asks a question from the altar, I'm not sure that he expects an honest answer. The Archbishop of Paris – we are talking about 1913 – was all set to ordain my Uncle Frank as a sub-deacon. He was standing at the altar of Saint Sulpice, the seminary on the left bank of the Seine. Frank was a thin, dark, clever boy from Cork, as pious as they come, and deep. He *thought* about things. The ceremony in Saint Sulpice was important. Becoming a sub-deacon involved the promise of celibacy. As seminarians used to say, 'This is the day we lock on the iron pants and throw away the key.' The liturgy was framed in formal Latin, but each candidate was called before the Bishop beforehand to speak for himself.

'Frank Mulcahy,' he asked, 'are you seeking ordination of your own free will, and without pressure from anyone?'

Frank thought for a moment. In the preparations for the formal ceremony, this exchange had been unrehearsed, taken for granted. The Bishop had asked a reasonable question and Frank gave a straight answer.

'It wasn't really my idea, my Lord. It was my mother's.'

A shocked pause.

'Then go back to your mother,' said the bishop calmly. Frank packed his bags, went back to Cork, and found his vocation as a businessman. He married my father's sister, who gave him two remarkable, much-loved children. The boy, also Frank, died as a missionary in a Brazilian shanty town. The daughter died before her time as the mother of twelve children.

Later in life, Frank would read Gibbon's *Decline and Fall of the Roman Empire*, then, disturbed and fascinated, read it again; and a third time. Family legend has it that by the end of the third reading he had lost his faith, to which, as a matter of interest, he returned at the end of his life. Those who knew him throughout his life remembered a happy man. On the brink of manhood, he had discovered just in time the distinction between his mother's dreams for him, and his own.

A MONK

Michael Harding

I have a young Tibetan friend, Losang Rabsal, who is a monk. He seems so happy in his monastic life, and in his celibate vocation, that I once asked him to tell me the circumstances of how he became a monk.

First he laughed.

Then he went silent.

And finally he became very serious and began speaking.

'There was always snow,' he said. 'In Tibet.'

When he was growing up.

He was his mother's only child, though there were cousins his own age in the nearby tents of his relations. It was a huge family of many people in many tents, surrounded by an abundance of sheep.

His father was old. He was small and thin and full of wind. Like a snake standing erect, with huge ears, and in his throat a constant whistle of wind. In those days, all the young children would eat dried fruit, which they called 'old people's ears'. Rabsal called them 'Father's ears'. They lived on the hills, with tents and animals. His father sat on the grass in summer, motionless, like a log of wood in the forest.

There was always something suffering in him that his son could not understand.

In the depth of winter, the extended family would all settle in one sheltered place. Sheltering the animals. The children playing with bells. The women stirring soup. The men smoking pipes and taking snuff.

The coldest part of the night was just after dark. Until bedtime. Rabsal's young cheeks burned with the cold air. And he sat in the corner of the tent dreaming of monasteries.

He did not desire cattle. He did not desire horses. He did not desire yaks. He did not desire a wife or child or to be famous or be praised by the village. The only thing he desired was a monastery.

How wonderful to be inside the walls of a monastery. Learning to read. With a warm stove and an old Mongolian teacher to shorten the evenings. With stories like 'The Empty Pot', and 'The Upside Down Pot', and 'The Pot with the Hole in the Bottom'.

At night, he would sometimes stand out with the horses and the horses kicked the wind because they were angry at the cold air.

'I am also disappointed,' he told the horses. 'You wish for shelter. But I wish for a monastery. We are not so different.'

He rubbed the horse's nose, and stared into its eyes until the horse settled and then he would fall into the snow laughing.

His father was withering away. Turning into air. A shadow in the corner. Always in the dark of the tent now. On the bed. Yellow in the face. And a putrid smell from his urine. He was in pain when he moved. His legs swelled with sores. And his tooth ached in the middle of the night. One day, he turned to his son and said, 'You were born dreaming. You will never get a wife.'

'I don't want a wife,' his son blurted out. 'I want to go to the monastery.'

It was not something he intended to say. The words just walked out of his mouth.

The old man laughed till it hurt his ribs and he coughed black phlegm up as his laughter turned to choking. That was the first time Rabsal had ever revealed his desire to his father, and he was glad, because it made his father laugh, and because the following day his father was dead. And because such words had walked out of his mouth, at such a moment, Rabsal knew they must be true, and he knew it was time to walk to Lhasa and enter the monastery.

A MORNING WITH AN
ORACLE IN LADAKH

Marguerite MacCurtain

In the Himalayan Kingdom of Ladakh, the April full moon cast an icy glow over the ancient town of Leh. Its buildings, glazed with frost and icicles, shimmered in the shadows of surrounding glaciers.

In the dining room of a local hotel, I joined a diverse collection of people gathered around large pots of bubbling hot food arranged along a rectangular table. The atmosphere was warm and chatty until a bearded man, who had been speaking in hushed tones, leapt suddenly from his chair and proceeded to dance wildly around the centre of the room. He touched his chin with his knees in the course of a frenetic limb-throwing perform-ance. A fellow traveller informed me that he had been miraculously cured by an oracle who was said to be possessed by the spirit of a god. Three weeks ago, according to my friend, the dancing man could not even walk.

Next morning I entered the crowded, smoke-filled kitchen of the oracle's house in the village of Saboo. A tiny woman with deeply lined skin and dark hair was raised on a stack of cushions in the corner of the kitchen. She was dressed in a red and turquoise silk cape lined with shocking pink and embroidered with Chinese cloud motifs. On her head she wore a narrow-brimmed top hat which was strewn with layers of white gauze prayer scarves. Her mouth was covered with a red trian-gular piece of cloth.

She clutched a bell and shook it violently and then she began to chant feverishly as she went into the rituals of her trance. Her face became contorted, her eyeballs flicked up, her body writhed and shivered, her voice shrieked.

She screamed for pilgrims. The crowd pushed a reluctant woman forward. She staggered half upright from her kneeling position to place an offering of a white gauze prayer scarf on the oracle's hat. Then she fell to her knees to outline the details of her problem. The oracle emitted some high-pitched rasping and hissing sounds, removed her mask and buried her face in the exposed flesh of the woman's abdomen. She raised her face and spat a black looking bile that she had apparently sucked from the women's stomach without wounding her, into a bowl of hot ashes which was placed beside her.

Pilgrim followed pilgrim. The oracle's responses grew more frantic. Her healing methods varied only to include the use of a bamboo tube for releasing the black bile of evil from pilgrims' necks, tongues, cheeks and abdomens. A mother with a very sick baby knelt before her. The oracle's daughter handed her a knife which had been reddened in the fire. She placed the burning blade on her own tongue until it sizzled. Then she gently blew over the head and body of the baby. Finally she prayed over some barley and handed it to those nearest to her. She also blessed the people who knelt before her by touching them on the shoulders, head and back with the dagger and *dorje* or thunderbolt symbol which are the sacred ritual instruments of Buddhism. She came out of her trance as noisily as she had entered it and slumped in an exhausted, frail-looking bundle amongst the cushions.

The pilgrims filed from the room. I sat in silence with some local women on the smooth mud floor. The oracle's daughter seized a bellows and fanned the yak dung fire in the great black stove. She offered large mugs of hot sweet tea to everyone in the room. We watched as the oracle folded her ceremonial clothes and placed them neatly in a box. She then turned towards us and dissolved the tension which had gripped the gathering with a wide smile.

She spoke to me through a Ladakhi friend who acted as an interpreter. We chatted about the hazards of mountain travel and I told her about the injuries that I had sustained in a recent car accident on a treacherous road nearby. Before I left she handed me some barley and a chain of coloured threads to protect me on dangerous trails and to keep bad luck at bay. In a land where paralysed men get up and dance, the westerner soon learns to adopt the native's ways.

DANCE AT AN ESKIMO SETTLEMENT

Gerald V. Kuss

The most marvellous dance I ever attended in my life was in a small Eskimo settlement called Umanak, on the west coast of Greenland. Umanak has a population of 800 souls and twice that number of husky dogs. It also has a dance in the parish hall every Saturday night, scheduled to start at midnight. I had to climb up about 2,000 feet from sea level to the dancehall, a timber building measuring about twenty-four feet by ten. On the way I ran the gauntlet of hundreds of dogs, all foraging for food, because the Eskimos do not believe in feeding their dogs in summer when they are not called upon to work. The hungry dogs, incidentally, are not averse to eating the odd human, an event regarded by the Eskimos as a kind of traffic hazard.

Inside the dancehall, the Eskimos waited patiently for the dance band to arrive. There must have been at least eighty persons crowded into the hall, and they were segregated according to sex, the males on one side, the females on the other. While the young men wore more traditional European clothes, the girls were anything but stereotyped in dress. Some wore stiff, sealskin, full-length boots, trousers make from dog-skins and blouses of string beads. When they walked, their gait was like that of some female Frankenstein monster. The pop group, called incidentally the Umanak Beatles, were an hour and a half late in arriving, but no one seemed to mind this. When at last they turned up, three young men, they got down to business immediately.

One had an accordion, another unwrapped a set of drums, while the third was unburdened: he was the group's canary. The accordionist slung the instrument across his shoulders, and his small and beautifully shaped fingers raced up and down the keyboard in a manner which, I considered, indicated the expert. The man on the skins, his Beatle-style hairdo sticking out in all directions like a terrified porcupine, faced his array of drums like an Eskimo hunter about to attack a polar bear. Suddenly a chord of music shattered the fog of the overcrowded room — we were off!

The young men on one side of the room rose and descended on the girls on the other side like an avalanche; they pulled them onto the floor and began to dance the first number which, although played in polka tempo, was instantly recognisable. I had heard it many times as a child and it went like this:

> When we are married we'll have sausages for tea, sausages
> for tea, sausages for tea,
>
> When we are married we'll have sausages for tea, sausages
> for te-e-e-e.

On they played, the Umanak Beatles, verse after verse. The man on the skins whacked away for further orders, bashing the cymbals noisily at the end of each verse, as though he were harpooning an elephant seal. The first dance lasted about twenty minutes — non-stop. Then there was a ten-second pause, after which the Beatles played a foxtrot that was already antiquated in the early 1930s. This too lasted for twenty minutes, and wore out many of the sealskin-booted Eskimo girls. Dance number three was a repetition of dance number one, yes, my old friend, 'Sausages for te-e-e-e'. One polka and one foxtrot comprised the total repertoire of the Umanak Beatles.

The dance continued for more than an hour. When the atmosphere in the room became as dangerous as that of the celebrated Black Hole of Calcutta, I struggled over to a window and flung it open. Outside, the night was rent by the howlings and yowlings of hundreds of dogs; one beast came right under the window beneath me, thrust his neck up into the air and bayed piteously. Apparently it did not think much of this new sound being produced by the Umanak Beatles. Just when the dancers were getting their second wind — and I was wondering if I would survive the experience — the musicians decided they were not being sufficiently appreciated. Without warning, they wrapped up their instruments, heaved them onto their backs and left.

No one seemed the slightest bit surprised by this sudden break-up of the evening's entertainment. They waited until the orchestra members had left, and then they, too, squeezed their way out through the narrow door and walked slowly downhill to the settlement houses perched on the rocks like shadowy toadstools. Doors banged noisily to indicate that, as far as the family was concerned, the day was over. Outside, the dogs howled and bayed and foraged, fruitlessly, for the sausages for te-e-e-e promised by the Umanak Beatles.

VERONA, 1990

Áine Mulvey

It was midday in August 1990 and I was seated at the top row of the steps in the Arena di Verona. The sun beat down fiercely on me and 3,000 other singers, arrayed in rows, spread out like an eagle in the Arena. Far, far down below us, the Moscow Philharmonic Orchestra sounded like a distant brass band, and our conductor, the internationally renowned Lorin Maazel, struggled to control an enormous choir that sounded more like a football mob than a group of musicians worthy of his baton.

I was one of 3,000 choristers from around the world who had come to perform Verdi's *Requiem* in Verona's Opera festival. Pavarotti was billed as soloist and, from my vantage point at the top of the Arena, I watched him arrive for the rehearsal. Old ladies leaned from balconies calling excitedly, 'Luciano!' and he waved back, magnanimous. His arrival inside the Arena disrupted the entire rehearsal for several minutes while the huge amateur choir went wild.

But the logistics of the immense choir and the enormity of the Arena were causing problems. There was a sound delay of several seconds from one side of the choir to the other – the fugue during the 'Libera me' was disastrous. Unable to hear the orchestra, we must have sounded like some lumbering mammoth, dragging along several seconds after the beat. Lorin Maazel became more and more irritated – I'm sure he must have regretted committing to this ludicrous idea. We were all on holiday, but his professional reputation was on the line.

By the following day, the sound engineers had performed wonders. We could hear the orchestra! The alto line still sounded as if it was coming from the other end of the universe, but it was better. I spent the rehearsal amused at the incongruity of the furious 'Dies irae' sung by a choir where the ladies were dressed in bikini tops and shorts and the men had handkerchiefs knotted over their bald spots.

The first of two *Requiem* concerts was performed against a backdrop of a beautiful Italian evening. As the sun went down, the audience of 25,000 lit candles, and we looked out at a perfect ring of glimmering lights. As the night grew dark, the candles went out slowly, until there was only the darkness of the night, the light of the stars and the mosquitoes that landed on our scores and refused to move before the page turned. It was a magical and funny atmosphere.

We bought the papers the next day and marvelled at the photographs. Someone attempted to translate the Italian review. The gist of it was that the enormous choir was more of a visual spectacle than a musical success, but we could accept this reasonably cheerfully.

After the final concert, a few of us joined dozens of other fans stationed outside Pavarotti's dressing room, hoping for an autograph. He made us wait and most gave up. An hour or so later, there was still no bribing the security guard. So we decided to sing – we were choristers after all! And some moments after our three-part arrangement of 'Danny Boy' had faded out, the message came through: 'Let the singers in.'

We entered his room, momentarily stunned to be in his actual presence. And a vast presence it was too – bigger than he looked on television, dressed in a loud, red and black smoking jacket. Pavarotti was the soul of benevolence, dispensing autographs with wry charm and patiently posing for photos – an occupation that must have been as dull for him as it was riveting for us.

Dizzy with success, we sang our way down the cobbled streets to the piazza where the rest of our contingent had retired for a post-concert glass of wine. Jubilantly we boasted of the photos we had taken and proudly displayed our autographed programmes.

When I look at the photo now, I smile at the girl with the mile-wide grin, arm around Pavarotti's huge shoulder, clearly delighted with herself. Still – it remains a beloved memento of the time when I sang Verdi's *Requiem* with the Moscow Philharmonic on a balmy Italian night lit by stars and candles.

SALOME AT THE
OPERA HOUSE, VIENNA

Kevin McDermott

Is it any wonder that Oscar Wilde was drawn to the story of Salome? I
see it appealing to his taste for the grotesque, all those lurid ingredients
– obsessive desire, eroticism, the fear of the flesh, revenge, a bizarre
dénouement. Salome addressing the severed head of John the Baptist,
kissing it, caressing it – and the gruesome, murderous ending. Right up
Oscar's street, wouldn't you say? Not one for understatement, our
beloved Oscar.

And when Richard Strauss used the play as the libretto for his 1905
opera, the effect was explosive – 'blasphemy', 'infamy', 'pornography',
the protesters cried.

Richard and Oscar. The odd couple. Both publicly humiliated –
Oscar for the 'crime' of homosexuality ('I never saw sad men who
looked/With such a wistful eye/Upon that little tent of blue/We prisoners call the sky') and poor Richie, in his eighties, undergoing a
process of de-Nazification.

How savagely our civilised world upholds its values; how deeply we
fear our artists.

I thought of Oscar Wilde and Richard Strauss when I sat amid the
splendour of the Opera House in Vienna, attending a performance of
Salome, as a shaft of blue light from the stage fell on the rapt and beautiful face of a woman in the audience upon whom my gaze was trained.

A week before, I had paid €7 to sit in a litter-strewn cinema in Dublin and here I was, having paid €9, sitting in a box in one of the finest opera houses in Europe. €9. A cinema seat in Dublin. A seat in the opera house in Vienna. *Quel dilemme.*

To be honest, I wasn't sure what our €9 had secured for us. So when we handed our tickets to a young hussar, we were delighted when he invited us to ascend the wonderful baroque staircase. To walk there, among the good citizens of Vienna, dressed up to the nines in their fur coats and gold jewellery, was worth the admission charge alone. And then, another hussar directed us to our box. We occupied the second row, with a full view of the auditorium and a partial view of the orchestra and stage.

No matter, for when the curtain rose and Strauss's magnificent music filled the auditorium, we were transported. An hour and forty minutes of enchantment. 'Your skin,' Salome tells the prophet, 'is as white as the snow of Judea.'

Afterwards, we followed the fur coats to a coffee house, The Landtmann, where Sigmund Freud was wont to sit of an afternoon, unravelling dreams. We sat opposite a maharajah, whose vermilion silk robes were embroidered with golden thread. It seemed apt, somehow, after the extravagance of *Salome.*

Snatches of conversation drifted our way.

'Had she not married him,' the maharani told her prince, 'she would have ended up a common housewife selling cosmetics in Bombay.'

I'm not sure what makes art great. I'm not sure what makes a great artist. I do know, however, that listening to Richard Strauss's *Salome* in the opera house in Vienna, on a weekend when the marble city was covered in snow, was a glorious reminder of the human capacity to create beauty – a reminder of the power of art to put us in touch with our best selves – and to take us beyond ourselves.

And I salute you and I thank you, Richard, Oscar.

I HEAR YOU CALLING ME

Marie MacSweeney

I admit to being a bit of a sceptic where car-boot sales are concerned. I distrust the tall tales of those who claim to have captured prize pieces at such events – a Meissen plate, for instance, unrecognised as such by the seller, and secured for just a few shillings, or a fine porcelain vase which made its way from the Orient over several, history-laden centuries, and was then offered to bored punters for peanuts. Such bargains never come my way. And why on earth, I ask, should they always bypass me?

Recently these thoughts came unbidden to my mind when I was invited to support a car-boot sale, and were instantly dismissed when I heard of the charity involved. I turned up at the venue, wandered around for a while until I came to a stall carrying a selection of records. After a nostalgic rummage among the 78s, I moved to more recent times – and vinyl LPs. It was there that I found my treasure – an early recording of our own Irish tenor, Dermot Troy. It was made by the Avoca Record company of Brooklyn, New York, and included such favourites as 'She Is Far From The Land', 'At The Mid Hour of Night' and 'The Lark In The Clear Air'.

When I played the record later that evening I was both thrilled and saddened to hear again the voice I had heard sing out over those famous crowds in Crumlin many decades ago.

You see, although born in Wicklow, Dermot was regarded as a 'home-grown' boy by the people of Crumlin. And after a short career in the RAF he began to nurture his vocal talent, studying at the Royal Irish Academy of Music and winning the prestigious Caruso Competition in 1952. As a result he was invited to join the Glyndebourne Chorus, and this was followed by a three-year stint at Covent Garden. He also carried out a successful tour of Germany over a period of several years, and his playing of Lensky in Tchaikovsky's *Eugene Onegin*, performed in April 1962, was his last performance. He died in September of the same year at the tragically young age of thirty-five. But on one of Dermot's visits home, his fame having preceded him, crowds collected outside his home in Cashel Road in Crumlin. And I was among the many youngsters there, attracted by the glamour and excitement of the occasion, and determined to help provide a decent 'Welcome Home' for the local boy-made-good. For his part, Dermot repaid his friends, neighbours and fans by singing for us. He stood just inside the open front window of the upstairs bedroom and sang, his sweet powerful voice rising like a prayer on the evening air.

I can't recall which songs he selected on that balmy night, but in listening to my newly acquired record, I fancied he finished up with the song 'I Hear You Calling Me'.

> I hear you calling me.
> You called me when the moon hath veiled her light,
> before I went from you into the night.
> I came, do you remember, back to you,
> for one last kiss, beneath the kind stars' light.

THE SHOFAR

Judith Mok

Ten thousand candles would be lit in the Portuguese Synagogue in Amsterdam. I promised my little daughter a feast of light during our walk from home to the synagogue. She wasn't exactly looking forward to sitting upstairs behind railings in the women's only section of that building. A religious ceremony was normally not part of our lives. But on this day of Yom Kippur, I thought it important for her to experience the spectacle of a Jewish feast day in one of the most beautiful synagogues in the world, as well as listening to the Kol Nidrei, the blowing of the shofar, the ram's horn, to soothe all evil spirits.

She met some of her girlfriends in the street just as I was pointing out the stone pelican above the side entrance. It was the symbol of Sephardic Jews during the seventeenth century. They had to get into this immense building through a side door, as Jews were not allowed to have a main entrance to their place of worship on a busy public road. The little girls shrugged and ran inside the courtyard through the now-open main entrance. I followed with the Mummies, all dressed up and coiffed for the occasion. In the obscure light upstairs there was a lot of gold on display around wrists and necks. Some women were wearing perfumed furs and old-fashioned hats that made me wonder what people would have looked like back then.

The synagogue was built by Suasso and Pereira and Da Pinto with the money they had earned by financing both sides in the wars between the Dutch and Spanish armies. These Sephardic aristocrats became wealthy supplying both armies and were allowed to build their mansions on the outer canals of the city of Amsterdam. The inner circle of canals remained closed to Jews until the nineteenth century. But their money was good enough for the Spanish King Philip or the Dutch Prince, William of Orange. Across the road from the Ashkenazi Shul, the other synagogue, a new and magnificent building, was erected. To this day there is no electric light in the main hall.

Some of my ancestors came to Amsterdam when they fled the Spanish Inquisition. Now, while I was staring down at the Orthodox men swaying back and forth in prayer and chant, I imagined my remote ancestors sitting up here with their daughters shifting impatiently in their seats. We were sitting so far away from the ceremony that there was plenty of opportunity for gossiping and sizing up each other's clothes.

I, who did not have the slightest notion of the religious aspects of this ceremony, was concentrating on my immediate surroundings. Now, a lot of the girls and women had curly, fair hair, but back then there must have been a lot of luscious, dark, Spanish hair and eyes behind the bars we were allowed to look through. And the women would have pointed out the future husbands to their daughters. I peered down intensely to see if there was some charming little boy hopping, or rather, swaying, around down there. But to no avail.

A bearded man came forward with the long ram's horn and blew the theme of Kol Nidrei. It was as if the sound haunted itself in between these ancient walls. Even my child grew quiet. For a moment, then, I had lost her again, in her red hat and coat, curls dancing on her back. She had disappeared down the rickety stairs. Probably to play hide and seek in the courtyard. I waved to my friends and left as well.

Down in the courtyard, a crowd had gathered. A group of older people dressed in their warm coats and hats, survivors of the camps or other atrocities, were chatting away and continuously turning this or that way to greet acquaintances and friends. Children and grandchildren were introduced and admired while I tried to get hold of my offspring.

And there he was; the wonderful, kind old man who recognised me and took my hands in his with tears in his eyes. And this is your daughter, he said, smiling at my pretty rascal, now hatless, who had appeared. He told her how he cherished the great books her grandfather had written. She seemed surprised and smiled at him, giggled when he told her a funny story about her grandmother. He stroked her hair gently, embraced me and walked away with the weight of centuries on his shoulders. I felt good. Just by remembering my parents, my own life had been lit up again. With at least ten thousand candles.

KALO PASKA

Fionnuala Brennan

Only sometimes do the Western Christian and Orthodox Easters co-incide; this year, 2008, there is a difference of over a month. Greek Easter is on 27 April and the next time that we celebrate Easter together will be on 4 April 2010.

The reason for the difference in the timing of Easter in the Western and Eastern traditions lies in different church calendars. We go by the Gregorian calendar, while our Greek and Russian Orthodox brethren follow the Julian calendar. In both traditions, Easter must be celebrated one month after the Jewish Passover, which is on the first Sunday after the first full moon after the Spring Equinox, not earlier than 21 March. As for calculating in either tradition when Easter will fall on any partic-ular year, one would need a degree in higher maths or the like to work out such, to me, mysterious factors as the Golden Number and some-thing called an 'epact' which apparently is to do with the age of the moon at certain times of the year. I am happy to leave such calculations to whomever it concerns.

A new method for calculating the date of Easter, discussed by the World Council of Churches and the Middle East Council of Churches in Aleppo, Syria in 1997, could have resolved the differences had it been put into practice in 2001 when the Julian and Gregorian Easters co-incided, but the Russian Orthodox Church especially was reluctant to change, having already experienced a schism caused by the calendar issue.

Another difference between the Eastern and Western practice of Christianity is the fact that Easter, not Christmas, is the major feast in the Orthodox rite. We will not be in Greece this year to celebrate *Paska* with our friends, but we will be with them in spirit. We will be thinking of our old friends, Maria and Arsenia, who, for the duration of Lent, do not eat meat, fish, dairy or poultry, nor does Maria cook with olive oil. They enjoy the end of the fast all the more.

As usual this year, they will attend all the great preparations during *Megali Evdomada* — Holy Week. Maria, who is a sprightly ninety, will go the magnificent fifth-century Byzantine Church of the *Ekatonapiliani*, the Church of the Hundred Doors, as it is colloquially called, with her daughter Arsenia and her many grandchildren on *Megali Pempti* — Holy Thursday. They will be back for the Good Friday ceremonies when the icon of Christ is taken down from the cross, wrapped in linen and placed in a flower-covered casket symbolising the tomb of Christ. With the rest of the congregation, they will follow the bier through the village streets lamenting the death of Jesus.

They will, of course, stay up for the midnight mass on Easter Saturday. On that night, the great church is in darkness until the Paschal candle is lit by the priests and the flame passed from candle to candle throughout the congregation until the church is ablaze with flickering gold. The priest sings out, '*Christos Anesti*' — Christ is risen — to which the audience replies in one voice '*Alethios Anesti*' — truly, He is risen.

Fireworks explode in the church courtyard and the congregation files out into the night, shielding the flames of their candles in the hope they will make it home before they are snuffed so that they can mark the sign of the cross over their door to protect the house for another year.

Then Maria and her family will sit down at a laden table to break their fast with *mageritsa* — a wholesome soup made with lamb sweetmeats and egg and lemon sauce. Later that day, the family will enjoy *kokoretsi* — lamb cooked over a spit. Maria will have baked the traditional Easter bread *tsoureki* in which she will have embedded *paskalina avga* — red-coloured hard-boiled eggs. The family will crack these with those sitting beside them at the table, and the one who holds the last uncracked egg will be the lucky one for the next year. The feasting will go on all day. The sun will be shining and the wild flowers will be blooming. I wish we were there to wish them all *Kalo Paska*.

EASTER

Pat Donlan

I sometimes find myself muttering that centuries-old chant, 'Ah, things were different then.' But they *were* different. Even Easter smelt and sounded different. The strange silence of Good Friday – my father swearing that even the birds stopped singing between twelve and three o'clock – followed by the bells of Easter day: St Patrick's Cathedral, Christchurch, St Nicholas of Myra... Did sounds travel farther then, or could I really have heard them all together? And then the smells...

There is a cold smell to Easter that is linked forever in my memories to furious activity as my mother, in a temper of spring-cleaning, attacked everything in sight. Floors were scrubbed with great cakes of Sunlight soap, to be polished with Mansion polish – and the only relief for a skulking child was to be allowed skate around with old cloths tied to shoes. There were seemingly endless days of this fierce activity, as tired curtains and cushion covers were laundered and mangled, leaving home a curiously denuded and comfortless place. This daytime activity was matched by the sound of the sewing machine whirring and clacking late into the night as old dresses were remodelled and new ones created, for custom dictated that we wear something new to mass on Easter Sunday.

One Easter we went shopping to Pims or Maceys to buy my first shop-bought outfit, a blue 'costume' with a dark velvet collar. Nothing since has matched the excitement and feeling of sophistication, never mind that its pleated skirt started down at my ankles (you'll grow into it) and ended up loathed and well above my knees as I feared I would never grow out of it.

I was a particular fan of *Girl's Crystal* and *Girl* comics, devouring their contents. *Girl* had a feature I loved as it fed my fantasy of being creative. it was headed 'Mother Tells You How' and starred a paragon mother, Superwoman's ancestor, and her perfect family of husband, clever daughter Judy and baby Robin. Each week Mother instructed in some crafty enterprise usually inspired by the seasons. For some reason Easter exercised her greatly and Mother told how to bake a simnel cake, make an Easter bonnet, create a clever brooch for your Easter outfit, make Easter decorations, greeting cards and Easter novelties — novelties for goodness sake!

All of these were shown to my dubious mother, who sniffed in derision at such nonsense and wondered out loud if all that reading was really good for me, and what in the name of all that's good and holy was a simnel cake, and by the way have you done your homework? But I hankered after all these things and years later when my own daughters arrived, baked my first simnel cake and loved the symbolism of the eleven golden marzipan eggs, one of each of the disciples, excluding Judas. And I learned the reason why such a cake full of eggs should celebrate Easter, for eggs were forbidden during Lent and brought to church to be blessed on Easter Sunday as a symbol of rebirth and resurrection. Best of all I added to that old cold smell of Easter new smells of cinnamon, almonds and marzipan.

ICE CREAM IN THE SNOW

Maureen Charlton

My mother had a strong aversion to the twentieth century. What she might have made of this one, only heaven can tell! An exile in the present, she imperiously disdained all the gadgets and labour-saving devices which a Dublin suburban semi had to offer when we were transplanted there from the country. She brought with her all the customs and ways of times past, familiar from her rural upbringing.

The move to Dublin had come about when my father had taken up a post as principal of a Dublin southside national school and our new home offered all the important inventions of modern times. Candles, after all, had long been obsolete!

Lights switched on and off, a three-ring electric cooker stood gleaming and pristine in the kitchen and yet — winter and summer, in heatwave or cold snap — a fire blazed in the dining room with an ungainly kettle bubbling on the hob. Potatoes were baked there in their jackets and often an Irish stew in an ancient black pot. Nor were pop-up toasters needed when you could skewer a piece of bread and in a flash have a most delectable slice of toast.

Electric blankets and the humble rubber hot-water bottle were unheard-of luxuries. For, to keep chilly little toes warm and snug on winter nights, a brick reposed in the glowing embers as exercises were got through around the dining-room table. When bedtime came the brick was wrapped in an old piece of blanket and accompanied us to our chilly bedrooms.

Our iron was, of course, made of iron and heated on that ever-gleaming dining-room fire. But children are natural conformists and, when I went to the homes of my pals, I used to watch with a mixture of wonder and envy as kettles were plugged in and miraculously boiled.

But the thing I most envied in those kitchens of yesteryear was that gleaming white cupboard humming away happily to itself in winter and simmer – the fridge. How lucky those kids were! I ruefully thought that they could have ice cream whenever the fancy took them, when we would have to cadge the money and scamper off to the local shop for a twopenny or fourpenny wafer.

But my mother even triumphed over this contraption. Only once in my memory, it must be said, and yet, what a delightful memory, viewed however mistily along the corridor of time.

A cold spell set in after one Christmas and that first night we could hear the snow falling faintly and faintly falling, as Joyce so memorably puts it. And next morning – a miracle. A gleaming, wonderful, white world. A soft, fluffy, white fitted-carpet which nature's workmen had obligingly installed over our back garden.

There was no time to be lost. My mother set to. Eggs and cream were whisked. The remaining drops of the Christmas sherry were added and the mixture was placed in a bowl and buried in the snow. And in a few hours it had turned into delicious ice cream.

The Italians are credited with the invention of this scrumptious dessert, as they are with so many other wonderful things – aqueducts and aeroplanes, Olivettis and Vespas. Manly creations. But I bet it was some Italian mama, deep in the heart of the Dolomites, who first thought of ice cream in the snow.

AT HOME WITH DIOR

Frances Donoghue

In the autumn of 1947 the fashion house of Dior lit up Europe's post-war austerity with something called the New Look. A female population starved of fashion for six years fell on it hungrily. Hemlines dropped from knee- almost to ankle-length, skirts were huge and circular, swinging in bias cut from tiny nipped-in waists. Blouses had dramatic puffed sleeves, or ruffled collars. Everything billowed, in fact, except at the strategic points where the female shape was indented. It was a mass expression of release after the harsh, tailored outlines of wartime clothes. Fabric was used in reckless quantity – I remember how guilty I felt at carving up a whole four yards of material to make one of those swinging skirts.

That summer I had been au pairing in France, the usual fundraising device of the hard-up student. En route back to Dublin in September I found Paris in a state of delicious anticipation of the Dior first showings; there had been hype and rumours in the magazines for weeks, but the actual clothes hadn't yet been unveiled. I conceived an outrageous ambition to be there on one of the famous little gold chairs at this moment in fashion history. It took ingenuity, neck and a couple of downright lies to achieve this.

I presented myself to the Madame of the salon, a creature of awesome elegance. I represented an important women's journal in Dublin, I said, whose readers were even now posted at every newsagent waiting for the revelations of Monsieur Dior. I provided the name of a real magazine, confident that no emissary from Dublin would be there to show me up as an impostor. I clutched my student briefcase authoritatively. Her scanty English discouraged her from enquiring too closely into my credentials. Anyway my youth and total lack of personal style (I think I was wearing my duffel coat) would not have suggested a fashion pirate. I was waved in with a mixture of hauteur and indulgence to join the élite on the little gold chairs.

The salon, quite tiny, baked under its chandeliers. No runway, there wasn't space. The models swooped and minced amongst us to a background of elegant string music. I had never imagined creatures so rarefied and beautiful, with their handspan waists and fragile ankles on three-inch heels. The make-up of the day was frankly theatrical – flawless pancaked faces, false eyelashes, scarlet slashed lipstick. Fabulous meringues of hats topped the tailored suits, nipped in or peplumed. The long pencil skirts flashed sexy seamed stocking legs through the deep slits which were necessary to let the model move. The extravaganza ballroom dresses had minimal glittering tops, like Barbie dolls, and skirts so voluminous that the girls had to scoop them in their arms as they swayed through us and then release them in one magnificent pirouette just before they disappeared offstage.

When the last model, in a puff-ball wedding gown, had released her frothy skirts and thrown her flowers into the audience there was a polite stampede on the portly Christian Dior, now bowing and embracing a couple of his most stunning girls and looking very complacent, as well he might. The fashion writers and the rich customers cooed and shrieked and kissed the air around each other's faces. I did not wait for the free champagne and canapés; I thought I had pushed my luck sufficiently for one day.

CHANGING TIMES

Tommy Sands

My father was not, by any stretch of the imagination, a violent man. With one rare lapse, however, in 1960, he managed to cut off all relations between our house and the rest of the world.

In August 1960, he coolly picked up the biggest knife in the kitchen and stabbed our old wet battery wireless in the speaker. He followed this up by throwing a cup of tea in its face, soaking such far-flung stations as Stockholm, Oslo, Frankfurt and London with hot, wet tea leaves. His general target on that occasion was Athlone, the headquarters of Ireland's national radio station, and Micheál O'Hehir, the brilliant sports commentator, in particular.

'Take that, ye karn ye,' he roared. 'And that, you knob-faced knur,' he shouted, delivering a bare-knuckled blow to its hitherto smiling dial.

It was all because of a Gaelic football match. Down was trailing by two points against Offaly. It had been a bruising All-Ireland Senior Championship semi-final. There were just a few minutes left in the game and James McCartan, the dynamic Down centre-half forward, had been downed in the square. Paddy Doherty was getting ready to take the penalty kick. All around Croke Park, you could cut the tension with a knife. Around our table, things were no less fraught and a bread knife that usually cut simple soda farls for quiet country people was lying relaxed and innocent nearby.

O'Hehir was almost hoarse with excitement. 'Paddy Doherty is now standing back to take the penalty. His socks are down around his ankles. The crowd is hushed ...'

At that moment, the whole population of County Down, it seemed, was either in Croke Park or gathered around a wireless like ours, teething prayers and threats alike to saints and other holy people who might have influence on Providence in such times as these.

'Can Doherty score this and save the day for Down and put them into their first-ever All-Ireland final in history?' O'Hehir went on breathlessly. 'He's placing the ball on the fourteen-yard line ... this could be the most important kick of his life ... the most important kick in the life of County Down ... he's stepping back now ... the crowd are holding their breath ... here he comes ...' O'Hehir lowered his voice to a whisper. 'He puts his head to one side in that familiar style ... a hush has fallen over the crowd ... here he comes ...'

There was deathly silence. We stopped breathing, waiting for the kick. We waited and waited ... and waited.

But Paddy Doherty never got the ball kicked in our house. Our wireless had stopped breathing too. The wet battery had run out. It needed to be charged again but not in the manner that it was being charged, battered, butted and knifed by my father.

'You dirty, rotten treacherous two-faced son of a bitch's ghost of an excuse for a wireless,' he roared, with lefts and rights to AFN Frankfurt and the BBC Home Service. 'If you were playing that pop rubbitch on Radio Luxembourg, you wouldn't break down. I houl ye, wouldn't ye not!'

Perhaps we had the volume turned up too loud. Liam Daly told us later that high volume could drain the power out of a battery. Others said that even a wireless could suffer the effects of tension, which, in turn, could have drained the battery. And then there was the weak signal from Radio Éireann. If the game had been broadcast on BBC Northern Ireland, it would have been clearer and less work for the old wireless, but the BBC never broadcast Gaelic games.

As it happened, Paddy Doherty scored that penalty and Down had qualified for its first-ever All-Ireland final, but we wouldn't know that until the next morning when Jack Grant would come with the *Irish Press* and the groceries in Gorman's lorry.

We decided that we would go to Dublin for the final, just to be sure, and hopefully we'd see for the first time a team from the Six Counties win the All-Ireland Senior Championship.

It would be an unforgettable expedition. Josie Shevlin from Armagh said she would take us in her car. We would all go, even my mother. With egg sandwiches, flasks of tea and a red and black flag we had sown together from a dress belonging to my mother and an old soutane belonging to Father Hugh, we headed for the border. All along the way, through the counties of Armagh, Louth, Meath and Dublin, Down flags hung from every tree, in support of the Wee North against the mighty Kingdom of Kerry. We went to the red church in Drumcondra, near Dublin airport, for eight o'clock mass. There were Kerry people in the congregation too, who would be expecting a different result from God. He had already delivered them nineteen All-Irelands. Down had been given none.

'Maybe,' I respectfully suggested to God, 'it is time for a change.'

We were waiting outside the gates of Croke Park from 9.30 a.m., along with thousands of others, singing and swapping sandwiches. At 1.30 p.m. we crushed in and got carried away with the crowd to a heavenly spot, right down beside the wire under the Cusack Stand, and there, in a kind of euphoric trance, we witnessed one of the most memorable spectacles in the history of Irish sport.

Through the two-inch mesh, twelve-foot-high wire fence, we roared, wailed, wept and cheered as these modern-day Cúchulainns leaped in the air like the very grass was on fire and swept up and down the field like waves of myth and magic. At the end, unable to hold back any longer, we scaled that fence like spiders and sped out on to the Croke Park grassland just to touch the hem of a red and black garment.

Down had beaten Kerry and, amid unimaginable celebrations, Kevin Mussen, the captain, carried the Sam Maguire Cup across the border. For a long time, there was no work done on the farms around Ryan, and that victory united Catholic and Protestant for many weeks and the whole of the County Down walked on air.

My father's attack on the wireless that year cut us off from the outside world for many weeks, until Hugh and myself walked the battery two miles up the Crossan Road to Mrs Linden's shop to get it charged. More than thirty years later, her grandson Mickey Linden would lead Down to further All-Ireland victories and I would write a song with my son Fionán as we watched a new generation train in Kilbroney Park, Rostrevor, under the watchful eye of Pete McGrath. Every evening they ran up and down the side of Slieve Martin to Cloch Mór, the big stone thrown there by Fionn mac Cumhaill to dislodge Benandonner, the icy giant from the wintry north. They seemed to be suffering sweatfully for the very hills that were rising around them, to bring a sparkle of light to a loved homeland in a year of hate and a time of darkness.

> The cheering like thunder rolled
> The flags they flew from every pole
> And we sang and danced the whole way home
> On the day we won the All-Ireland.

When the wireless returned, however, it was never the same again. The newsreader, Charles Mitchell, seemed to be talking through his nose, or like a man who had been shocked by a sudden 'dig in the bake'. But he talked on regardless, and we heard news of John Fitzgerald Kennedy being elected president of the United States and scientists talking about exploring the moon. The whole world was changing.

SWIMMING LESSONS

Leo Cullen

We had moved to Dublin, my father, brothers and sisters and I, in 1967. He had bought an enormous old house in decline near the sea at Monkstown and his idea was that he would convert it into flats. We would live in one of them and he would let out the others for an income. There was one flat in the basement with sitting tenants. That was a part of the house that could not be converted. The Sullivans would not budge, but I was not aware of that. I had become friendly with them that summer. In their kitchen I ate Maltana, a juicy loaf soaked with sultanas – the staple diet of Dubliners, as far as I could tell – and I sang with them from their radio the songs of Engelbert Humperdinck – the staple songs, as far as I could tell. My father employed a man named Oliver, a Longford man who claimed he could put his hands to anything, and that included ridding a house of dry rot, of rising damp and of unwanted tenants. I was supposed to be Oliver's helper and henchman.

Then came a late summer day when, baked by the heat and feeling suddenly hot right into the very core of my being, an idea flew into my mind. It came slap in the middle of a Maltana afternoon with the Sullivans. It was not just the heat that had got to me. It was more; maybe the long summer of dry rot and rising damp had got to me at last. Maybe I'd had enough of Maltana and inactivity and the criticisms of Oliver who, right at that moment, I was supposed to be helping with the knocking of a wall. Maybe I resented the Sullivans making implications about my father and about his designs for the house. Maybe I'd had just enough of my own disloyalty to him. I don't know what it was. But the moment the words came out of me, I knew I had made a mistake: 'Let's go for a swim,' I said, even as I remembered I could not swim a stroke.

'Good idea,' said the Sullivan boys. 'Let's go.' The Sullivans could swim. And the Sullivans' friend Luggy, who went everywhere with them and who was my mortal enemy since I'd come to live in Dublin at summer's beginning, could also swim. Luggy, whose name came from the lugworm bait he dug out of the sand. Down we descended with skimpy togs and towels, down on a tide way out on the flat beach of Seapoint, out, it seemed, as far as Howth. A cold breeze ripped in, skinning my white legs. After the sticky heat of the Sullivans' flat, I felt the sudden chill. I walked out until the water was halfway up my thighs. Stringy lengths of floating seaweed kept getting in my way. It was a slow business. I wasn't sure of my footing and the waves splashed up at me, making me draw my breath while I tried to keep my balance. Then I ducked down, and after a wave swooshed into my mouth, I thought I'd had enough and might return to the shore. But Luggy was behind me. The sawn-off trousers he wore for togs were now wet and hung from him, making him look like a salty, partially dressed scarecrow.

'You're not swimmin',' he said. And he was right. I had been crawling, hands and feet pegging along the muddy sand at the sea bottom.

Maybe it was because of the new element of salt water all about me, but I did not think of it as surrender when I capitulated to Luggy. 'No, I'm not able,' I said. 'Will you teach me?'

It was an admission, yes, but a clever one. By asking for his help, I was defending myself against his jibes.

Luggy taught me how to swim. He was just as vicious in the sea as out of it, but in there I was somehow buffeted from him. In the gulpy cold water and with the cries of the strand only a faint rumble in my ears each time I went under, the lungs took over from the thinking parts of the body. Every day for the remainder of a week in September that my father called an 'Indian summer', we went swimming and I had lessons. Luggy's face went black with cold and his arms around my waist holding me up in the water went hard as wire ropes. 'Kick, kick, you culchie,' he said. 'I'm not leaving the sea until you swim because you are only a culchie.' He was punishing me. By the end of that month, when only elderly people came down to bathe, in what I heard them say was the iodine, I had learned to swim and also to dive. It was no good just swimming with the Sullivans. Diving on the full tide was the business.

Luggy still hated me. Given half a chance he would still have had a crack at me. He was one of the world's great haters, and nothing much could be done about it. But I had learned to swim and learned to dive. The sea was my element. The sea was the place where all ... what was it ... all responsibility washed away. Learning to swim, after all, had not been a mistake. Oliver from Longford looked at me each day on my return as though I were a strange animal with fins and a tail.

'Swimming,' he said. 'Getting into that sea. I don't know what this world is coming to. And all the work here waiting to be done for your father.'

Swimming. That was only the start of it. All through one's life one is bullied, or one bullies oneself, into the learning of diversions that become essential to survival.

THE DEVIL WALKS

Fachtna Ó Drisceoil

> Now over Polegate vastly sets the sun;
> Dark rise the Downs from darker looking elms,
> And out of Southern railway trains to tea
> Run happy boys down various Station Roads,
> Satchels of homework jogging on their backs,
> So trivial and so healthy in the shade
> Of these enormous Downs.

For me, John Betjeman's poem, 'Original Sin on the Sussex Coast', always brings to mind the seemingly innocent scene of two boys playing football on the lawn behind a large Victorian-era house. One of them, tall, handsome and fair-haired, about ten years old. The other, a bit older, dark-haired, large and overweight, but strong. But there is another boy here, hunched glumly on a garden seat at the back of the house, fair-haired also but smaller than the others, watching them warily and making no move to join them. It is my ten-year-old self.

While the other boys are bathed in sunshine, I am in the shadow of the house, its redbrick walls looming high behind me. The tall fair-haired boy we will call Edward, not his real name, the son of friends of my parents. My mother works outside the home, so I am often collected from school by Edward's mother and spend much time in his house. My parents are very grateful to Edward's mother for this. The other boy is Robert, a neighbour of Edward's. I can tell from the recurrent whispered conferences on the lawn that they are plotting against me, so I ignore their pleas for me to join them. They put on an obviously staged diplay of laughter and enjoyment in an attempt to entice me, but still I hold out. They even appeal to Edward's mother in the kitchen, but she doesn't intervene.

Finally, they abandon their pretence and make their way over to me. 'Come with us or else,' they command, their fists threatening, their voices menacing. I could have shouted out to get the mother's attention, but I didn't. Meekly and fearfully, I surrendered myself to their custody, allowing them to escort me down to the back of the garden. Perhaps Edward's mother saw us and smiled at the seemingly benign scene of childhood friendship. They forced me to climb a wall with them into the back garden of Robert's house. There was an old shed here, one door allowing access from the garden, the other opening out into a laneway behind it. I was taken in and Edward locked the door behind me. It was a dark and dirty place, the single window covered in grime, rusty paint tins on the shelves and a bunch of yellowed newspapers on the ground. My captors began ridiculing me, hurling abuse at me. I stood mutely in front of them, humiliated, scared.

Eventually, they tired of this sport and looked for a new way to use me for their entertainment. In one corner was a large, blackened and oily wooden box turned upside down. There was something alive inside it, for the sound of scraping claws and growling could be heard from within. Edward went over to the box and lifted it up. A pair of frenzied eyes leapt forward out of the darkness but fell back again in a whine of pain as Edward kicked at them. I could just about make out the dirtied white and shaggy fur of some type of mongrel, a dog bred in terror, stench and darkness. Edward turned his attention towards me.

'Get in there quick,' he shouted. My first reaction – shock, for even I was surprised at how far they meant to go this time. I had known fear before, but now my stomach was sick, my body tense with a new and unfamiliar terror.

What happened next took all of us by surprise.

I heard myself shouting at them that I wouldn't do it, I wouldn't get in the dog's box and, as the older and bigger boy came at me, his arms reaching out to grab hold, I found myself striking him as hard I could on the side of his face. He reeled back in pain and shock, calling on Edward to stop me escaping. But not only did Edward step aside, he actually opened the door to let me out, suddenly afraid of my new found willingness to fight back. Suddenly, I was in a blaze of evening sunshine, running up the back laneway, out of harm's way, running home.

> And when they're home,
> When the post-Toasties mixed with Golden Shred
> Make for the kiddies such a scrumptious feast
> Does Mum, the Persil-user, still believe
> That there's no Devil and that youth is bliss?
> As certain as the sun behind the Downs
> And quite as plain to see, the Devil walks.

A SENSE OF PLACE

RETURNING TO THE WEST

Tom Mac Intyre

When I met a Mayo man in Paris who poured out a story to me about fishing for sea trout in Clew Bay – and catching a shark instead – and how a Colonel who was in the punt with him reached for his gun and lost his wooden leg, which leg then hopped over the gunwale and into the water – where the shark dug his teeth into it – and couldn't get free – and how they had to coax the shark home with them then – and so on and so forth – hearing that saga in a room near the Seine, I knew I was on my way, this was The West coming to meet me, with a flourish of wooden legs and shark-teeth and the natural zest of the true tellers of tale and myth.

Other signs and portents: Dublin, town of 'red mackerel and lovely ray' and tricolour over the GPO. I'm not much on patriotism – the national anthem tends to leave me weak at the knees – but the second I hit O'Connell Street, that flag takes my eye. It's likely stretched flat out in a straight westerly: I stop and look up – tranced, wondering, 'What's the strength of that wind? Force five, six, seven? What's the force of it in Connemara? Is there rain before or after it?'

> When the rain's before the wind,
> then your top-sails you must mind.
> When the wind's before the rain,
> hoist your top-sails up again…

And this cluster of questions and calculations inclines towards one key question: will there be a boat? Will the sea be up or the sea down?

It doesn't, mind you, look too bad, four or five at the moment. And, believing in tomorrow, I saunter on.

And, at my ease, because I have eternity, I wander out into the midlands, tasting again the drowsy plenitude of Kildare and Westmeath, and I settle in Portumna – a fine spot – for the night, and in the evening's crack there I realise one thing I've been missing in the few months abroad. A simple matter (the scene is a comfortable and hospitable pub) of a Tipperary man who's come in over the border for the night – and who might sing for us. A stout carpenter and joiner – born for the job – is in charge of the persuading.

'He had a voice,' the carpenter tells me, 'a man's voice, only it left him. Didn't mind it – no matter. If we can persuade him now, you'll get a glimpse of what was. Come on, Mick, give us "Alice Benbow"...'

Mick's a true artist: if he's to be seduced in this matter, then let the seduction scene be a fitting one. The carpenter is in tune with this demand; his blandishments as exquisitely modulated as Mick's responses which move from 'I'm thick with the 'flu', through demi-semi-quavers of willingness to gallant surrender: 'I'll sing for that lovely lady there among ye.' And he sings the three-act tragedy of 'Alice Benbow', weaving and dancing among his listeners as he does, weeping one phrase and laughing the next – while the carpenter, in the wings (but barely) conducts this command performance, his face silently telling me – but that's lost, because the man from Tipp, done with Alice and now into his stride, is singing gaily of the necessity to 'look yourself in the eye' at regular intervals, and as the action unfolds, whirligig, I hear John Synge saying 'there's wonders hidden in the heart of man' – and agree with him – and head for Connemara in the morning, refreshed from Portumna in the vein.

In Galway I buy seed potatoes. In Oughterard a spade. In Clifden a fishing line and lures. I'm in Cleggan and there's a boat, the sea flat calm. I hear a woman say of the weather, 'No harm in it, shure, it's only dry rain.' And a man saying of a woman, 'A delicate woman all her life, and very healthy, if you know what I mean.' The spade is spotted.

'Wonder you didn't get the seed potatoes when you were at it?'

'How'd you know I didn't?'

I like these voices and the colours of expression they have. I let them take me. I'm in The West again, next parish to the enchanted Land Under Waves, and I'm quite at home.

TRAVELLING WEST

Anne Enright

It is easier, they say, to travel west, and I believe them. I have just been around the world, quite literally. Last week, I was around the world. I took a plane to Heathrow and I took a plane that stopped over in Hong Kong, then I got back on it and flew to Auckland, New Zealand, home of the writer Witi Ihimaera, whom I met the last time I dropped into Hong Kong – in March when it was just as smoggy as this time, in May. I was travelling east, the plane was ploughing through the night, and then through another night – you could see it on the little video screen, the plane was overtaking the spin of the earth beneath it. At least I think it was. But I might be wrong, I have little enough grasp of relativity.

I had a lovely time in New Zealand, blinking in the wrong light, at the wrong time of day, waking up bellowing with hunger at 4 a.m. and then fasting through dinner time. A few kilometres outside Auckland, they told me, is the point on the globe that is farthest away from London. I tried to think where the farthest point from Dublin would be, the farthest point from my house in County Wicklow – had I already crossed it? But God knows I can't tell even my left from my right, which is no help at all when you are on the other side of the world, watching a fat moon rise over Auckland and wondering if your children see the same moon, or a new moon, and how can you be so stupid about the world and how it spins and tilts? How can you miss this essential tendency: living meanwhile in the silence that happens when everyone you love is fast asleep, an electronic silence when you lift the phone and put it down again, because you cannot figure out the hours until they wake. You are mathematically lonely. You are, in your brute ignorance of time and tide, all at sea. You cannot tell your North Star from your Southern Cross, despite which, they have let you go off to circumnavigate the globe.

I nipped back west to Australia for a while and then got on another plane east to Auckland and from there east again, crossing the International Date Line on the way – and please don't try to explain the International Date Line to me, whether I lost a day or gained a day – and why it was, for so many, many hours, still Saturday. I have no idea what has happened to my time in the past couple of weeks; am I younger now than I should be, or older?

Auckland to LA where I got off the plane, queued for an hour to be fingerprinted by the American Department of Homeland Security, and just had enough time to dash up to departures and back on to the same plane, same seat, to go to Heathrow. This time, although I might be wrong about this, we stayed in daylight. We seemed to do this by flying towards the North Pole, where light is plentiful at this time of year. The map said that we were skirting the night – there was the shadow of night, in a curve, just south of us – at least there it was on the map. I looked out the window to see where night began, but I could not tell where dusk edged into dark – I could not see the night that tried to approach as we flew away from it, up over Nova Scotia clipping Greenland, and falling with the curve of the earth towards home.

A long-haul flight is a very emotional space. I had a little cry at *Chariots of Fire* and the person in the next seat thought maybe someone had died, maybe that was why I was on this plane home. In fact, I was just avoiding the film *I Am Legend* which featured a vampire race in Manhattan: creatures who were afraid of the light, as I in my jet lag – you know it's easier if you travel west – flinch and blink when the sun shines in the middle of the night, even when I am home. In which state – full of alarms, little flickering lights in the corner of my eye – I sit and write this, and wait for my soul to catch up with me, so I can scoop it up and take it with me, west, at last, west to County Kerry.

BRAY REMEMBERED

John Ryan

Bray, that Wicklow watering place in the Dublin suburbs (as it seems) owes its existence as a holiday resort to the extension of the Dublin-to-Kingstown (Dún Laoghaire) railroad back in 1851. In that date there was no esplanade nor orderly terraces of private hotels and guest-houses or, for that matter, Funland and Dreamland – just a rude track that ran between the shingle and the sand-dunes and meandered its way toward Bray Head.

I who spent all my childhood summers there find it hard to visualise that primordial scene, because I remember Bray well as an ancient, much lived-in place, well worn and slightly battered – but comfortable, like an old pair of shoes. Yet eighty years before there had only been two habitations on the whole seafront. One was a charming rose-wreathed cottage, the sort that tea-cosies were once knitted to resemble; while the other, by way of contrast, was a small mud hovel which was occupied by an eccentric, solitary tar-begrimed fisherman who took delight in surrounding his unattractive abode with ill-smelling heaps of manure, offal and other abominations that came within his reach. To what end he accumulated these 'malodorous tumuli', mused the author of *The Neighbourhood of Dublin*, none who knew him could surmise.

Bray was by far the most English-looking of Irish resorts. It sold candy rock and jellied eels and might have been copied from a *risqué* seaside postcard – the one with blue skies and yellow sands and naughty, funny, fat bathing belles and ageing roués with red billiard-ball noses.

Even Bray Head itself seemed to be the work of the same designer who had produced the 'prom' and the bandstands and made possible the ghost trains, the dodgem cars, the rollercoasters and the walls of death that crowded the slopes. Only the sea retained its primordial innocence and virginity.

Bray in the 1930s and the long, hot, dusty summers of childhood was a crowded, uninhibited holiday place, always full, but brimming over when Sunday brought a motorised army of day-trippers. Indeed the memory of columns of bull-nosed Morrises and Model T Fords bumper to bumper, together with overheating and other concomitant calamities of the internal combustion age, comes back strongly after these many years, as indeed does also the memory of all the Scots who came with their pipe bands and the sound of whose nocturnal revelry often kept us awake at nights.

There was an open-air theatre in a converted bandstand on the esplanade and here a famous comedian of the day, Mike Nono, dispensed a particular brand of humour which, in retrospect, seems to have been halfway between Percy French and Will Rogers. Among his supporting troupe were two little girls who sang and tap-danced to such current hits as 'The Good Ship Lollipop'. They were billed as 'The Two Maureens' and one of them still sings and taps. She is Maureen Potter.

There was a cinema, which from the outside might have been taken to be the harem of a sultan in greatly reduced circumstances. Inside it reeked of disinfectant and echoed to the shots of Tom Mix and the guitar of Gene Autry.

Down by the harbour, where I remember black Arklow sailing schooners discharging coal, were the special sea-water baths my mother used to take, which in turn were next to the house the Joyce family lived in and which is the setting for the most glorious family row in all of literature – the Christmas Day one in *A Portrait of the Artist as a Young Man*. And I wonder if there is any Joycean connection in the seafront guest-house named The Ulysses?

About the beginning of September the gales of the equinox would start to blow, sending great seas crashing over the esplanade, and this would herald the day we dreaded most: when we were packed back to school. Perhaps then we would take a final look at the familiar scene which now, in sympathy it seemed, was a wet and windy shambles. And thus would end abysmally what had begun so hopefully way back in June – our interminable summer holiday.

GREENE'S BOOKSHOP

John Boland

The first genuine books I ever read – not *The Secret Seven*, not *Biggles Sweeps the Desert*, not even *The Wind in the Willows*, but real books with adult thoughts and feelings – came courtesy of Rathmines Public Library, where I spent too many evenings of my teenage years. Yet even though a library is a fine and private place, for real lovers of literature, there is nothing to compare with a shop that sells second-hand books, and the first such shop I ever entered was Greene's on Clare Street, which closes its doors next Friday after 164 years in existence.

Samuel Beckett, who lived across the street from it above his father's business premises, frequented it often, as did his mentor James Joyce, and not just when he was waiting for Nora Barnacle to finish her working day at Finn's Hotel almost opposite. I used to imagine, as I was poring over dusty volumes on its stairway shelves, that the ghosts of these men were brushing by me. We wouldn't, of course, have talked because there's something about the atmosphere of a second-hand bookshop that invites the willing silence which libraries famously demand – an atmosphere that says that reading is a serious business and that we who are perusing these books are serious people, searching for something with which to provide solace for our solitary hours.

Part of the pleasure of this quest – a large part, I would say – is its uncertainty. You enter a second-hand bookshop usually having no idea what you are looking for or, indeed, if you are looking for anything at all, and suddenly there on the shelf in front of you is an old Everyman's Library edition of George Herbert's poems or Montaigne's essays and, years later, you look at these volumes on your own shelves and realise that, for a few pence or a few shillings or a few euro, you discovered in these bookshops writers who were to become your companions for life.

Or, but this is rare (though it's the rarity that gives the thrill), you suddenly find yourself face to face with a book you've been seeking all your life and you stand for a few seconds with giddy disbelief at your amazing good fortune before hurriedly seizing the treasured object just in case anyone else suddenly snatches it out of your grasp – even though it's been standing, forlorn and forgotten, on these shelves for months or years. I had that sensation when, after twenty years scouring through bookshops in various cities, I found myself in Los Angeles and happened upon a book that had been my bible as a teenager in Rathmines Library – Kenneth Tynan's 1961 book of theatre reviews, *Curtains* – now miraculously there before my eyes in mint condition and for a mere $10 in this rambling warehouse of a bookstore on the edge of the world.

Nowadays, I can go onto the internet, where this week on the Abebooks site I found forty-four other first editions of Tynan's book at prices ranging from a ridiculous $1 to a more daunting $167, but though this is a wonderful online service and I use it regularly, somehow it's not the same – you don't experience the delirium of discovery or the feel of the spine of the book or of the smell of its pages or of the whole inimitable ritual of entering the shop, the proprietor nodding at you, the other customers glancing round from their silent reveries at the shelves to size up the demeanour and perhaps the moral character of this newcomer, this fellow explorer who has decided to embark on the same voyage of discovery.

I went back to Greene's last week to say farewell to it and to imagine it soon sharing some Valhalla with Webb's on the quays and the Dublin Bookshop on Bachelor's Walk and those other irreplaceable emporiums that no longer exist in this supposedly literary town of ours. While I was there, I browsed among the depleted shelves on the stairs, leafing through old Reprint Society editions of Neville Shute and Nigel Balchin and Elizabeth Jane Howard and all those other writers who, like Greene's itself, have had their day.

I finally came across and bought, for a mere €2.50, a lovely compendium called *The Musical Companion*. The scrawl in fountain pen on the flyleaf informed me that it was once the property of Dorothy Beattie, who acquired it at Christmas in 1946. Years later, she or her family, for whatever reason, banal or heartbreaking, felt obliged to dispense with it. Was she one of the ghosts I sensed as I walked back down the stairs of Greene's for the last time?

1 SEATOWN PLACE

Conor O'Callaghan

For a country not renowned for snow, Ireland has produced more than its fair share of polar explorers: Kildare's Ernest Shackleton's race with Scott to the South Pole has been captured for the small screen by Kenneth Branagh; Annascaul's Tom Crean can be seen nightly on a TV ad mumbling 'The Kerry Dances' in a snowbound cave, dreaming of one more pint of famous stout. Arguably Ireland's greatest polar explorer, however, does not enjoy such popular renown. There are no dramatisations of his heroism, and he does not feature in any marketing campaigns. I know about him only because he came from my hometown, Dundalk.

A little over ten years ago, myself and my wife moved back from Dublin. Between the jigs and reels, we ended up buying a new house in the oldest section, called 'Seatown'. I fell in love with name and place. It is on reclaimed land and has a feeling of being both here and elsewhere, moored and adrift all at once. The short walk to the centre of town passes a Georgian terrace. Last house on the left has a blue plaque with a knighted name, nineteenth-century dates and a description of a profession that intrigued me so much I went researching.

Sir Leopold McClintock was born in his family home, 1 Seatown Place, in 1829. His father was the inspector of taxes. He was educated at Dundalk Grammar School until, at the age of twelve, his uncle secured a naval commission for him. In 1845, when McClintock was still a young officer, Sir John Franklin captained the *Erebus* in an attempt to become the first known ship to navigate the Northwest Passage: that fabled sliver from Atlantic to Pacific across the uppermost coast of Canada. For fourteen years Franklin's whereabouts remained a mystery. McClintock, having been in the crew of two previous failed rescue voyages, captained a third commissioned by Lady Jane Franklin. He departed an ambitious young officer and returned two years later one of the most celebrated men in Victorian public life. In the interim, through chattels found littering the barren landscape and Inuit sightings of strange men battling the elements, the last days of the crew of the *Erebus* were pieced together.

After Sir Leopold's father died, his mother moved to Gardiner Place and 1 Seatown Place went out of the family. When we arrived back ten years ago the house was flats, then a B&B. Its most recent and current incarnation is as a hostel for asylum-seekers from other continents. Some evenings I walk past with my kids and they are sitting out on the steps: talking, laughing and beneath it all probably wondering what strange twist in fortune has washed them up on this shore. Occasionally I have a strong urge to tell them who once lived in their present home, if only to give them hope. Perhaps they know the story anyway.

Upon his return in 1859, McClintock was knighted by Queen Victoria and granted the freedom of London. One month later, at a civic reception in Dundalk, he accepted an award from the townspeople and told them he would 'cherish it always more than any other honour, as it comes from the town where I spent my youth, from the friends of my boyhood days, from my home.' He died in 1907 at the age of eighty-eight and is buried in Westminster Abbey. To this day a giant stuffed polar bear he shot can be seen in the Natural History Museum on Merrion Street. The strip of water between Victoria Island and Prince of Wales Island in Arctic Canada now appears in every atlas as McClintock Channel.

I write all this in that golden no man's land between late spring and early summer. The evenings are getting warmer and brighter. As I write, I can hear the faint echoes of gospel music wafting over Seatown. This is a new song in these parts, and one I welcome. It suddenly occurs to me how fitting it is that 1 Seatown Place now houses those who have travelled several continents to find safety and new lives. I like to think Sir Leopold McClintock, a man who made his name in search of the lost, would have approved.

GROWING UP
IN NO MAN'S LAND

Mary O'Donnell

As a child in the 1960s, I was a true-blue fan of most things British, seduced by glimmers of Carnaby Street, by names like David Hockney, Mary Quant and The Kinks. If the choice was British music versus Irish showband, between *Fab 208* or *Spotlight* magazine, there was, simply, no choice. *Spotlight* was scanned for its liberal problem page but little else. The Republic of Ireland, *Spotlight* magazine, the showband scene and indeed the infant RTÉ television, were essentially pale and ineffective imitators of things which our former colonist was simply better at.

I grew up quite happily in our no man's land on the southern edge of the border, never certain of who the border people were or what we were supposed to be. Aware of being pulled hither and thither by rarely articulated passions and forces outside myself. County Monaghan straddled two opposite cultural traditions. Ulster people we certainly were, yet sometimes it seemed we were a forgotten sidekick of the *real* Ulster. We had our own writer, of course – Patrick Kavanagh, who by virtue of his banned novel *Tarry Flynn* had obviously done something right – but *real* Ulster seemed to mean the Six Counties, where things seemed brighter, more efficient and, in an unspoken sense, better.

As well as having the MI motorway, the shopping experience in the North – for housewives from south of the border – offered greater variety; hence the convoys which regularly crossed the border on a

Thursday afternoon, Monaghan's half-day, to buy provisions and clothing. These would be smuggled smoothly through the customs post on the return trip, though this too depended on the mood and outlook of the Customs official on duty on any particular day. For children, Armagh, Middletown and Aughnacloy were like ships, regularly plundered for their cargo of Mars Bars, Milky Ways and Maltesers.

Other things, too, worked to subtly alter our world and parish view. South of the border, when most of the Republic had to put up with RTÉ television and radio, we could choose to listen to the BBC and UTV, as well as BBC Radio 1 and 2. England was bursting at the seams with new music, with maddening themes of freedom and new fashion that pulsed its way excitingly down the airwaves.

Living as many of us did under a false sense of cultural inferiority, something quite different occurred on family holidays at my father's home in Kilkenny. Once south of Dublin I'd watch out for familiar landmarks: the Wicklow glens with their oak and beech groves, deep-banked rivers that contrasted with the slim sparkling line of our local river, the Blackwater. Finally, the sight of the Blackstairs Mountains, which meant the journey was almost at an end, for on the other side of that great sun- and cloud-swept immensity, lay Ballyneale, with its limestone pillars; the house with its unique, paraffin-oil odour; and outside again, a rushing stream; deep, bosomy pastures. For me, this was *the* bucolic idyll.

Once I heard my grandparents' rich southern voices, or caught the thread of local sayings and expressions in and around Ballyneale, I felt as if I had come home. I was bewitched, partly because I sensed unconditional acceptance in that house, but for another reason too: the place, the people, these voices, these ways of living, conveyed themselves to me – unpretentiously and naturally – as *really* Irish. On an unformed level I picked up the automatic ease of the cultural habitat in which my southern grandparents and aunt lived. There were, quite simply, no influences, there was no pull towards foreignness, otherness and the different ways which distinguished us in Monaghan from communities in both North and South. That independence charmed me. I have never forgotten it.

BLAEBERRY SUNDAY

Padraig McGinn

Whether you approach Castleblayney from east or west, you'll know you are near the town when you see Conabury Hill. It is a steep, drumlin hill, crowned by a mane of old beech trees, visible for miles in every direction. From this hill you can see the spire of Annyalla Church four miles to the west, Sliabh Gullion in Armagh thirteen miles to the east and Mullyash Mountain four miles to the north. And whenever we mitched from school, we always hid on Conabury Hill, because from there we had a commanding view of the two national schools and could time our arrival home to coincide with those who had attended school that day.

It was one of those days when I was mitching that I met Mick, an old bachelor who was walking his dog on the hill, and he told me about Blaeberry Sunday on Mullyash Mountain.

'Did ye ever climb Mullyash for blaeberries?' he asked. And when I answered that I'd never heard of blaeberries, he said that some people called them bilberries and others whortleberries. I had never heard of either, so he took it upon himself to enlighten me.

'The first Sunday in August was Blaeberry Sunday,' he began. 'People for miles around climbed Mullyash to eat blaeberries or to gather them for jam. There'd be fiddlers there and melodeon players and young people dancing sets and lancers at the crossroads below, in the evening. Some people would bring new potatoes and eggs and boil them, and have a picnic. Many a boy and girl met their future wife or husband there. It was a great place to meet a woman. The custom went back to ancient times. 'Twas a pity it died out.'

I asked him why it died out if it was such great fun and the people enjoyed it so much.

'The clergy and the Gaelic League,' he spat out. 'The people danced foreign dances, sets and lancers and barn dances, and the league didn't like that. But it was the clergy that gave it the knockout. The bishop declared that crossroads dancing was a sin. And the bishop himself often appeared at the open-air dances, a big ash plant in his hand, and stopped the dancing. It was amazing the power he had. Nobody would go against him.

'There was another reason, too, why the clergy were against the cele-bration of Blaeberry Sunday. It was originally a feast in honour of the pagan god, Lugh. His name is remembered in the month of Lughnasa and in Lughaidh, the Irish for Louth. It was time to kill off the last traces of pagan culture in the new Ireland.'

Although I was only ten or eleven at the time, I wondered if Mick's bitterness at the ending of Blaeberry Sunday on Mullyash was related to the fact that he never got a wife. I kept my unspoken question to myself. I resolved to climb Mullyash as soon as I was old enough and taste the blaeberries. They say that the way to hell is paved with good intentions and it was sixty years later before I made my way, last August, to Mullyash in search of blaeberries. Alas, the blaeberries, like the ancient customs, were long gone and a forest of spruce trees covered the land where lovers once danced and shared wild berries.

IN A GARDEN

Sinéad McCoole

Should you ever have met Catherine Kennedy, who died in 2000 in her eighty-seventh year, you might perhaps have glimpsed in her animated gestures the actions of her famous grandmother, Lady Gregory. Certainly there were those who insisted that they could see the similarity in the tilt of the head, as captured in Epstein's bust of Lady Gregory. It was not merely an obscure ancestral link that Catherine shared with her grandmother. Her earliest years were spent in her care, living at Coole.

Catherine Kennedy's ashes were scattered on Coole Lake. One of her last wishes was to return to the place which, once upon a time, she had called home. But with that last act, her presence did not completely disappear from Coole – if you know where to look, you will find her garden, a garden within a garden.

Her grandmother had laid out three tiny gardens for her grand-children, her 'chicks', as she called them. They had all been born at Coole – Richard in 1909, Anne in 1911 and Catherine in 1913. By encouraging them to tend their own gardens, Lady Gregory wished to instil in her grandchildren the love she had for nature, for her native Galway, for Coole.

Richard, Anne and Catherine were the children of Lady Gregory's only child, Robert, and his wife, Margaret Graham Parry, whom Robert had met when she was a fellow art student at The Slade in London. The couple had no interest in living in Coole, and even after the birth of their son they departed from Galway, leaving the infant Richard in his grandmother's care.

Richard was sent off to boarding school at a very early age, but Anne and Catherine were always at Coole. It was in Coole they heard of their father's death. Robert, aged thirty-seven, had been killed in 1918, shot down over northern Italy, another casualty of the First World War.

Shortly after that, the girls were taken away from Coole for the first time, brought to England by their mother. Knowing that the girls were desperately unhappy away from Coole, their grandmother sent them great parcels of moss and little red toadstools on twigs from the Nut Wood, which the girls made into great flat dishes, and sniffed and sniffed the lovely wet mossy smell and imagined that they were back at their beloved Coole. It was not long before their mother, aware of their loneliness, sent them back to Ireland, to Coole.

Something of the time, that golden childhood, is captured in Anne's memoir, the enchanting *Me and Nu*. The voice of the child, who called her little sister Nu, brings characters of the literary renaissance to life. Stories of a grandmother, a very different lady to the one imagined as one studies images of a stern-faced woman in widow's weeds. George Bernard Shaw had played with *and* cheated them at 'hunt the thimble'. So indignant were these young girls at his antics that despite their grandmother's urging would not address him as their 'kind playmate', even when he wrote a poem in their honour, addressing them grandly as 'two ladies of Galway.'

Yeats 'always seemed to be there' and they could remember him 'humming' away for hours while he wrote his verse. They also remembered his bad manners; he never said please and thank you. The girls met Sean O'Casey and witnessed him carving his name on the autograph tree at Coole. The tree is still there in the garden, standing proud.

Two years after Robert's death, Margaret told Lady Gregory that she wanted to sell Coole. She finally agreed to keep the house, the garden and 350 acres. But this was only a short-term respite. In 1927, Lady Gregory acted as a witness to Margaret's signature on the deed for the sale of Coole to the Department of Agriculture and Lands. The new owners formally took possession of the estate, but they did permit Lady Gregory to lease the house. It was some consolation to her, an old lady who was dying. She had already undergone two operations for her breast cancer.

Lady Gregory lived to see Richard's coming of age in 1930, but it was not what she had imagined. Shortly before her death in 1932, Lady

Gregory had written of Coole: 'I have lived there and loved it these forty years and through the guests who have stayed there it counts for much in the awakening of the spiritual and intellectual side of our country. If there is trouble now, and it is dismantled and left to ruin, that will be the whole country's loss.'

The house has been gone for a long time now. Ironically, the property, that great historic house, had belonged to the Irish people, but a local official felt that it was better to be without the encumbrance of the house and sent in local men to undermine the roof. In time it was knocked because it was an unsafe structure. The lands of Coole had been saved because of the rare trees that had been planted by a Gregory centuries before.

The magic of the place still lingers in the garden and woods. If you have never been, I urge you to go. I am sure that you will find your way to look at the autograph tree and view the initials of the famous who visited Coole. Lady Gregory's grandchildren never carved their names on that tree — they were not famous — but if you look really carefully, you will find three tiny hedges that surround three areas of earth — and just imagine the children digging there a long time ago in a garden.

THE HOUSE
THAT EILEEN BUILT

Patricia O'Reilly

It's a warm summer's day in 1926. The woman drives her MG roadster into the train station at Roquebrune, parks, and reaches into the back for her rolled-up towel. Anticipating the pleasure of a swim, she crosses the low stone wall and walks along the narrow pathway, looking for a way down the cliff to the beach. After a few minutes, the path fizzles out.

Intrigued by the isolation of the area, she clambers over crumbling walls, through the scattered Levant pines and brushes of wild rosemary and euphorbia, before arriving at a small natural terrace cut into the honey-coloured limestone rocks.

The woman is Eileen Gray, born in Wexford in 1878 to an Anglo-Irish family whose ancestry dated back to the fifteenth-century English peer, Lord Gray. For a decade she has been the toast of Paris for her lacquer work, furniture and interior design.

She is in the south of France looking for a suitable site to build a summer getaway for herself and her current lover, Romanian architect Jean Badovici. For the past three weeks she has been searching up and down the Côte d'Azur. Without success.

Today – and when she wasn't even looking – she has stumbled across the perfect site on which to build her perfect house. She calls it the E-1027. E for Eileen. 10 for Jean. 2 for Badovici. 7 for Gray. And she gifts it to him.

The house was tiered and, carved from rock face, it embraced the natural contours and used light and wind to best advantage. With walls of glass, it looked out towards the ever-changing turquoise of the Mediterranean.

During three years of construction, Eileen remained on or near the site. Dressed in a trouser suit, silk shirt and a jaunty bow tie, she buzzed up and down the treacherous mountain roads checking on details, ensuring every aspect of her design was adhered to, refusing to compromise.

Seen from the sea, the finished villa, complete with masts, looked like a ship at anchor. Sailcloth membranes protected the terrace from the sun; life preservers hung from the balcony deck and reclining chairs suggested a cruise. On land the design was equally impressive. By using the same wooden floors, plain white walls, shutters and lights, the exterior terrace seamlessly converted to a secluded living room. The furniture was chrome, leather, wood, glass and cork.

Into this house she poured her very soul and she and Badovici spent many summers there, frequently with house guests. One was modernistic architect Le Corbusier who painted – without permission, Eileen maintained – eight sexual murals which she called 'an act of vandalism'.

After the break-up of her relationship with Badovici, she left E-1027, never to return. She was amused to learn, however, that the German soldiers who occupied the place during World War Two used the murals for target practice.

Seventy-eight years later, on an equally warm summer's day, I walk in the footsteps of Eileen Gray. I've come by train from Nice. Crossing the tracks, I climb over the same stone wall and wander the quarter mile or so along the now-asphalted pathway. It's dirty and dusty. Littered with wrappers, beer and coke cans, cigarette butts and dog faeces.

A vandalised telephone box and padlocked gates mark the entrance to E-1027. The smell of urine predominates. Yet the Mediterranean, barely visible through the tangled overgrowth and chicken-wire fencing, is still turquoise and still dashing against the honey-coloured limestone rocks.

The E-1027 has become a shipwreck of a house. Crumbling concrete. Staircase off-kilter. Smashed windows.

Recently it has been designated by the French government as a historical monument. Ironically, it owes its salvation to the murals. Without them, rumour has it, it would have been left to rot.

THE GRAVE OF SYLVIA PLATH

Michael O'Loughlin

When we think of England, or at least when I think of England, I think of cities and motorways, the London Underground with its multicultural crowds. So, as I sat in the little train that runs between Manchester and Leeds, that idyllic green heartland of hills and valleys, woods and quaint villages came as a revelation to me. Moston, Rochdale, Smithy Bridge, Todmorden; the solid Anglo-Saxon names of Yorkshire delighted me. But when I reached my destination, the small village of Hepden Bridge, it all began to seem familiar. The canals and sturdy stone bridges, with the brown moors in the distance, the mist on the small chimneys tucked into river valleys, these I knew from the poetry of Ted Hughes, in particular his book with photographer Faye Godwin, *Remains of Elmet*.

This was no coincidence, as the reason I was in this literary area was directly related to Ted Hughes. I was to give a reading at his former home of Lumb Bank, not far from his birthplace in Heptonstall. The old mill owner's house is now a branch of the Arvon Foundation, providing week-long creative writing courses for people from all over the world. As I sat sipping a glass of wine in the library, surrounded by thousands of poetry collections, the director introduced me to a large black tomcat.

'This is Ted Hughes,' he said. 'We're now on our seventh.'

After the reading, I remarked to the director that the group included quite a few Irish people. He told me that they were being inundated with applications from Ireland.

'It's those SSIA government savings things,' he told me. 'People now have money to develop themselves.' It's an ill wind that blows no good, I thought.

After a restless night, in which I dreamt that the stream flooding the valley below was a hurricane, I woke in the dark just before dawn. I had a special task to do before returning to Dublin.

It was a grim, damp morning. The sheep huddled on the moors and the clouds enveloped the trees. As I sweated up the hill, I passed the occasional square stone farmhouse, with an old Land Rover invariably parked outside. Everything seemed old, neat and untouched for centuries, in contrast to the jumble of visual styles you would see in the Irish countryside.

In the small village of Heptonstall, people were just waking up. As I walked along the wet, narrow street paved with large slabs of stone, I could see into the old weavers' cottages, where people were preparing breakfast. There was no one on the street. Then a door opened and a young man emerged. He was wearing jeans and a leather jacket, but the front of his head was shaved and a long blond plait hung down his back. His face was half-covered by tattoos and half a dozen piercings. He looked like he had stepped straight out of an ancient Saxon chronicle.

The churchyard wasn't hard to find. A beautiful old church, with a ruined medieval monastery beside it. When I stepped into the ruin, a crow, perched on one of the exposed roof beams, cawed loudly and flew off. It was very quiet in the rain; there wasn't a living soul about. The church itself was surrounded and hemmed in by a jumble of large stone gravestones. But what I was looking for wasn't there.

Poets are inveterate sniffers around graveyards, I suppose because a lot of the work has already been done for us. I crossed a country lane into a windswept, flooded field on the outskirts of the village. This was the new graveyard, which took the overspill from the village. After a few minutes patrolling the densely packed rows of almost anonymous graves, I found what I was looking for: the grave of Sylvia Plath. It looked the same as all the others; if anything, more neglected and anonymous. The small stone was decorated with a string of carved pearls, as seemed to be the custom of the graves around here. The simple stone gave the name Sylvia Plath Hughes and her dates but, below it, these lines: 'Even amidst the fiercest flames the golden lotus can be planted.'

As I shivered in my unsuitable clothes in the mud, I could not help thinking that the fierce flames would soon have been doused by the low-lying clouds and the golden lotus was nowhere to be seen.

I retraced my steps through the village, with mothers arriving to deposit their children at the local school. And after breakfast at Lumb Bank, I left Yorkshire again.

A few hours later, when I sat in the gleaming modern glass and steel of Manchester airport, it all seemed like a dream. Had I really been to England at all? And then I looked down at my shoes and saw they were still caked with the mud and grass of Heptonstall churchyard, a souvenir to bring back to Ireland.

GRANADA

Anthony Cronin

The other day a chance encounter with some young Spaniards in a café set me thinking of Granada, a city from which one of them came. I remembered clearly the heat and the mountains and the gypsy caves in the slopes above and the contrasting coolness and the unexpected all-pervading smell of box hedges in the gardens of the Generalife. Granada resembles Dublin in one way, at least, and that is that you are often surprised by a vista of mountains at the end of the street. The difference is that the Sierra Nevada are snow-capped all year round, majestically indifferent to the summer torridness of the city. It is because of these mountains, rising to ten thousand feet or more, that Granada became the last stronghold of Moorish power in Spain, falling to the Christian monarchs Ferdinand and Isabella only as late as 1491.

Granada's most famous attraction is of course the Alhambra, the great pleasure palace of the Moorish Kings which towers over and disdains the valley in which the rest of the city is built. I call it a palace, like almost everyone else, but it is really a sort of fortified suburb, a complex of separate palaces and gardens within a huge fortified wall of red brick. The Alhambra was begun by Mohammad I of Granada at a time when Muslim culture in Spain far surpassed that of the Christians. It is, in a way, one of the wonders of the world and it has lasted for more than seven centuries, but its present-day fame has a curious history.

For centuries after its abandonment, nobody paid much attention to it and it was allowed gradually to moulder. Carlos V was so insensitive as to build himself a separate edifice, a piece of sixteenth-century classicism, impressive only for its weight and bulk, right in the middle of the intricately laid-out grounds. The Napoleonic army almost blew up the whole affair before they retreated from the city.

Then, in 1892, a young American consular official, Washington Irving, found himself in a room looking onto a patio with tall cypresses and a lovely fountain in the middle of all that marvellous decaying splendour, and there, in a few weeks, he wrote a book called *Tales of the Alhambra* in which he evoked what he imagined to be the episodes out of the palace's romantic Moorish past. The time was the height of the romantic movement and Irving's book, which seemingly evoked the centuries of caliphs and harems and beautiful Christian princesses and court poets, swept the civilised world. And just in time too, for the Spaniards were moved to begin the long process of restoration and preservation which has kept the Alhambra intact.

It is not, of course, the only tourist attraction which owes its original fame to a literary man. The Lake District owes its to Wordsworth, while Killarney was originally largely due to Sir Walter Scott.

I must say, beautiful as much of the delicate abstract plasterwork is – and enchanting are some of the courts with their pools and fountains – I found the Alhambra almost a bit too well-preserved, too much of a monument to a totally dead civilisation. But then Granada is in many ways a city of death. Dead poets, dead bullfighters, gypsies reduced to an almost utter dependence, relics of Spain's greatness in the days of empire abound.

It was here that Granada's great poet Federico García Lorca was murdered in the first days of the Civil War and buried no one knows where. My friend Gerald Brennan has written a fascinating essay on an unsuccessful search for his grave and the reasons for his killing. In a footnote to his book on the Civil War, Hugh Thomas suggests that an unsuccessful fellow poet who hated him may have been a member of the Falangist gangs who were out in lorries that night, a thought which certainly ties in, however terrifying. Both knew the psychology of revolution and of poetic jealousy. Cyril Connolly has said that Lorca loved Granada because it was a symbol of the Middle Ages and that suddenly the Middle Ages were reborn and struck him down. However that may be, Yeats's great line, 'a drunken soldiery rides the night' probably conveys it all.

In the main square of Granada, probably now called the Generalisimo Franco or the José Antonio, I forget which, there is a market, and here the male gypsies carrying the horse or mule whip which is a mark of their caste congregate for converse as well as commerce of a sort. The first thing one notices about gypsies in Spain is, paradoxically, their pride, for the men at least bear themselves with an outward arrogance, which is in strange contrast with their position of beggary and dependence. Of course the actual begging is, for the most part, left to the women and children.

Most of Granada's gypsies live in the caves in the hills above the town on the opposite site of the river valley from the Alhambra. Some of these caves are, in fact, quite large and decently equipped as dwellings; others not. In the larger ones, flamenco dancing is done for the benefit of tourists. A gypsy I met in a bar one night asked me to join a party to see some dancing. To please him I said yes, but when the party assembled the following evening I found to my horror that it contained only four persons, including an American judge and his wife. There were six dancers to entertain these four people, none of whom knew anything whatever about flamenco. It was a sad occasion.

Many things about Granada are sad and yet, by a not uncommon paradox, that sun-baked city, with its relics of departed prides and departed glories, its dead Moors and its tombs of the Christian kings, has a power over the imagination that other places lack. Even if the Alhambra is a bit too perfectly preserved, Time, the sole philosopher, rules it all.

MY FIRST BASQUE VILLAGE

Paddy Woodworth

Itziar was the first Basque village I ever saw.

Its enormous church swung abruptly into view, set high on a hill above the road, as I was hitchhiking from San Sebastián to Bilbao on my very first day in Basque country.

Those were stirring times. The old dictator, General Franco, lay dying in Madrid, still signing death warrants as if the execution of his enemies might somehow further postpone his own wretched and lingering departure. A great wave of democracy was waiting to break over Spain, but the heavily armed police at checkpoints I had passed along the road were a reminder that change would not come easily.

The noisy and overheated political side of my brain suddenly went silent, however, when I was dropped off on the old main road, which ran between Itziar and the sea. I thought the great Gothic church above me was like a stone ship anchored to the steep green hillside. I thought that this was an original thought until I found, years later, that it was a commonplace in Basque writing.

That day, other images seduced me: a brace of oxen, their chunky wooden yoke blazing with woollen decorations in primary colours, and the wiry man in blue overalls and a black beret urging them on, almost pushing them up the slope; the tang of freshly cut young bracken, the sweeter smell of mown grass; and, everywhere and yet nowhere in particular, the echoing of sheep bells. Itziar became my image of a Basque pastoral Eden.

Two years passed before I returned to the same spot. It was an exceptionally bright June day when I turned off the main road and took the long sweeping S-bends up to the village. The great white farmhouses with their sloping red roofs gleamed like another country, more North African than Basque. And it was Sunday lunchtime, so not a soul was stirring outside the family home. But it was far from silent in the shimmering heat.

From one of these centennial farmsteads, someone was playing Pink Floyd's drug-fuelled 'Wish You Were Here' at full volume. Oddly, it did not seem inappropriate to the setting. Wandering off through the woods which dipped up and down towards the townland of Lastur, I saw a little bull, a very little bull. I thought the bull was funny when he started tossing his head aggressively, but I stopped laughing when he charged. I climbed a tree very fast. It gave me a glance of bored contempt and abruptly dashed off again.

Looking back, I wondered if the whole day had been a dream, some bizarre mixture of nostalgia for student psychedelia and a childhood fear of cattle. Itziar remained as remote and desirable as ever.

About ten years later, I began reading Joseba Zulaika's landmark book about ETA's social roots, *Basque Violence: Metaphor and Sacrament*. I was amazed and disturbed to find that Itziar, of all places, was the object of a masterpiece of anthropological fieldwork. The book also tells the story of the author's youth at a time of great crisis — which happened to be precisely the time I had first seen the village. It contained much stranger, more wonderful and more terrible things than I had imagined in my idle fantasies about Itziar.

Zulaika made vivid the nearby caves, with their masterpieces of Neolithic cave painting hinting at ancient Basque ancestors. His mother had seen the Basque goddess Mari flying like a ball of fire through the sky. The old ways were fading in Zulaika's youth, but, even as an adult, he could still interview someone who saw a witch sitting beside his tape recorder, quite clearly in broad daylight.

The social world of Itziar in the 1970s was equally strange, and more tangibly dangerous. Zulaika's youthful companions had included an active service unit from the armed Basque separatist group ETA. This is a much more secretive group even than the IRA. Many people in Itziar admired ETA at this time for giving the dictatorship a bloody nose, yet they were deeply shocked to find that it was local teenagers who had made the headlines for several weeks by kidnapping a businessman. After sharing many sociable meals with him in an isolated farmhouse in the townland around Itziar, they had shot him in the head.

The village, Zulaika wrote, encompassed both a rich tradition of Basque oral poetry and distinctive rural sports including rock-lifting, and a disco where the callow sex-and-drugs lifestyle was much the same as in Mullingar or Madrid.

When I finally met Zulaika, I told him about my dream day in Itziar. He could explain it all. His brother Xalbador, who has sadly since died, was a big Pink Floyd fan, and always played their music very loud. And Lastur, it turned out, is famous for its puny but pugnacious bulls.

Today, another of Zulaika's brothers, Bixente, is struggling to bring Lastur back to life. Its tiny scattering of houses now forms an extended restaurant and hostel, which enclose two sides of an earth arena. Here, the little bulls again do battle with youths, in the Basque style, on Saturday afternoons. This is a kind of burlesque bull-fighting, in which the animals are taunted but rarely harmed physically. It's very popular with stag parties from nearby towns.

Bixente jealously guards the authenticity of the old rituals. He knows the intimate history behind every faded photograph in his restaurant: the bohemian-tragic life of the itinerant accordion players; the brilliant but alcoholic folk healer who lost his daughters to typhus; the rock-lifter whose record has never been broken. Leading poets come to 'sing' spontaneous verses in bersolari style at the communal meals Bixente organises; champion rock-lifters and lumber cutters perform at fiestas.

Itziar and its townlands today, and yesterday, are a far cry from the garden of Eden I had once imagined them to be, but somehow I feel at home there, and perhaps that makes it a kind of paradise.

MEDICINE BOW AND THE RED DESERT OF WYOMING

Benedict Kiely

Twice in my life have I passed through Medicine Bow and the Red Desert of Wyoming. And it isn't likely that I'll be back that way a third time. Not that I've anything against the Red Desert or Medicine Bow. But if you live half an hour's walk from St Stephen's Green, you are not likely to find yourself too often in Medicine Bow unless you have urgent business there, or very hospitable friends.

The first time round I went through Medicine Bow by train, going east. Far across the coloured desert, which is by no means a monotony of sand but a wonderful, living, changing patchwork, you could study for miles and miles an enormous snow-covered mountain actually glittering in the sun; a mountain that, the story goes, inspired the great Edison when he was out there game-hunting and gave him some new ideas about electricity.

There wasn't much movement in the railway station the day I passed through and few people got on or off the train. On a bench against a wall sat four Indians wearing tall black hats, and with their chins resting on their chests just the way you'd see them in western movies. For the five minutes the train was there they didn't make a move, didn't even raise their heads to look at the train or the people in it. They could, of course, have been asleep, but I don't think so. What they were silently saying was,

I feel, something like this: 'We and the desert were here before you came. We and the desert will be here long after you are long gone.'

Next time through Medicine Bow I was heading west and on a greyhound bus. Back somewhere in Nebraska – or rather in Nowhere, Nebraska – the bus had been unduly halted while an altercation went on between the driver and a passenger in the seat behind me. The man had a few drinks taken. He wasn't roaring or shouting, or even singing, but he was still sipping out of a bottle, and to take bottles, even bottles of Coke, aboard a long-distance bus is strictly verboten. So the row began.

The driver said, 'Gimme the jug, bud.'

The man said, 'Aye got no jug.'

This went on for some time with no altercation whatsoever in the dialogue ('jug' meaning bottle of booze) until the driver said: 'You don't give me the jug, man, I call the police.'

Which, indeed, he did, and the hapless traveller was hustled off the bus by three enormous cops and taken away in a screaming car to somewhere in Nowhere, Nebraska. For all anybody knew a dying mother might have been waiting for him at the end of the journey. Back home here in Ireland you wouldn't know who to put off first, but those long journeys impose a heavy strain on drivers and passengers and all the strict precautions may be necessary. For later on, I read in a newspaper that, the very day after I had passed through Medicine Bow, a bus had pulled into that very same station in the early morning, and one of the sleeping passengers had woken up shooting, and before they could deprive him of his pistol and his rights as a US citizen, he had shot four of his fellow passengers dead. He was an Ozark mountaineer and perhaps in the Ozarks they *normally* wake up shooting. Yet I selfishly thanked the God of Greyhound that I hadn't made the journey a day later, not that nowadays we can afford to talk.

It was early morning also when I passed through Medicine Bow and in the dawning light the desert wind blew sand along the streets, and revolving water sprayers were already at the struggle to keep the lawns green. No lawns to be seen there eighty or so years ago when a traveller who was also a popular writer came there by train. This is what he saw:

> Some notable sight was drawing the passengers to the window...I saw near the track an enclosure and round it some whirling dust, and amid the dust some horses plunging, huddling and dodging. They were cow ponies in a

corral and one of them would not be caught no matter who threw the rope.

That was the opening of Owen Wister's celebrated novel, *The Virginian*, which I have recently been re-reading: a theme that in our own decade we have seen peter out in a television series with James Drury as the Virginian being pushed into the background and Trampas, originally the bad guy, becoming a Grade B and very watery class of a hero. The copy which I now possess was bought for me in a second-hand book shop in the lovely New England village of Suffield, Connecticut, and the previous owner (to whom a title page inscription tells me it was given as a present in 1913) thought enough of it to paste inside the covers and on the fly leaves, clippings taken from a magazine at the time (in the 1940s) when Paramount made the movie with Joel McCrea as the Virginian. This was the first movie to be based on Wister's book. I quote from those clippings:

> It is the greatest piece of Wild West fiction ever written. In four decades the book has sold well over a million and a half copies and become a textbook in many high schools. Made into a play, it ran three years in New York and had unnumbered road engagements. Aside from appearances in the movies in which the first three Virginians were Dustin Farnim, William S. Hart, and Gary Cooper in 1929, *The Virginian* has been a fountainhead of inspiration for the 5,000 horse operas to have reached the screen since the cinematograph was invented. All the traditions of Western fiction – tough but kindly cowboys, cattle rustlers, school marms, stampedes – owe their existence to the novel, written in 1902 by Theodore Roosevelt's friend and dedicated to the President.

Bret Harte and Mark Twain had already written seriously, if also humourously, about the West. But when Owen Wister, pal of Teddy 'Rough Rider' Roosevelt, went to Medicine Bow, he invented the popular western.

He'd be horrified if he could see what has happened to it in seventy-odd years. For not so much since 1902 but since 1942, the Wild West has, particularly on the cinema screen, changed from being a primeval heroic paradise to being a blood-soaked wilderness. We are better informed now about what really happened to the Indians and that's a good thing. But the Wild West was not all blood and murder; and what we have done is impose on it the imprint of our own minds in one of the bloodiest half-centuries in history. Even when the movie people tried foolishly to do a remake of John Ford's classical *Stagecoach*, the screen has to be, in the first few moments, as blood-boltered as Banquo's ghost. What Owen Wister wrote, though, was a perfectly normal novel about a simple rural society, and it's still a pleasure to read – although I'm glad that I wasn't in the bus in Medicine Bow the morning the man from the Ozark Mountains woke up shooting.

A SMALL TOWN
IN WYOMING

Leo McGowan

We wouldn't have stopped at Green River in the ordinary course of events. But it was too far to drive back to Salt Lake City in one day and Green River looked like one of the few places we could stay in a state that is still largely prairie.

We spent the night in an unremarkable motel. The following morning, Annabel was feeling upset.

'I didn't sleep well,' she said. 'There are bad vibes in this place, like someone was murdered here. Or maybe several people.'

I shrugged. 'It could be, I suppose. This was part of the Wild West.'

From past experience I knew better than to dismiss her feelings out of hand.

'Let's not hang around,' she said, 'we can stop somewhere on the road and get breakfast.'

But on taking the cases out to the car we discovered a flat tyre. No quick exit now. The spare wheel turned out to be one of those modern skinny things that looked as if it came off a scooter. I fitted it anyway and gingerly drove to the nearest garage to ask the young man there could he fix a puncture.

He looked at me strangely.

'Oh, you mean a flat?' he asked eventually.

'Yeah, one like this,' I answered, pointing to the punctured wheel to make sure we had achieved a meeting of minds.

Sure, he replies slowly, he can fix a flat but not until later, why don't we folks have breakfast while we're waiting? It is the kind of question to which there is only one answer, so still in our three-and-half wheeled car we drove down the main street in search of breakfast.

The waitress had emigrated from Liverpool many years before and was glad to chat to people from close to the country she dimly remembered. But Annabel was still feeling the dark vibes of the town. On impulse she asked:

'Was there ever a mass killing in this town?'

'Oh yes,' came the reply, 'the massacre of the Chinamen.'

'When was that?'

The waitress was unsure. 'Sometime in the last century, I think.'

Breakfast over, we made our way back to the garage where the young man replaced the wheel, tightening the nuts pneumatically with a lot less effort than it had taken me to get them off. We were ready to roll again but somehow couldn't leave without finding out more about this massacre which still seemed to hang in the atmosphere. In the town's history museum we found the sad story.

Green River's nineteenth-century economy revolved around the local mine. The miners were of many nationalities, including a group of Chinese, who always worked together and kept to themselves. It wasn't clear why the management decided to allocate this group a different section of the mine, but the other workers felt it would enable the Chinese to obtain greater output and so earn more money. The perceived injustice, linked to xenophobia, flared into racial hatred. A couple of Chinese were shot. Instead of bringing people to their senses, it triggered a killing rage that swept through the town. The homes of all the Chinese were invaded and the inhabitants killed, about thirty in number, it's reckoned. A small-scale crime by the standards of world genocidal atrocities. But enough to leave a tragic wound in the air a century and a half later.

Although we aren't particularly religious in the conventional sense, we nonetheless felt moved to say a prayer for some kind of release for the town. Sombrely we got back into our rented car and headed out across the prairie.

VISITING DACHAU

Thaddeus O'Regan

As a child, I knew little about the reality of war. I read *Victor* and *Hotspur* where military combat was often portrayed as an extension of the sportsfield. The hero would yell 'Share that among you' or 'This one's for Chalky' as he successfully stormed a machine-gun nest, thus paving the way for the entire Allied advance. I built up a sizeable collection of toy soldiers, planes and tanks and we replicated such comic-book heroes in our boyhood games.

When I was eleven, my father asked me to help him prepare an attic for conversion. The premises had once been a lending library. I was still small enough to crawl out towards the eaves and retrieve memorabilia from the cobwebs and the mists of time. It was there, in a damp, mildewed box, that I encountered pictorial histories of the First and Second World Wars. I started to turn the pages, staring intently at the graphic images. Time and space blurred and, with a childish addiction to know ever more, I continued until I came upon the liberation of the concentration camps, late in World War Two. I still vividly recall the contrast between the liberated and those who came to free them. Robust, burly Americans grinned or forced a smile for the cameras, while alongside them, the shadowy, skeletal remains of European humanity seemed frozen in a rictus of incomprehension. They gazed out at a world that had finally found them, but for many, perhaps too late.

In time, I read more about the Holocaust and while my intellect absorbed the material, my heart still found it hard to understand how it could happen. Then, one beautiful, autumn afternoon, I visited Dachau. The sky was a strong, cloudless blue. The trees in the vicinity had lost few of their varicoloured leaves. The sun was warm as I walked through the gates and along a pathway beside the former administrative buildings, now a museum. I rounded a corner and found myself on the edge of the Appelplatz, a grey, open, gravelled rectangle where the prisoners mustered twice daily. The boundaries of this huge space are formed by the museum, the camp walls, complete with watchtowers and two long, wooden huts. Originally, thirty-two such huts housed the prisoners. Their concrete foundations still exist and occupy the remainder of the huge rectangle that forms the overall camp. I strolled down the long space between these foundations to the far end. Small birds flew across the silence. The concrete seemed as fresh as if it had been poured the previous day. The administrative block did not look unduly harsh. It had many graceful features, typical of Bavarian architecture. Try as I might to visualise the countless prisoners, I could not. The blue sky and distant, golden foliage defeated me. Then I entered the museum.

Huge black and white photographs dominate the rooms. They depict every aspect of camp life. Like the boy in the attic, I was drawn inexorably from image to image. But this was different; I could now recognise the walls, the huts, the building I was in, and went back out into the sunshine with new eyes and ears. Now, in my mind's eye, uniformed figures strutted about, orders rang out, prisoners assembled. I could see what had happened in this very place at another time. I began to understand, to grasp the wisdom of maintaining the camp as it is. Standing in lovely, leafy suburbs outside Munich, the Dachau Camp Museum embodies the worst excesses of perverted humanity. The deep, deceptive silence that pervades it is like the surface of a placid sea. For those who look beneath this calm, the lessons and the wreckage of the past are clearly visible.

WORLDS AWAY

Matthew Byrne

It was a sultry day in Greystones. August 6, 1945. Woolly clouds ambled across a summer sky. Even the sea was lazy, no more than shingle-whispering on the long beach. Up at the house, a group of people on a well-mown lawn idled at a game of croquet.

It was a lazy day. And yet, for all its dreamy listlessness, there was an uneasy feeling to the day. As though there were something hidden in the quietness.

The newspapers in the next week gave substance to the shadowy feelings.

They had dropped the bomb on Hiroshima.

In the next few weeks, John Hersey's report ... column after column in *The Irish Times* ... put names and human faces on the brutality.

But, for all the reading, Hiroshima was still no more than a name I filled in for myself on my school atlas. An island of sorrow that was worlds away. A lament whose throbs soon lost their melancholy in the bedlam of a teenager's summer.

The summer passed.

And the years.

Now it was 1954. I was an Army Chaplain on leave from Korea.

And I was in Hiroshima. Standing at the spot just above which the bomb had burst on that fateful day a few years earlier.

Noise and city sounds drifted towards me. Out beyond, the darkening river. And the bridge, thronged with bustling people putting shape on their day.

But here, where I stood, was desolation. Devastation, tidied after the shadow of the mushroom cloud had gone.

A shanty-town landmark on the road of history.

In the huddle of sacks, stretched tins and bits of wood, I found the building that stored the artist's impressions of the inhuman night.

Burnt yellows, blacks and gory reds painted scenes that seared your eyes. Faces screamed. Great buildings buckled. Bodies, bleeding, burning, raw on their desolated homesteads. Women and children, men mangled in the debris. Or running frantic through the streets where raging fires burnt out a pathway for them.

Outside this gallery of torment, the stalls where they sold the weird paraphernalia salvaged after the explosion. In aid of 'Atomic Bomb Casualties'. A roof-tile charred by the bomb flash. A bottle melted by the heat and reformed into a cruel shape. A piece of soap turned to stone as an old man washed his hands at the time the bomb burst.

Dominating this dereliction was the Peace Building. In its former glory it was the Industrial Promotion Hall. But now ... jagged against the sky, twisted, raw, a ruin browsing in tatters enclosed by a wire fence.

Along the road, a little lad squatted at his mother's feet. His intent face followed every movement of his hand across the drawing-block resting on his knees. Every now and then he'd look up, scanning the scene before him. And then he'd dig his pencil, carving, as it were, into the paper the cruel outlines of the Peace Building.

From where he sat he could clearly see the great, modern plinth set up outside the fence. But he couldn't read the message it bore in Japanese and English.

In fact, it said:

> Once a stately building serving as the nerve centre for the development of industries in Hiroshima Prefecture, it was turned into ruins by the first atomic bomb that exploded 570 meters above it on August 6, 1945. Of the thousands of buildings that met the same fate, this alone, marking the centre of the explosion, is now being preserved to symbol-ise our wish that there be no more Hiroshimas.

Above the panels, in concrete letters, the word PEACE.

A DREAM OF MANDARIN DUCK

Norrie Egan

I wasn't expecting a lot from our visit to Wuhan – capital of the Hubei Province in China. We had arrived there late the previous evening after a cruise on the Yangtze that took us through some of the most awe-inspiring scenery in the world. We had negotiated the rapids in the beautiful Three Small Gorges, and at Yichang had visited the construction site of the controversial dam which will displace over a million people and destroy this premier scenic area. After all that Wuhan seemed very small beer. Surely a chance for a much needed snooze on the bus.

I had reckoned without our new guide, Wei. She was tiny and frail with greying hair, but her voice compelled our attention. In perfect English she welcomed us to her city, one of the most beautiful in China and Mao Tse-tung's favourite. It was *en fête* for the fiftieth anniversary of the founding of the Republic and the streets were decorated with flowers and lanterns and lights.

The museum she was bringing us to was new – specially built to house the treasures recovered from the tomb of the Marquis Liu, who had ruled the area over two thousand years before. The most significant find was a set of chimes, sixty-six in all, ranging from enormous bass bells to small treble ones. Each bell, when struck with a hammer, produces two notes, a tone apart, depending on whether it is struck in the centre or at the side. The chimes, now restored to their original magnificence and re-hung as they had once been on a three-tiered wooden frame, are on display in a huge glass room that forms the centre of the museum. I was fascinated. My snooze would have to wait.

In the museum, Wei showed us a mock-up of the tomb. It consisted of four chambers. In one were chariots, weapons and armour. In another, enormous amphorae and food containers, cooking utensils and a primitive barbecue! In the third were the chimes and other musical instruments. And in the fourth and largest, the remains of the Marquis himself in a gigantic double sarcophagus. This was displayed nearby, the colours on the outer casket still amazingly fresh.

In this chamber were also found twenty-three small coffins. Each contained the body of a young girl. All had been poisoned. Wei paused and her voice became dreamlike.

'Who were these maidens?' she wondered. 'Concubines? Servants? Or were they musicians needed in the afterlife to make the chimes sing again?'

In one coffin a mandarin duck was found.

'These are very special in China,' Wei continued. 'They mate for life, and so replicas are traditionally given to young girls on marriage as a good-luck charm. Who was this girl's husband? Had he placed the duck beside her in death, or had she died alone in agony, clutching it for comfort?'

I was hanging on every word.

Wei sighed. 'I like to dream,' she said softly.

Later, in the basement theatre, eight musicians in period costume gave a recital on a replica set of bells and other instruments like stone chimes, zithers, mouth organs and two-stringed fiddles.

In the shop on the way out I bought a wooden, hand-painted mandarin duck. It will always remind me of Wei, who turned just another visit to another museum into an unforgettable experience. At the appropriate time I will give it to my daughter, and hope that its magic will work for her – even if it failed that little Chinese girl two thousand years ago.

AN ENCOUNTER IN IRAN

John Heuston

My initial impression of Urumiah was of a totally Islamic city. Dozens of mosques dominated the skyline and any women I saw on the streets of the city wore the obligatory *chador* – the all-enveloping black garment which conceals every part of the body except the eyes.

But appearances can be deceptive in Iran, as in any other place, and I was soon to learn that Urumiah and the surrounding region is home to a long-established and sizeable Christian community. Known as Nestorians, after the fifth-century bishop who broke with mainstream Christianity in a now long-forgotten theological dispute, the Nestorian Christians of north-western Iran have lived for over a thousand years in a society dominated by Islam.

I learned this interesting aspect of Iranian life when, by chance, I found myself speaking to one of these Nestorian Christians as I queued patiently in the local equivalent of the GPO; waiting for a phone call to Ireland. He was a pleasant young man in his mid-twenties, a farmer who had several acres of apple orchards outside the city. We had a long and interesting conversation about the position of the small Christian minority in Iran and, after helping me to make my telephone call, he invited me to see his church, which, he assured me, was not too far from the post office.

I accepted his kind invitation but, as he led me down some very narrow back streets, I was beginning to have a few misgivings about this unscheduled part of my visit to Urumiah.

At last we arrived at a large compound surrounded by a high wall. As we entered by a narrow gateway, I saw hundreds of men, women and children walking about the compound or squatting by the walls – and I soon discovered that they were Kurdish refugees who, just a few days before, had fled in terror from the helicopter gunships and chemical weapons of Saddam Hussein.

My guide introduced me to the elders of the community and I spent several pleasant hours as their guest, answering many questions about Ireland and discussing the likely outcome of the refugee crisis which was growing more acute by the hour.

When it was time for me to leave, the leader of the community beckoned me to follow him to a large, carved wooden door in a nearby wall. Unlocking the door with an enormous key, he led me down several flights of steps until I found myself in a small chapel with a vaulted ceiling supported by high, whitewashed walls. He explained that the chapel was built in the second century after Christ and, as such, was believed to be the oldest place of Christian worship in the world. He told me that it was built on the site of a building in which one of the Magi – one of the Three Wise Men of the Christmas story – lived and died almost two thousand years ago.

He explained that the Magi who brought gifts of gold, frankincense and myrrh to the stable at Bethlehem are believed to have been followers of Zoroastrism – a religion centred on the study of the stars which was dominant in that part of the world at the time of the birth of Jesus.

And almost as an aside, he remarked that Marco Polo had prayed in the same chapel of St Mary of Urumiah as he made his way to China in the fourteenth century.

The atmosphere was cool and refreshing. But to me, the most striking aspect of all was the silence in that ancient building. And yet there was something else which I will always remember. The little chapel was filled with sleeping bags, clothes, shoes and other items intended for the refugees.

It was explained that the chapel was only used for worship on very special occasions – such as Christmas and other important feast days – but that outside of those, it was put to good use as a secure place in which to store the supplies so desperately needed by the refugees.

By the time we made our way back up a flight of steps worn by the footsteps of almost two thousand years, it was getting dark and the stars were beginning to twinkle over the city. Then the leader of the Christian community at Urumiah bade me goodbye and as he wished me a safe journey back to Ireland, he handed me a small container filled with a whitish substance that looked like coarse-grained sugar.

'What's this?' I asked.

'Frankincense,' he replied with a smile.

TORTOISE TEARS

Madeleine Going

I looked into the eyes of the tortoise – shiny, opaque eyes, like choco-
late drops, then at his wrinkled face, receding chin and scaly neck. Tears
began to roll down his leathery cheeks.

Sympathy? Crocodile tears? Tortoise tears, perhaps – but that was
fantasy, for they flowed down well-worn channels. Secretions from
ancient and almost certainly dim eyes. We had been told that he was well
over two hundred years old.

And no ordinary tortoise. Upright on short, sturdy legs, he reached
my waist. About as broad as he was long, he was one of the several
dozen that roamed the tiny island, off Zanzibar. The contrast between
his vast bulk and his gentle expression was very moving.

We were spending a week on Zanzibar. Warm, spicy scents – clove,
nutmeg, vanilla – intoxicated us. In the small harbour, *dhows* (Arab
sailing ships from the Persian gulf) dipped and swayed at their moor-
ings like ballet dancers practising at the barre.

'You must visit Tortoise Island,' friends had said.

I hesitated. I remembered once, driving around Kenya's Tsavo
National Park, coming upon a tortoise, asleep in the middle of the
track. I jumped out and picked him up. He rewarded me with a copious
stream of urine splashing over my legs and into my shoes. I was so star-
tled, I just stood there, making no effort to avoid the cascade. But these
Zanzibari tortoises were giants – quite different from their Kenyan
cousins.

The visit to Tortoise Island sounded fun, so we made up a small party and hired a boat. After about two hours at sea, we were deposited just before noon in a narrow, rocky cove. We told the boatman, in stumbling Swahili, to return at six o'clock — *saa sita*, the sixth hour, we said firmly.

It was a day of a lifetime. Spice-laden breezes fanned palms and baobabs fringing the coral strand. The sea ebbed and flowed, rattling the shells on the beach. The water was crystal clear and sun-warmed. After a long swim, we found the deep shade of a mango tree, picnicked and snoozed.

As the sun set in a blaze of red, gold and turquoise, we walked around the island — catching glimpses of these amiable creatures who went about their business with such stately dignity. It was hard to believe that some of them were born when America was just getting her independence.

Darkness swept over the sky and night fell. We scanned the crumpled sea again and again, but no boat arrived. We were benighted. Nevertheless we were soon settled around a makeshift campfire, with a few boiled sweets and a battered banana. We tried to open a couple of coconuts but they defeated us. We were pretty incompetent Robinson Crusoes.

But it was wonderful. Attracted by the fire, the tortoises gathered, settling motionless, just beyond the ring of firelight, watching and waiting, the flames burnishing their enormous shells or glinting in their tiny eyes.

Towards midnight, rescue arrived. We'd been missed and an ancient motor boat had been sent to pick us up. Later, we were told what had happened. In East Africa, the first hour — *saa moja* — is daybreak (our 6 a.m.). The last hour, the twelfth, is nightfall (our 6 p.m.). By this reckoning, *saa sita* — the sixth hour — is midday for the boatman; that would have been the following day. But — no regrets — it had been an unforgettable experience.

Before the boat left, I ran back to the fire to thank the tortoises for letting us get to know them a little. Several were weeping and I promised that I'd go back. But I never did.

EXOTIC FLOWERS

Hilary Boyle

Once, when going down to Tenerife, we stopped for a whole day in Madeira. So with a boardship acquaintance I went up to the top of the island. Suddenly, she grabbed me.

'Look,' she yelled, pointing. 'Who on earth can have planted cinerarias up there?'

Sure enough, upon a plateau on the rock face was a mass of this lovely flower, and I shared her excitement. But of course the answer to her question was no one had planted them: they are indigenous in the South Mediterranean and the islands. I have always been thrilled to find plants we grow in pots here, growing wild with abandonment in other parts of the world. Cinerarias are really a senecio, a close relative of our humble groundsel, but how gorgeous they looked there against the grey rock background. On reaching Tenerife, everywhere there were kniphofia, or red-hot pokers, in enormous clumps. This was long before the Canary Islands became tourist playgrounds and materialistic money spinners, and I have never forgotten the pleasure that wild begonias gave me in the hills in Jamaica, peeping out of the clefts of the rocks between Newcastle and Greenwich, a mass of rosy blooms.

Even aspidistras took on a different look when they were in sheets under the trees beside the roaring river. They were far bigger than Gracie Fields's 'Biggest Aspidistra in the World' and even sported sprays of tiny lily-like flowers and they looked so right, which, in a horrid yellow-bepatterned jardinière, they never do.

In Malta we had lots of thrilling flowers. Jonquils in all the fields in November, cream-coloured ones which one could smell before one opened the door when Toni's wife came to sell me the bunches she had picked on Sunday afternoon. In March, all the fields were scarlet with the Adonis anemone, and in a wadi was the greenest grass, grey boulders belonging to bygone ages, and vetches galore and magenta clover four times the size of any of our closers, and gladioli.

Both magenta and pink lifted their delicate heads erect in the warm air. Earlier in the year I had found asphodel, the real asphodel of the ancient Greek gods, and could easily believe it was a sacred flower. In the damp crevices of the wadi grew maidenhair fern in masses. But the Maltese flower I loved best of all was the tiny iris that grew on the grass near the sea, a place gentian blue and the stalk no bigger than a matchstick and flowers perfect with golden centres and falls just like the huge iris of our gardens, all in fairy size.

Then in Italy one autumn in the woods were patches of the little *cyclamen europaeum*, all red and lovely. Sadly, the peasant children used to gather big bunches to sell to passing tourists and I fear they will soon be gone. Indeed in the Italian alps, edelweiss was picked to sell also, but in next-door Switzerland there is an on-the-spot fine for picking wild flowers, even the pheasant-eye narcissus which grew by the field-full. I very dimly remember wild wistaria hanging from the rocks in China and asters and single chrysanthemums growing wild, but we seldom left the house and the court of the children. I have always yearned to go to the foothills of the Himalayas at the right time of year and to see the glorious blue poppy, *meconopsis bailii*, in its natural environment, to say nothing of all the million different varieties of primula. In Kashmir, violets were not single clusters but carpets of yellow as well as purple. Spring burst there after the last 'sister ten days death' of the winter snows, and the almonds flower bravely against the blue sky in the snow-covered ground.

Flowers. Nature's healers of tired souls and minds, and my favourite of them all are our own heather-covered hills and little white violets of the hedgerows at home. One can bear anything if one has flowers to look at and love, so although I should not do so and cannot afford to do so, I have pots of bulbs hidden away in the dark press under the stairs to bring me joy before anything can get out in the garden. *Iris reticulata*, daffodils, paper-white narcissi and hyacinths. Expecting them will shorten my winter.

WILD FLOWER WOMEN

Michael Fewer

The first wild flowers I can remember noticing and getting to know were the bluebell – that Keats so well described as 'Sapphire queen of the mid-May' – and the delicate primrose, that herald of spring, probably because these were the earliest blooms to appear in abundance after the long Irish winter. At the first taste of mild weather, we had family expeditions to a favourite place we called Bluebell Valley, to pick bunches of powder blue and pale yellow blossoms for our little May altar. While I never became expert in any way on botany, I have always remained a devotee, and have found endless pleasure during walks discovering species that were new to me, and later seeking to identify them and searching for what folklore had to say about them.

My mother showed me that even common wild flowers, dare I say weeds, have a wealth of history behind them. Who would have thought, for instance, that the dandelion – named from the French '*dent de lion*', recalling the golden teeth of the heraldic lion – was richly praised by many seventeenth- and eighteenth-century poets, that its roots were used by poor peasants in Germany as a substitute for coffee and that it is a proven medicinal remedy for liver complaints? Even the little daisy that suburban gardeners abhor in their lawns was Chaucer's favourite flower, and had its unique uses. It was said to encourage pleasant dreams of loved and absent ones when placed under the pillow, to provide a readily available salve for soldiers' wounds on the battlefield, and in the days of chivalry the little much-maligned flower was a symbol of romance: a knight had a daisy tattooed on his arm to signal to all that he was in love.

In those days, when plants were used for medicinal purposes, their accurate identification was all the more important. I no longer have my mother to name the unfamiliar plants I find, and although nowadays bookshops have whole shelves devoted to publications that show a myriad species in perfect, sharp images, even they can sometimes let us down.

Years ago, on a May morning on Carlingford Mountain in County Louth, I came across a tiny plant with a purple flower I had never noticed before and on returning home, I consulted my wild flower books, poring over many photographic illustrations to try to identify what I had found, without success. I finally turned to an old, much-treasured book and in a short time found a clear image of what I had seen: its name was the common butterwort. A penned note under the illustration stated that the book's original owner had come across the plant 'near Carlingford, County Louth, on the 25 May 1927'. The feeling this little discovery gave me, the sense of communicating across all those years with Annette, was exhilarating.

The book concerned, the 1924 edition of Hooker's *Illustrations of British Flora*, contains over 1,300 black and white line drawings of plants, and I had bought it for £1 at a jumble sale some years before. The inscription penned inside the cover reads: 'Annette J. Spence, from her loving pupil Iris Ainsworth, 9th of August 1926.'

I wonder, had Annette retired from teaching? The volume had been lovingly bound with stitched canvas for use out-of-doors, and it seems that, for the next few years, as Annette explored the countryside around Dublin, she lovingly, delicately and accurately coloured in the line drawings of plants she found with watercolours. Under each little masterpiece she noted where and when she found it: at a glance it can be seen that she came across wild strawberries at Abbotstown in September 1926, and the fragrant orchid near the Dodder River in the Dublin Mountains in July 1927. Only a small proportion of the plants in the book are so coloured, and the last 'entry' noted is the water dropwort she found beside the canal near Castleknock on 31 July 1928. I often wondered what became of Annette and her love of wild flowers, seemingly enjoyed for such a short time, but since that Carlingford day, as I wander in perfumed boreens, I somehow know she has joined my mother at my shoulder.

A SENSE OF HUMOUR

YOU DON'T GIVE A CURSOR

Nicola Lindsay

You have gone down in my estimation
Because you just don't give a cursor.
I will be bold and highlight how I feel.
I'm feeling double-spaced
After failing to keep tabs on you
For I'm not quite sure of your alignment.
Just what is on your menu?
I saw you zoom in there and merge
In a deadly embrace. I'm not blind, you know!
It made me flush right
To the very font of my being.
I saw you scanning the options,
Selecting new texts, editing without justification.
I have displayed all the tools in my bar.
Did I not have the right accessories?
I used to be your icon.
Booted up, I tried hard to head your footers,
Inserting where I thought best,
Scrolling around for things to interest you,
Searching through the windows,
Dodging all those damn bullets.
But I was no I.T. superstar.
I tried my best to cut and paste

Over the cracks but, perhaps,
What we had was not worth saving.
I asked for help but your screen's gone blank.
I view the situation with regret.
You just refuse to shift. I'll not return
For there's no point in underlining things.
All I can do now is close down
And, quiet as a mouse, make my exit
While you backspace-delete my memory.

THE TOWERS

Sheila Smyth

Miss Martin came from Galway, and like the Connemara goats, she had high notions. In 1824 she married the nouveau-riche Arthur Kiely-Ussher. Since the fancy name of Kiely-Ussher was newly acquired and was an imaginative variation on plain old Kelly, and since her husband was thirty-five years her senior, the proud lady felt she had bestowed an enormous favour on him by agreeing to marry him. Perhaps the tight-fisted Kiely-Ussher felt so too, for in 1834 he allowed her to persuade him to build a new and magnificent home to replace the very ordinary one they lived in at Ballysaggartmore, County Waterford.

As the plans were being drawn up, Mrs Arthur Kiely-Ussher had a brainwave. Using all the wiles at her disposal, she wheedled her husband into building the entrance first. She had seen what had happened at Strancally Castle and she was determined the same fate would not befall her. Her sister had married John Kiely-Ussher, her husband's brother, and he it was that built the fairytale Strancally Castle overlooking the glorious Blackwater. When he was finished, however, there was not suffi-cient money left for gates worthy of such a stately pile, and her sister had to be content with riding in her carriage through an entrance that lacked a lodge and a gatekeeper.

Mrs Arthur Kiely-Ussher had always envied her sister's fabulous home at Strancally. Now, at least, she had the chance to own an equally beautiful castle, and in the matter of entrances she would completely outshine her sibling.

Fired with her jealous obsession, she persuaded her gardener, a competent architect named Smith, to design an amazing castellated bridge that spanned a gurgling mountain stream. Florid towers and turrets were silhouetted against the romantic background of woods and waterfalls. This was the main entrance, but it was not the only one. Further up the avenue, this ambitious woman insisted on another phenomenal Gothic building of massive proportions. On either side of the second arched entrance stood a lodge, each one large enough to house a good-sized family, and both were adorned with their quota of cut-stone castellations.

Mrs Arthur Kiely-Ussher née Miss Martin of Galway, was ecstatic with her follies. They spoke of wealth and power, a foretaste of the opulence that was to come at the end of the avenue, and even more importantly, they would make her sister pea-green with envy.

History doesn't tell us how her husband broke the news to her that his money had run out. Just as work was due to begin on the castle of her dreams, fate stepped in and decreed otherwise. History is also mercifully silent on her humiliation in the long years ahead as her guests swept up the impressively long and winding avenue, passed through the truly awesome entrances, and arrived at, well, a very ordinary house.

This plain building was demolished in the 1930s, but the follies remained. They are known today as simply 'The Towers' and tourists often stop when they see the sign on the Lismore Road. They are invariably astonished when they discover that these extraordinary portals lead to nothing, but they are also fascinated when they hear the story of the woman who had a castle with no gates, and her sister who had gates but no castle.

MILKING THE VICEREGAL COW

Gregory Allen

For a period in my Garda service thirty years ago, I was in charge of the headquarters' Central Registry, a dusty domain crammed with the files of half-a-century of history. In my next reincarnation as Organisation and Methods Officer I recommended the creation of an archive. My proposal for preservation of historical papers resulted in my appointment as Archivist – a consequence I hadn't foreseen.

Reading myself into my new job, I called at the old State Paper Office in Dublin Castle. I was brought on a tour of the Record Tower. Up the winding stone steps, on each level, the papers of the British Government in Ireland in the nineteenth century were stacked to the ceilings in identical green document boxes. Selecting one of the brass-handled boxes at random, among the perfectly preserved papers I turned up a complaint of unbecoming conduct against a constable of the Dublin Metropolitan Police, stationed at Cabra barracks – then located at the back gate to the Viceregal Lodge in Phoenix Park.

The background was this. Early one morning, a military gentleman attached to the Lord Lieutenant's entourage, taking the air in the grounds, had found a police constable milking one of the viceregal cows. Over the breakfast table the equerry reported what he had seen. A request for an explanation was sent in the first instance to the Chief

Secretary for Ireland, who in turn passed the viceroy's note to the Under Secretary, head of the civil service in the Dublin Castle administration.

The Under Secretary passed the note to the Commissioner of Police, who directed an investigation. In time-honoured tradition, the Dublin Metropolitan Police closed ranks against a common enemy. The culprit's Section Sergeant extolled his efficiency and dedication to duty. The Station Sergeant respectfully described the burdens for a constable of having to provide for a family of ten children on a wage of one pound a week. The Inspector pleaded that the extra milk was a lifeline for the children's mother who wasn't strong. And so on back up the ranks.

In the shorthand of civil servants transmitting a file when there's no more to be said, the Commissioner marked the file to the Under Secretary with the words: 'To see'.

When the Under Secretary had seen it, he sent it on to the Chief Secretary, again marking it: 'To see'. The Chief Secretary, in turn, handed it on to His Excellency the Lord Lieutenant with the same laconic message: 'To see'.

After a reasonable delay for consideration of the case, His Excellency, with good-humoured tolerance, wrote on the file: 'I see'.

THE WILY TURK

Maureen Keane

Dublin in the late eighteenth century had its share of lively characters, but it is hard to think of one more colourful than Dr Achmet Borumbad. He was lately arrived from Constantinople and he strode the streets in his Turkish robes. A fine figure of a man, he was over six feet tall and his high turban made him even taller. Although much of his face was hidden by a bushy black beard, he was handsome and his manners were exquisite. His English was good and his foreign accent added to his charm.

The doctor had a mission. In his travels in Asia, Africa and Europe, he had noted how frequent bathing in supervised baths improved people's health. What he wanted was to set up an establishment in Dublin where the public could immerse themselves in hot baths, temperate ones, medicated ones and cold ones. There would be a reasonable charge, but the poor would be allowed in free and he himself would treat them for nothing. He convinced the College of Physicians of the merits of his plan and persuaded them to back his application to the Irish parliament for funds. Parliament granted him the money to set up baths in Bachelors' Walk and his successful career was underway.

The baths were instantly popular and the doctor kept his word about treating the poor for free. Society loved him and he was welcome everywhere. The only problem was that he needed more and more money for capital expenditure and the best place to get this was from parliament.

To keep his supporters there happy he threw lavish parties for them. This proved to be the doctor's undoing.

During one particularly rowdy evening, one of the guests decided he had had enough and left the gathering to go home. The merry, drunken crowd followed him, begging him not to go and clutching at his coat-tails. Unfortunately, he opened the wrong door and fell into a vast cold bath. One by one, those after him fell in too – a scene worthy of the Marx Brothers. Doctor Achmet and his servants fished them out and revived them with brandy and mulled wine, but the experience cooled their enthusiasm for public baths. After that night, the doctor got no more funds from parliament – he could sink or swim on his own. Actually, it did him no harm in the public's eyes and the business continued to be good.

What happened next was an old, old story. Doctor Achmet fell in love with a girl of good family who loved him in return. There was only one problem. Her family insisted that he must convert to Christianity and shave off his heretical beard. He agreed, and on Sunday morning he appeared before her, clean-shaved and in European dress. As she gaped at this newly westernised figure he embraced her and said 'I'm Patrick Joyce from Kilkenny county, the divil a Turk any more than yourself, my sweet angel.'

Her love survived the revelation and they married. It soon became clear, however, that the public no longer believed in the doctor's skill. It had disappeared along with his beard and his foreign faith. The baths closed down and Patrick Joyce, alias Doctor Achmet Borumbad, vanished from history.

DESERT BARBECUE

Arthur Reynolds

I had gone to Tory to record a method of herring-netting from open boats which was rapidly dying out elsewhere. While virtually all herrings caught around Ireland are taken by trawlers using bottom or floating trawls, the Torymen set a buoyed net in a circle around shoals often located by birds diving. This was because the fishermen were compelled to use boats that could be hauled out of the water by tractor when the bad weather threatened. That's what I had gone to record, but the story I brought back from that rain-drenched County Donegal island proved to be much more interesting.

There were no other visitors there at the time, so the resident priest was keen to invite me into his home on a few evenings to talk about almost everything under the sun. As it turned out, the story he told me certainly had to do with very hot sun – never experienced near Ireland.

He said that before he came back to his native Donegal he had been a chaplain with the Royal Air Force stationed in the Gulf of Aqaba. With not much to do, he had learnt Arabic well enough to speak with the many nomadic desert Arabs who came to the base with their camels from time to time.

So, when the RAF needed to extend its premises, it was decided to ask the Arabs if they would bring along their camels in six weeks' time to help unload a ship, which would carry the building materials. A few days before the vessel came, the nomads arrived with many camels and set up camp at the base. Forming a continuous train, they used the haughty beasts to carry the bags of cement and blocks to the site. They certainly did not need to bring in sand, for there was scarcely anything else there.

When the task was finished some days later, the base commander arranged a night-time barbecue, with lambs roasting on spits over big fires, and the priest was given the task of making a speech to thank the nomads for their willing help.

Then came a surprise.

One old man with a face wizened from the harsh desert winds, who owned the most camels and the biggest tents, stood up and replied in English, saying that they were glad to help the airmen, as the base had always been helpful to the desert wanderers, particularly with mechanical repairs and medical attention. He had taken on the job of organising the operation.

And when he sat down, the priest went up and embraced him saying that he was sure from his accent that the man had learnt his English from a Donegal man.

'Indeed I did,' he replied. 'I'm from Stranorlar. I came out here with Lawrence of Arabia in 1924.'

IRISH BULL

Eric Cross

A few days ago, whilst turning out a drawer, my eye caught sight of a heading on the old newspaper which lined the bottom of it. 'Government Sends Irish Bull to the Pope'. It is amazing how much more interesting old newspapers are than the current ones. Without reading any further I pondered on the possible significance of this particular heading. Could it mean, for instance, that the government had actually acquired a sense of humour and, after hundreds of years, was returning a *quid pro quo*, a tit for tat, with the long-disputed papal bull *Laudabiliter* in mind? Or was it perhaps a communication to the Pope in that peculiarly Irish form of humour – the Irish bull?

For all of the many forms of wit and humour, the Irish bull is probably the most distinctively national. Most other forms of humour or wit or mental play such as puns, riddles or double entendres, are common to all nationalities but no other nationality produces the 'bull'.

Like humour itself and any of its forms, it is difficult to define, and what definitions there are take its own form – both defining and illustrating at the one time. There is, for instance, Lynn Doyle's definition: 'An Irish bull is the saying of something in an obscure way in order to make your meaning clearer than if you had put it into plain language'. There is also the definition, attributed to both Professors Tyrrell and Mahaffy of Trinity: 'An Irish bull differs from all other bulls in that it is always pregnant with meaning.' It is not sheer nonsense, nor is it sheer sense, but a form of nimbleness of wits with which words cannot keep pace — an exuberant verbosity.

Sir Boyle Roche, the member of the Irish Parliament for Tralee in 1775, was the most famous breeder of Irish bulls, which he introduced to the world during the otherwise solemn debates of the time.

'Mr Speaker,' he exclaimed on one occasion, 'I smell a rat. I see it floating in the air and if it be not promptly nipped in the bud, it will burst into a conflagration so vast as to deluge the whole country.'

Perhaps even more memorable was his contribution to a debate concerning a grant which was proposed, to benefit posterity.

'Are we, Mr Speaker, to beggar ourselves for the fear of vexing posterity? Now I would ask the honourable gentleman and this still more honourable house, why should we put ourselves out of the way to do anything for posterity? What has posterity ever done for us?'

This pronouncement was, quite naturally, greeted with roars of laughter. Sir Boyle Roche, however, had not yet finished. When silence was restored he explained that by posterity he did not at all mean our ancestors, but those who were to come immediately after them.

The Irish barrister, John Philpot Curran was another well-known breeder of bulls and one of his most famous related to cattle. Winding up a case concerned with a dispute concerning cattle, turning to the jury, he said, 'It is for you, gentlemen of the jury, to say whether the defendant shall be allowed to come into this court with unblushing footsteps, with the cloak of hypocrisy in his mouth and draw five bullocks out of my client's pocket with impunity.'

Even Daniel O'Connell, either in truth or in repute, took part in this trade. In the House of Commons, while pleading Ireland's case, he produced, 'The cup of Ireland's wrongs has been overflowing for centuries — and is not yet full.'

The bull has an ancient history. A very old statute book records 'An act to provide that the King's officers may travel by sea from place to place within the land of Ireland'.

I finished reading the paragraph. It turned out the Irish bull which the government was sending to the Pope was an Aberdeen Angus.

BORROWING

Stephen Rynne

Times have changed. I hate to say that: it's a platitude of monumental size. Times have been changing all the time. But one special change rather interests me: the fading-out of the borrowing era. Thirty or forty years ago we used to borrow like mad. Country people, I mean. Objects and articles and sundries, I mean. Not money – there wasn't any.

The subject is vast – neighbours borrowing from neighbours – but I have no inclination to research it properly.

Clucking hens were in great demand at about this time of year. If you were to be approached for the loan of one, and had one to lend, you'd want to take a hard look at her before she left the premises. Three weeks sitting on the eggs, six to ten rearing her brood: she'd be in the moult and off the lay by the time she was back – if back she came at all.

Borrowing was a good game when fairly played. It is a pity it is a thing of the past.

In our locality, there were three famous items.

Mrs Dunne's crochet-bordered linen sheet, for wakes. Poor thing, it was used for herself in the end. People came for miles to borrow it. I don't know if I am drawing on my imagination or not, but I think Mrs Dunne's crochet sheet was sort of proverbial.

'How's poor Johnnie?'

'Bad. He had the priest *and* the doctor. I'm thinking it won't be long before one of them will be facing up Mrs Dunne's avenue for the sheet.'

Then there was Murrays' teapot. They were very obliging people. The last word that ever came to their lips was 'No'. It was an outsized teapot, of course. It was so big that it had two handles: a front one as well as a back one. Don't ask me its capacity, but you would be pouring tea out of it until the cows came home. We had it on loan many times – all the neighbours had it. It served a parish and a half at least. For threshing dinners and teas, of course; other occasions too. If it could talk, it would spout of weddings and wakes and whist drives and functions to raise money for parochial funds. The Murrays were very obliging. I heard that the teapot was in circulation long before I came to these parts, and that's well over forty years ago.

'You never saw it new,' people used to say to me. 'I think it came from the Curragh Camp after the British left. It was lovely...' I had to take their word for it: the teapot I knew was dinted and bulged and had a black bottom and the look of the morning after the night before.

The next of the famous borrowing items I am talking about belonged, curiously enough, to ourselves. Chimney-sweeping brushes – a wheel-like brush head and a dozen or so interlocking rods. I bought the set at a farm machinery auction the first year I was here. Two shillings. There was snow on the ground that day and the brushes were lot number three.

'How much will I say for the chimney brushes?'

'Two shillings,' I shouted.

Of course I had to pay commission on top of that. Trust those boys – auctioneers look after themselves.

Two shillings. Not bad, really, but we were never what you might call the *owners* of the brushes: we were the trustees. Talk of the Murrays' teapot and a parish and a half – the brushes were borrowed by the barony.

How and when the news got out after the auction I don't know. But in no time, everyone had it.

'Is it sweeping brushes? Go up to the Rynnes and ask...'

It was somewhat seasonable – like the clucking hens. Everyone took the notion of chimney cleaning in the late spring or early summer months.

'Me mammy sent me up to know would you lend her the brushes?'

'Sorry, we haven't them. Try O'Farrell. He might have them. If he hasn't try Murphy. Or Kennedy...'

'I will and thank you.'

The boy is about to step on his bicycle when an urgent message comes from the kitchen: 'Hie, wait a second. When you are finished with the brushes, leave them back here, will you, because we want to borrow them ourselves.'

They were good old days, those bad ones, when nobody had everything and borrowing was part of the spice of life. Can anyone tell me this? What's happened to the spice of life?

BALDY BOY IN DUBLIN

Benedict Kiely

The first time I ever saw North Richmond Street in Dublin, one of the two things I was, at the time, told about it was that the biggest Christian Brothers' School in Ireland was there – just *there*, where I could see it. I was not quite ten years of age and the information made a great impression on me. There were only six Christian Brothers in my own school in my own Northern town, but a fine body of men they looked when they stood up for the gospel in the parish church, in the front seat to the left of the nave. And one of them (a lovely old man) would whip out the largest white handkerchief I had ever seen and blow his nose with a trumpet blast that would set the wooden angels on the rafters dancing. The thought of the population of the biggest Christian Brothers' School in Ireland all blowing their noses like that was awe-inspiring.

The other thing I was told about the street was that the Christian Brother who had written the poem about Hy-Breasil, the Isle of the Blest, had lived and died down there. The poem I already knew by heart, with an inexact comprehension of the meaning, to say the least. But the result of being told of the author's association with North Richmond Street was that, to this day, when I think on the lines:

Rash dreamer, return! O ye winds of the main,
Bear him back to his own peaceful Ara again.
Night fell on the deep, amidst tempest and spray,
And he died on the waters, away, far away!

To this day, I say, when I think on those lines and that poem I see not the Aran Islands, not the illimitable ocean but the cul-de-sac off the North Circular Road as it seemed to me more than forty years ago.

It was some years after that when I opened James Joyce's *Dubliners* and read:

> North Richmond Street, being blind, was a quiet street except at the hour when the Christian Brothers' School set the boys free. An uninhabited house of two storeys stood at the blind end, detached from its neighbours in a square ground. The other houses of the street, conscious of decent lives within them, gazed at one another with brown, imperturbable faces.

Thereafter, North Richmond Street had a new dimension and Joyce's story 'Araby' made that modest place the symbol of the first disillusionment of life in the feelings of the boy when, after much travail, he gets to the fancy fair to find only that the booths and the bazaar are silent, the shutters going up, the lights being turned off. Yet no impression, no feeling, no thought that we have is ever unmixed or unadulterated; and now, when I read 'Araby', I remember also the way I felt when I first saw North Richmond Street.

For that was also my first visit to Dublin, something long looked forward to, and something that, because of a jovial barber who had taken a drop too much, and because of a loose iron tip on the heel of my left shoe, became a more or less tragic disaster. Once, I attempted to get the memory out of my system by writing a story about it and the story was printed in an American magazine, in, of all places, Texas. But that only made matters worse instead of better, because in the making of a story, you mix lies with truth and truth with lies and in the end you can't tell which is which, and you wind up with a very confused mind indeed.

Try it yourself. Hear a funny story in the morning and tell it to seven people separately in the course of the week and you'll find that you've told seven different stories, none of them quite the same as the one you originally heard. We're all novelists, or short-story writers, or just plain liars. Or slaves of the imagination.

Because there was a man in our town who kept a cow in the house I called the story 'A Cow in the House'. More or less! The reason why the cow went in and out of his half-door was that his back-garden ended at a wide river and the only way to get the cow from its byre, which was at the back of the house, to the field, where the beast grazed, was by walking her through the pantry and the kitchen and a long hallway right out onto a busy street. The river was too deep to be fordable. The towns-people understood, but to a stranger to the town it was always a bit of a surprise to see a cow stepping out of a respectable hall doorway.

When I wrote the story I suspect that I meant the cow in the house to be a symbol of absurdity, and nearly everything that happened on that, my first visit to Dublin, was absurd. The following, as far as I can now work it out, is the backbone of the truth of what happened.

My father and myself came up on an excursion train. The previous day my mother sent me to the barber to be made respectable for my positively first public appearance in the capital city. The barber was boozed. Two of his pals who had come in from the pub with him were also boozed. Not violent or anything, just talkative. They talked and talked, about football and greyhounds and the usual, and the barber clipped and clipped…until he balded me, clean naked bald, and all my efforts to halt him were unavailing.

At that time it was a terrible disgrace for little townie boys to be bald. Only little country boys were bald, either completely so except for a sinister fringe, or with the unmistakable mark on them where father or elder had snipped around the edge of the bowl.

The agony of getting home through the town to the safety of my school-cap, I will never forget; and next day, on the journey to Dublin, and all that day in Dublin, indoors or out of doors, eating or walking or visiting the zoo, nothing could get that cap off my head. All Dublin, I thought, was watching the Celebrated Baldy Boy from Tyrone fresh from his recent successes with Duffy's Circus.

Then, just as I stepped off the train in Amiens Street the horror deepened. Clink-clink-clink it went, the iron tip on the heel of my left shoe, having (as I thought) the general effect of a leper's bell, telling all the Dubliners that the phenomenon was approaching. The agony of the day meant that I had little to tell about Dublin when I came home to my pals at school, except lies about the things I had seen and done. That was why, when I came to build a story around that day, I added bits and scraps about other visits to Dublin and even, God help us, about visits to Belfast.

Years afterwards I told the tale to Brendan Behan and said: 'Brendan, I thought every person in Dublin was looking at me.'

'They were,' he said, 'I was there myself looking at you ringing like a cracked bell all along the North Circular.'

The thought of the ghost of a little fat city boy watching the ghost of a gaunt bald boy from the country can affect me at times almost to the point of tears, and you may now see why, when I read 'Araby', I get the Joycean boy mixed up with the boy who was balded by a boozy barber; and somewhere, on a vast backdrop, a luckless Aranman sails westward, forever vainly searching for the Isle of the Blest. No little boy nowadays is bald. Nobody nowadays keeps a cow in the house.

THE GENTLE
CLASSICS MASTER

Sam McAughtry

For most of my life I have been mixing with men who look back on
their schooldays with great fondness. As someone who hated nearly
every day at school, it's a state of mind that I have always found absorb-
ing. I once jumped at the opportunity to travel in a bus full of educated,
nice, mature, erudite men, on their way to see the boys of their old alma
mater play rugby, so that I could study the breed at close quarters. On
the way down to Dublin from Belfast, the conversation was delightful,
ranging from literature through history to politics to society and back
again. It showed the benefit of a grammar school education. It's no
wonder they hold such loyalty to a school that, instead of going horse
racing, they'll go and watch a new generation play rugby.

In the company was the sort of figure I'd never met, but had often
read about – the old, revered, classics master. White-haired, serene,
gazing absently out of the bus window, I couldn't take my eyes off him.
What was he thinking about, I wondered. I liked to imagine the old chap
linking the coming game with the odes of the Greek lyric poet Pindar,
an early sports writer, I suppose you could call him, who celebrated the
winners of the Olympian games in his odes. The idea of being taught by
truly learned teachers is one that I have a problem in handling. I saw in
the classics master a gentle Latin and Greek scholar who taught his boys
to face up to life honestly and never to take the easy way out.

In all the years that I spent at St Barnabas Public Elementary school not one teacher ever tried to persuade me to face up to life honestly, or never to take the easy way out. Indeed when the bell rang to end school it was risking broken bones to get in the way of the sprinting teachers.

Although I say it myself, I was a whizbang at English; my stories sold around the class for two caramels a reading, and while the other kids in the class were sucking their pencils, labouring over the first page of a piece entitled 'The Main Places of Note in Belfast', my essay had to be ripped from my grasp when the time was up. I didn't go for nominating places like the ropeworks, the shipyard, or the City Hall; instead I heartily recommended a visit to a dockside sawmill, where a man once lost two fingers of his right hand on a circular saw, and a week later lost the same two fingers on his left hand, showing a workmate how it had happened. After the second accident the doctor asked the man if he'd brought the severed fingers with him.

'No,' said the patient, 'I couldn't pick them up, d'ye see.'

Mr Morton, who taught the only four subjects we studied, didn't once compare my imagination to Homer or Horace, as a gentle classics master would have done. Instead, he told me that I was a head-case. And as for Shakespeare? He once took me by the lapels of my jacket, flattening me against the wall and snarling: 'We'll get this correct should the two of us have to stay here till midnight. Right — to be or not to be, that is the question...'

When we arrived at the Dublin ground, the college old boys hit the bar smartly. They were probably all taught to hold their drink by the gentle classics master, I surmised, comparing it to the way I took my first mouthful. It was in the RAF and when I got back to camp I was going to fight the cook. You wouldn't have got a grammar school man doing the like of that.

The college team won; they had saved themselves from relegation. We all got into the bus, and I started up a conversation about Beckett with the gentle classics master.

'Did you see an allegory with *Endgame* in today's match?' I asked him.

He completely ignored me, stood up, and with his eyes wild, pulled the shirt out of the front of his trousers, and yelled, 'Who's going to beat us?'

Next thing I knew he was leading the whole bus in singing the first verse of 'O'Reilly's Daughter', unexpurgated version.

After I got over my surprise, I saw the point. What I was watching was the gentle classics master's updating of Jason and the Argonauts, in search of the Golden Fleece. His version was actually more arresting than that of the original by Appollonius Rhodius. You talk about college education? You can't whack it.

BIRTH-SHARING

Tadhg Ó Dúshláine

Do you remember *Helga*, the first technicolour sex education film to hit this country in the mid sixties? Remember the excitement, the sensation as John's Ambulance Brigade members patrolled the aisles, and ambulances stood by outside the cinemas across the nation to attend the weak-hearted and the fainting, as the facts of life and birth in all its gory detail was publicly revealed for the first time?

For us teenagers it blew the theory of the stork and the cabbage patch and the millions of angels flying around up there in heaven waiting to be born and when your number comes up, it's down the hatch and out the tube like the lotto numbers.

We've come a long way since then and sex education is now as much a part of junior curriculum as tables and spelling, and partnership is the 'in' thing, not just in education and employment but from the very beginning in the labour ward.

My wife and I were on sabbatical leave in America in the late 1960s, when the traditional taboos surrounding childbirth began to topple. Expectant mothers and fathers went hand in hand to prenatal classes to learn all about partnership in birth, contractions, breathing exercises and stopwatches.

Íde told me not to take all this theory too seriously, that in the real life situations a lot of this went out the window when the pain came, and not to take it personally if she cursed me from a height as I mopped her brow, and held her hand trying to soothe her and she in the throes of it.

'Tis like a hard camogie match,' she said, 'hanging around beforehand is the worst part, the real business is all blood, sweat and tears and when it's over you're just knackered.'

She was right. The build-up to the big day was desperate. Clíona was in no particular hurry to leave the security of the womb and had to be induced. It was a long night of sweet nothings and empty chit-chat about house renovations and holidays and the best films we ever saw as we attempted to run down the clock without a mention of labour or birth or baby, as we had done on the births of our first two. To make matters worse, next to us was a young expectant mother on her first, in all her finery there, looking her best, while her husband, a vet, thumbed through a massive illustrated tome of gynaecology, smiling and nodding wisely and reassuringly to his wife as if to say 'no bother, been there, done that, a piece of cake'. This guy had it all apparently, theory and practice.

Then, all of a sudden, Íde felt something stirring. Clíona had decided her time had come – fast. Yer man, the vet, looked horrified as we were whisked off to the delivery room where all civility, gentility, decorum and etiquette went out the window. We were down to the fundamentals of life here and the actions and sounds were suitably primitive; screams and grunts and passionate pleas while beads of sweat, not of the romantic Keatsian variety, like bubbles in a late disturbed stream, mingled with tears and running noses of pain and effort. And then the exquisite slimy beauty of it all as Clíona popped out like a pea and we hugged and sighed in relief and exhaustion.

Soon afterwards they brought us tea and toast and as we sat blissfully content and grateful for the miracle of life, we heard the clatter next door. Apparently things had begun to happen for the vet's wife immediately after us and as he sat there on the stool, holding his wife's hand in one and his handbook in the other, he took fright at the real thing, fainted and fell backwards and clocked himself on the hard, tiled floor. Alarm bells sounded and when they got him out of the way to the Accident and Emergency room, his wife had no bother getting on with the real business in her own natural way.

When I met him that evening on the stairs he was no longer carrying *The Partner's Complete Guide to Birth*, but a huge bouquet of flowers and I gave him a wink and a nod, as much as to say: you know, sometimes a little learning is a safer thing.

LIFE, DEATH AND FOOTBALL

Catherine Brophy

Ireland had got to the World Cup for the very first time and the TV, the radio and the newspapers were making an unmerciful fuss. Big deal, I thought. It's a game, lads, it's only a game. However, it was an international competition and Ireland was playing, so I kept an eye on it. Then came the day that Ireland played Romania in Genoa. I was all set to watch the match when my mother became very seriously ill.

She'd taken several turns in the past year, but this one looked the most serious yet. The life seemed to drain from her. She couldn't eat, she couldn't drink and she could barely speak. We called the doctor and he immediately ordered an ambulance to take her to hospital.

I sat by her side, waiting and watching. Every breath looked like it might be her last. Outside, the sun shone and the road was deserted because everyone was watching the match. I waited and waited; no sign of the ambulance. My mother looked haggard and grey, her eyes were closed and she seemed to be barely breathing. I was afraid she would die before the ambulance arrived. A neighbour came in and insisted that I take a break while she sat with my mother.

I made coffee and turned on the TV to see what was happening to the match. Extra time had just finished and the score was Romania nil, Ireland nil. Well, at least we hadn't been beaten. They were standing around on the pitch waiting for the penalty shootout. Jack Charlton prowled about, clutching his cap behind his back. Packie Bonner pulled on his gloves and stretched. I began to feel nervous.

Packie's first up in goal. He blesses himself. Hagi places the ball on the spot. He kicks...boom! One-nil. Yeah, well, even I knew that Hagi was good.

Lung, the Romanian goalie, replaces Packie. He looks experienced and crafty. Kevin Sheedy comes up, and boom! Yes, yes, you little jewel! One-all.

Packie returns. He's looking better this time. Lupu places the ball, he kicks...two-one. Oh well, that's to be expected.

Lung looks meaner this time, but Ray Houghton looks good, he looks springy. Yes, yes, yes! You're a jewel and a diamond, Ray! Two-all.

By now, I swear, Packie has grown a couple of inches but Kotariu looks dangerous. And he is. Three-two.

Lung, too, has grown and looks look positively vicious. Tony Cascarino is up next. Tony has Italian blood, and he is in Italy.

I can hardly look. He kicks. You darlin', you pet! Three-three. Yes, yes, yes! I can hardly breathe.

Packie looks edgy but determined. Timofete comes to the spot. He looks as cool as all get out. He runs, he kicks...Oh my God, oh my God, Packie's saved, Packie's saved! Oh Packie, I love you, I love you. The crowd's delirious, I'm delirious. I'm trying not to scream too loud and upset my poor sick mother upstairs. Besides, we all have to settle down once again and bite our nails. It's the last Irish kick and it's David O'Leary.

Lung takes his place in the goal-mouth. He looks like Mephistopheles. He seems to take up all the space. Oh please God, please God. David places the ball, cool as you like. He runs up, he kicks and he scores, he scores, he scores. Oh David, I love you! The crowd is dancing and screaming. I am dancing and screaming. I dash up the stairs two at a time.

'We won, we won, we won!'

My mother opens her eyes. She is looking bleary and puzzled.

'We beat Romania, Ma, we're into the quarter-finals!'

'Ireland won?'

'Yes, yes, yes, we won!'

'I never thought I'd see the day.' She smiles and she sits up in the bed.

The colour has come back to her cheeks and she can't keep the grin off her face.

'I think I'd like a cup of tea,' she says, 'and maybe a bit of toast.'

Two days later, when I went to bring her home from hospital, the doctor told me that patients were leaping out of bed, fully recovered, with 'Olé, olé, olé' on their lips.

The following Saturday I found myself watching the Ireland–Italy match and explaining the offside rule to a visiting American. Now, finally, I understood what Bill Shankley meant when he said, 'Some people think that football is a matter of life and death, but it's not, it's far more important than that.'

IT'S NOT THE WINNING THAT COUNTS

John Fleetwood

Any gathering of sports fans will be sure to produce stories of fantastic scores, wonderful saves, record-breaking performances and occasionally of incredible flops. Goalkeepers in any game tend to feature in these last tales of failure but Isadore Trandir of Brazil, who was never likely to feature in that country's World Cup team, must get first prize for letting in the fastest goal ever. A deeply religious man, he knelt down for a brief prayer to the patron saint of goalkeepers, whoever that may be, before every match. So intent was he on his devotions that on one occasion he missed the referee's starting whistle. Three seconds later the ball whizzed past him for the first goal of the match.

I don't know what the final score was but it could scarcely have been worse than the twenty-one-nil defeat inflicted on a Wolverhampton amateur club from England whose secretary had written to the wrong address. He had written to Maintz, then one of the top German teams. Their secretary, in turn, got things wrong, for he thought he was arranging a friendly with Wolverhampton Wanderers, then one of the leading English First Division teams.

If a boxer fails to come back fighting within ten seconds of being floored he is counted out. The record for attaining this state was achieved by Ralph Walton in 1946. As he was still adjusting his gum shield, his opponent Al Couture bounded across the ring to give him one mighty wallop half a second after the bout, if one can call it that, had started and flattened him for the necessary ten seconds. On this side of the Atlantic, some sort of similar record was recorded by Harvey Gartley and Denis Outlette. After forty-seven seconds of the first round, during which neither ever looked like landing a blow at all, Harvey let fly with a haymaker which missed Outlette by a good twelve inches but had so much power behind it that its would-be deliverer spun round so many times that he became dizzy, fell on the canvas, was unable to get to his feet for well over ten seconds and was counted out.

Racing may be the sport of kings but for at least one aristocrat, the Duke of Albuquerque, the annual visit to Aintree for the National usually included a side trip to the local hospital for running repairs. Seven times he started the race but came off at an early fence. Bookies were offering sixty-six-to-one that he would not finish the course and in 1974 you could have made a nice profit if you had put a few pounds on this unlikely event, for two days before the race started he had broken a leg and a collar bone. Still, he climbed aboard, plaster and all, to complete the course for the only time in his life. Interviewed afterwards, he said in heavily accented English, 'I sit like potato sack and not help thee 'orse.' Maybe that's how he managed to finish. Horses can do great things if you just let them get on with it.

One doesn't have to be in the international class to break records and lots of other things as well. At a small sports meeting at Cumberland in 1952, the hammer thrower worked up such a momentum that when his unguided missile landed, it caused £150 worth of damage to his own car, bounced off that and through a window where it flattened one of the organising committee. This athlete was a one-man disaster, for in previous throws he had hit a police car, a petrol pump and a portaloo, the occupant of which dashed out minus his trousers believing that his tigeen had been struck by lightning.

Still the Olympics can always be relied on to produce records of all sorts like that of Eddie the Eagle who carried the idea of competing rather than winning to extremes. He became world famous in 1988 during the Winter Olympics in Calgary when he finished last in the ninety-metre ski jump, which wasn't surprising, for his only previous experience had been on the artificial ski run in Cheltenham.

But the prize for the biggest para-athletic clanger of all time must surely go to Mayor Jean Drapeau of Montreal, the city which hosted the 1976 Olympics. He nailed his colours to the mast and declared 'the Olympic Games can no more have a deficit than a man can have a baby'. Three weeks later, Montreal was three billion dollars in debt and twenty years later is still in the red. How wrong can you be?

RESCUE

Helen Skrine

Long ago, in the age of chivalry, the troubadours of France and the Don Quixotes of Spain regarded it as their vocation and privilege to rescue damsels in distress. Virtue was its own reward. I felt something of the same satisfaction when I received into my household twelve displaced ladies. Actually, I'm wrong — there were thirteen, a baker's dozen. Somebody had added the thirteenth for luck, I suppose, and good riddance. She was very lame and bumped along rhythmically like a bicycle with a flat tyre. They were all extremely quiet and timid, being unused to a country place where there was only the sound of the rooks in the trees.

Where they had come from there had been a constant noise like a permanent scream and now the quietness was, yes, *frightening*. They huddled together for reassurance and spoke little amongst themselves. The sunlight, too, seemed to make them cringe, but on entering the house they seemed reassured and more relaxed, though still too intimidated to chatter even quietly in their own language. Also, it was warmer inside, for the clothes they had arrived in displayed enough bare skin to qualify them as models for the Paris Fashion Week. It would take time to tog them out in country clothes.

As always happens, a leader soon appeared amongst them and it was she who blazed a trail into the great outside world, while the others followed with tentative steps. Having so little in common with ordinary folk, they embarked with great anxiety on what we would call a steep learning curve. The first shock was to sample the non-prison food and the second was to make acquaintance with green grass. They examined it with astonishment. But the most agreeable sensation by far was, I think, that released at last from their solitary confinement in very small cells, they could now 'swing a cat', or whatever the equivalent is in their own terms.

After a week of the getting-to-know-you phase, the sun came out one day in its full mid-summery glory and, after breakfast, out they went to enjoy it. And I came upon them, all thirteen of them, lying stretched out on the grass, sunbathing, with their eyes shut, oblivious to everything but the happy conviction that they had arrived in paradise.

After three months they were looking smart in their beautiful new fine feathers and at last I was rewarded by finding an egg for my breakfast. Soon there were enough for an omelette. To celebrate, I introduced a fine cock with handsome green tail-feathers, a shiny orange scarf and a tall red comb on his head. I must admit he received the frostiest of welcomes, and his strutting and crowing were a bit subdued.

But now we're all friends and my reward is a *daily* reward. Their love for me is probably all of the cupboard variety, but mine for them is of a higher order. Or is it? If there's no egg for my breakfast I do feel a bit hard done by.

'I must have eggs,' I shout at them, 'or else — back to the battery!'

But it's an idle threat and they know it, as they sing a reply and pluck at my shoelaces.

A SUBLIME MOMENT

Michael Judge

Now and again there comes a sublime moment which makes everything seem worthwhile.

We were holidaying in the little port of Puerto Rico in Grand Canaria. It was a package holiday, the cheapest we could get, and our apartment was halfway up the side of a mountain.

We lived in little holes in the whiteness of the apartment block; like kittiwakes on a cliff face. And we were happy enough. The apartment, though small, was comfortable. There was a large swimming pool, with sunbeds around the edge. The sun shone every day, God was in his heaven and everything was more or less right with the world.

Then came the yacht... like the serpent dropping into the Garden of Eden for a chat.

One morning, there it was, anchored about half a mile off the port, gleaming and resplendent in the brilliant sunshine.

Now, I'm no expert on such matters, and I couldn't even attempt to give an estimate of its tonnage. But it was big. Brass fittings glinted and glittered, the snowy whiteness of the paintwork reflected the sunlight blindingly back at us.

And then we noticed two astounding facts. The yacht was carrying a helicopter... *and* an aeroplane with its wings folded back.

This was serious wealth, we told ourselves. It was as if the king of all the islands had come to visit us.

For two days the yacht stood off the harbour. Now and again the helicopter rose in the sunshine and disappeared on mysterious errands to important places, before returning and squatting down on the immaculate deck again.

As we stared at the boat from our hole in the cliff-face, a gradual change came over us. Our apartment no longer seemed comfortable. It got smaller, the beds got harder, the sparse furniture became increasingly Spartan. The swimming pool shrank into a sordid soup of suntan oil. Even the ubiquitous sun seemed to lose some of its warmth. Our conversations became dark discussions on the inequalities of life, the vulgarity of wealth, and the psychological damage which must inevitably be suffered by the rich of this world.

Then, on the third day, the yacht came into the harbour. Various other boats already moored there had been cleared out of the way to leave space for this most important visitor. We troglodytes rose in our sweaty hundreds and descended the sloping streets to the water's edge. The air was heavy with suntan oil, sweat, aftershave and envy. At the harbour we sat on the wall and waited, a resentful, muttering multitude.

The splendid yacht arrived at her mooring. Men in white uniforms bustled about the deck. A ramp was dropped. Two jeeps thundered up from the depths and stood panting on the quay. Whistles were blown. A personalised gangway with a white awning over it was lowered. More whistles were blown.

Then he came. A small, fat man, in immaculate white ducks. A white cap with gold braid stood jauntily on his head, gold epaulettes framed his portly chest. He saluted, skipped onto the gangway... and fell into the water.

A huge sigh of satisfaction washed over the assembled troglodytes. We rose and made our way back up to our caves, without waiting to see the captain being fished out of the sea.

God was safely back in his heaven.

BED AND BREAKFASTING IN THE COUNTRY

Melosina Lenox-Conyngham

My wee cot is sited in a glade of trees; a twist of smoke curls from the chimney, honeysuckle entwines the pillars of the walls, peeping through the windows. The roses also tint my spectacles, blotting out the fact that bindweed is an even more invasive climber and that goosegrass, too, is a keen contender for wall space. The lavender bush is but a raggedy specimen and the curl of smoke is from the firelighters that I have thrown in desperation on to the damp wood of the fireplace. But Conrad Hilton said that enthusiasm was everything and, when I nailed a 'bed and breakfast' sign to a tree, I felt that already he must be feeling the cold wind of competition, for soon my name would be synonymous with Ritz and Waldorf.

This was some time ago, when there were very few B&Bs, so my optimism was rewarded when an unwary youth on a bicycle fell into my net, or rather into my cobwebs – the olde worlde look is not only on the outside of my house but is also part of the interior décor, as I am no great shakes with a duster. Oh, what a great Irish welcome I gave him! I laid before him plum cakes, sponge cakes, three kinds of biscuits and tea out of a huge, brown pot. My friendly conversation was like a waterfall about his ears, and at supper, I was so excited that I practically got on to the plate to see how he was enjoying his food.

He was terrified, for even when he had gone to bed, having locked his door, I carolled through the keyhole enquiries as to whether he needed a hot-water bottle or more blankets – and this was on one of the hottest days of the year.

While I was in the midst of cooking an enormous Irish breakfast for him, he slipped away, leaving the money on the table. I ran after him calling that he had not yet partaken of the devilled kidneys and kedgeree that I had imaginatively added to the menu. But this made him pedal faster than ever.

The next people were treated very differently as their arrival coincided with the disappearance of my horse, an experienced escapologist who, the previous month, had galloped up High Street and had been caught just about to enter The Monster House, Kilkenny's leading department store.

The guests, a Canadian couple, and their car, were immediately commandeered to take part in the search and capture. And by the time we had successfully accomplished this mission, I was so exhausted we all retired to a pub where they had to sustain me with strong drink. They told me happily that it was just how they had imagined Ireland would be and booked to stay another two nights.

From then on I became more confident and was positively blasé when the Arts Week administrator asked me to put up the quartet that was to play a concert of medieval music and wanted a quiet place where they could practise. It stretched the capacities of my hostelry to the limit, or rather to the walls, and I even had to vacate my own bedroom. The guests arrived in two huge Mercedes that were considerably longer than my house and their musical instruments took up all the space downstairs; a clavichord blocked the fridge door, a couple of viols were laid across the chairs and music stands and cases were strewn over the floor.

At dawn, Professor Ulsamer was in the garden tootling on his *dudelsack* – a herd of cows his entranced audience – while his wife harmonised on her *glockenspiel* in the little wood nearby, but I think it was the *krummhorn* that brought a neighbour hotfoot to ask if I was in trouble. I emerged sleepily from my lair under the kitchen table to explain.

'How sour sweet music is when time is broke and no proportion kept!'

DORMANT ACCOUNTS HOW ARE YA!

Arthur O'Reilly

Not long ago, the Irish government introduced measures to ensure that monies held in bank accounts that had been inactive for some time would be invested for public use. The funds are guaranteed safe for their owners when, or if, they turn up. I forget the amount of money in these dormant accounts, but it would appear to be a drop in the proverbial ocean compared to the funds sitting in a number of African bank accounts just waiting for someone – anyone – to claim them.

During the past twelve months, I reckon I have received, through email, at least thirty different propositions offering me a generous share of, in total, about US$1,000m. All I have to do to get this windfall is to allow the funds to be transferred from bank accounts in various African countries into my bank account in Ireland. For this simple service, I have been assured that I may keep anything from 15 per cent to 65 per cent of the amounts involved. The sums of money in these different accounts range from a paltry $9m (my share in this particular case would be merely $2m) to a more decent $126m (of which I would receive the not unreasonable sum of $50m).

As I have lately been getting at least one such offer every week, you can see that the culmination of just a few of these proposals would put me at the top of the Irish rich list quicker than my bank manager could think up my new banking charges.

The main beneficiaries would, of course, be the generous individuals who are making me these offers. These are (a) bank officials, usually a manager or auditor, who have discovered a large deposit in an account, the holder of which has died leaving no heir, or (b) a diligent public servant who has uncovered sizeable overpayments by contractors as a result of careless over-invoicing by less diligent colleagues in his government department or agency, or (c) the sole heir of an extremely rich, but now extremely deceased, former minister or similar high-ranking official, whose methods of accumulating wealth must have been such as to make a tribunal blush.

To enable my extraordinarily trusting correspondents to transfer this lonely lucre to my bank, I am asked to provide them with details of my account, passport, home and business address, phone and fax numbers.

My head tells me that getting these riches so easily would put winning the national lottery literally in the ha'penny place. My conscience assures me that because the people making these offers are undoubtedly con artists, any money I would receive would be tax-exempt, given the artistic nature of the enterprise. But my heart says, like Chesterton, that to be clever enough to get all that money, one must be stupid enough to want it.

Still, it gives a whole new meaning to foreign aid.

THE BOY SOPRANO

Bernard Farrell

When I was growing up in Sandycove, the back garden of our house backed onto the bigger houses and bigger back gardens of Spencer Villas. In these houses lived richer people, more aloof people, people we seldom saw and, when we did, we silently and respectfully passed them by. The house at the end of our garden was owned by Mrs Brennan who, despite her Irish name, was a most aristocratic lady – 'Like the Queen of England,' my father would whisper whenever we saw her, as she promenaded down Adelaide Road with an air of majesty and entitle-ment. She spoke to no one, ever – but all that changed the year that my sister began to take singing lessons, the year when I turned twelve.

In our family, my sister Margaret had an exceptionally beautiful singing voice and, in her early teens, she was already taking lessons in operatic interpretation, vocal training and choral work. And every afternoon, in that last summer of my pre-teen years, she would be out in our back garden, practising her scales, rehearsing her exam pieces and occasionally, with so little effort, soaring into something by Puccini or Offenbach.

And this was the time that Mrs Brennan and I first met and spoke.

I remember I was walking up Adelaide Road when suddenly she was standing in front of me, saying loudly and firmly: 'Good morning, Bernard.' I stopped in wordless amazement but now, more like Lady Bracknell than the Queen, she was continuing, 'I was in my back garden yesterday and I heard you singing and I must say that you have the most beautiful boy-soprano voice I have ever heard.'

I looked at her, knowing that I should immediately explain that she was listening to my sister, not to me, but, at that time of my life, I was so starved of compliments that I suddenly heard myself humbly saying, 'Thank you very much, Mrs Brennan.'

And so began our relationship as, in the weeks that followed, whenever she appeared, she consistently praised me, encouraged me and assured me of how gifted I was. As I accepted these compliments, my youthful confidence continued to grow and grow, as weeks turned into months and the seasons changed, and winter drove us indoors, and spring reunited us, and then we were into a new summer. And it was at this time, with my confidence at its zenith that my voice broke.

Suddenly, I was speaking hoarser and harsher and in a tone lower than I thought possible. But as I self-consciously monitored these adolescent changes, I never once questioned the effect they would have on my relationship with Mrs Brennan – until, quite suddenly, I met her again.

She greeted me with her usual enthusiasm and it was only when I replied, 'Good Morning, Mrs Brennan', that she stopped and asked what had happened to my voice. I politely told her that, over the past few weeks, my voice had begun to break and this was now how it would be for the rest of my life. She looked puzzled.

'But,' she said, 'I heard you singing yesterday, in your back garden.' I was trapped. I had to think quickly – and I did.

I said, 'Ah yes, Mrs Brennan – what has happened is that I have had to stop singing – but my sister, Margaret, has now started and it was probably her you heard.'

She looked at me for a moment and then said, 'Well, she does sing quite well – but she will never be as good as you.'

In the years that followed, I saw less and less of Mrs Brennan – she no longer promenaded along Adelaide Road and then I heard of her illness and, soon after, that she had passed away. By then, my sister's singing career had begun to blossom and, for many years, she revelled in the appreciation and the applause, until she relinquished it all for love, parenthood and family. And some months ago, at too young an age, she too died. At her funeral, as I remembered her, I also remembered Mrs Brennan and I wondered if they were now together, speaking to each other at long last. And I smiled at the thought of Margaret telling her who was really singing in our back garden all those years ago – and Mrs Brennan now knowing that the boy soprano never really existed, that he was just a young, insecure impostor who had once tried to live in the shadow of his much more gifted sister.

IN SPACE, NO ONE CAN HEAR YOU SMOKE

James Cotter

I was doing what all the hip, beautiful people do these days. I was huddling outside a pub, trying to shelter from the arctic winds, and have a smoke at the same time.

It was as glamorous as it sounds.

The doors swung open and I was joined by an old man. At least, I think he was a man. He looked like a cross between a pixie and a walnut – tiny, gnarled and gleeful. He coughed, spat blackly, flashed a toothless grin and lit up a cigarette.

'At this rate, buddy,' he said, 'the only place they'll let us smoke will be in space.'

He was wrong. Of course the government wouldn't let us smoke in space. If we were that far away, they wouldn't be able to tax us. Me, I reckon we'll be banished to underground caves, damned to live a lightless life, bitterly puffing on our heavily taxed death-sticks and working non-stop. While above us, in the clean air, the beautiful, clear-skinned, pink-lunged non-smokers skip merrily through life, living off the labour and taxes of us cigarette-chugging under-grounders.

Of course, there'd be a revolution. And us under-grounders would rush towards the surface to overthrow the oppressors, but by the time we'd climb all those stairs we'd have run out of breath and need to stop for a rest, and maybe a quick fag.

Anyway, chain-smoking walnut-man did have a point. We should really explore space.

We need to get off this planet.

Something's going to go badly wrong with it, soon. We know that at some point in the distant future, the sun will turn red and expand to a massive size, probably engulfing the earth. Or it'll just explode.

Not that we should worry about it, because before that happens we're bound to be hit by an asteroid.

Or a comet.

Or maybe a meteor.

But by then global warming will mean the oceans are up around Everest and we'll be too busy standing on each other's heads to worry about asteroids.

Of course, that's all assuming we don't just accidentally-on-purpose nuke each other to nothingness.

So wouldn't it be nice, while we're waiting for these catastrophes to fall on our heads, to explore outer space, so we can find somewhere else to live?

'Cause, when the world ends, it'd be good if there were a few of us elsewhere to, you know, keep the human race going.

But there's not a lot of exploring going on. It's been thirty years since we last set foot on the moon. The space shuttle was old technology when it was built, and that was twenty years ago. Now it's grounded for safety more often than it flies.

So we send robots to other planets instead of people, and like Beagle 2, they often don't work because they're being built on shoestring budgets. And then people say space travel's a waste of money. That's like giving someone 50p to build a car and then complaining that it isn't fuel efficient. Space travel is big and it is expensive. And I'll tell you why: because it's rocket science.

Governments say we can't waste money on something as frivolous as space travel, because there're taxes to be cut and health care to be given and wars to pay for and, and, and, and, we just need the money for more important stuff!

But wasn't it always like that? When we first flung men into space, weren't there other, more pressing things to spend the money on? When Armstrong landed on the moon, wasn't America busy fighting a war? That wasn't important, was it?

Exploration is vital — it's what we do, what we've always done; we explore. We go further than our parents; it's in our blood.

Well, if nobody else will do it, I've got a bold suggestion — Ireland should. We could build our launch pad under O'Connell Street. The Spire could tilt over to reveal a gleaming spaceship, just like in the Thunderbirds. It's bound to boost tourism. Anyway, what else are we going to put in O'Connell Street?

I know it's going to be expensive, maybe even as expensive as the Luas. But if we scratched and scraped and skimped on a few bits and pieces, I'm sure we could afford it. All we need do is raise taxes…or we could just make smoking mandatory.

A SENSE OF POIGNANCY

ST PATRICK'S DAY

Seán Ó Faoláin

Years ago, I wrote a short story that I liked very much at the time and that now rather haunts me, for a reason that you'll see in a moment. It's called 'A Touch of Autumn in the Air'. It's about an ageing businessman — hard, tough, successful, normally bristling with self-confidence — who's badly shaken one autumn morning by the memory of a trivial little thing that happened to him in his boyhood.

He's reminded by the smell of a sweet shop that he's entered of a toisin, or a tiny bag of sweets, that he had once shared with a girl of fourteen or fifteen when he was about the same age, about sixty years before. Those sweets were called 'conversation lozenges' — flat sweets, shaped like a heart, or a circle, or a hexagon — with a word or a motto stamped into them in another colour. Mottoes like 'Always do right' or 'Never look back' or 'Love is blind'. These sweets were called 'conversation lozenges' because they were supposed to start a conversation.

Now as the old man remembers back to that sunny, autumn morning some sixty years before, to an innocence that he has long since lost, he looks about him, he realises that there is 'a touch of autumn' in the air; in short, he has at last become old and signs on that he has started to become preoccupied with memories of things past.

Well, as I became seventy-five last month, you can see why I've said that my own story haunts me a little.

What interests me about memory is, not that it's often false, but that it's always fickle. As with that old man, it can hang on to tiny little things of no seeming importance, and let us down about things that, at the time, must have been of very real importance. Now, it's not at all easy to test this idea of mine, for the simple reason that we know what we remember but we can't realise how much we have forgotten. But we are sometimes forced to admit a blackout of memory.

For example, I happened, last week, to be going through a bundle of old diaries and I came on several references to a tour that I made in 1955 to four Italian cities – Turin, Milan, Rome and Genoa – in each of which I had to give a public lecture in Italian, which was a bit of an ordeal. So I ought to have remembered those visits to those four cities vividly, and I did remember three of those cities clearly enough anyway, in a general way. But as for Genoa, I have no least recollection of that visit, although my diary records it and it even notes the name of the hotel where I stayed – the old Columbia Excelsior on the Via Balbae. In other words, a total blackout.

But what's much more interesting to me about that little tour is that my only recollections of it that I retain with what I would dare to call absolute clarity, and precision, the only recollection that I really have clearly in my mind is of a painting of Cavour – the great nineteenth-century Italian statesman, virtually the creator of united Italy – that hung, as it probably still hangs, in the restaurant called Del Cambio, just beside the theatre where I gave my talk. Well, that's twenty years ago, and I still have no least idea why I've so completely forgotten Genoa, and why one portrait, and not a very good portrait at that, alone stands out stereoscopically in my mind against a general pleasant haze of nostalgia.

I have my own ideas about this seeming fickleness of memory – leaving aside practical affairs and science and scholarship, and keeping to the purely personal side of life – I think that we latch on most vividly to those things, often very small little things, like my old man's 'conversations lozenges', that prick a pinhole in the partition between our public selves and our private selves. I think if we only had enough of those pinholes and could interpret the significance of what we see through them, we could know ourselves whole and entire.

You know, if you take a card, and if you prick the tiniest hole in it with a pin, and hold that card up to your eye, you can see a whole landscape through it; and in fact that's what a short story is. It's a tiny aperture, pricked in the outward appearance of things, through which one sees the whole secret landscape of life hidden behind.

Unfortunately, we're generally much too busy with big things to catch on to these tiny things, tiny but precious messages, that are occasionally, none too often, alas, tapped out from some unidentified flying object hovering, like a dragonfly, on the farthest edges of time and space. So, we never do get to know ourselves very well.

Perhaps poets and musicians, artists in general, tune in best and most often to those messages from the UFOs of the imagination. Coleridge, who went into this question rather deeply, thought that when memory becomes emancipated from the order of time and space, it turns into mere fancy, or what we nowadays call fantasy. Rather rashly I suppose, I venture to disagree with Coleridge. I think that when memory seems to fail us, it just passes, disembodied, into our imagination, which then always keeps searching for some local life, local time, local place, person, who will act as its messenger. That is the time when we really begin to see things properly, when the memory is heightened, warmed, charged by the voltage of the imagination.

Now, all this is to do with my discovery that whenever on St Patrick's Day I try to think of St Patrick, nothing comes, just as I'm sure when the Italians of America celebrate Columbus' Day, none of them think of Christopher Columbus. The men are forgotten as men, yet not wholly forgotten as long as they can return through the imagination as symbols. I once did see a Columbus Day Parade in Boston. It was touching, but rather funny too. The drum majorettes rather fetching, a bit sexy; two priests marching behind them gallantly, under a wide banner identifying the band, the blaring band, as the Sacred Heart Rockets.

It was moving, to me very moving, because there were Italians who, like our famine Irish, had at last made good. And then, suddenly, around the corner came another blaring band – this time an Irish band – because they'd insisted on being in this parade too, led by a great, floating Irish tricolour. I confess I had to withdraw into a shop door to hide a sudden upsurge of tears. We, too, had made ourselves a nation. Perhaps that's all that St Patrick's Day is about – a buried memory speaking.

ALL QUIET
ALONG THE POTOMAC

Ted Goodman

Visiting Arlington National Cemetery, in Washington DC, a few years ago, I was following the path of many another Irish pilgrim to the graves of John F. Kennedy and his brother, Robert. I also wanted to see what I knew to be America's greatest shrine to the dead of all its wars, where they lie at peace by the banks of the mighty Potomac.

It all began with Mrs Lee's rose garden, in the grounds of a rambling old house called Arlington, set in 200 acres just two miles from the centre of Washington DC. How her little garden became the centre of one of the most memorable sites for any visitor to the American capital is a story replete with many of the elements of Victorian melodrama – hatred, vindictiveness and a dispute about property which was to last for more than twenty years.

When the American Civil War broke out in 1861, Mrs Lee's husband, Colonel Robert E. Lee, resigned his commission in the United States army to follow the cause of the South and his beloved state of Virginia. But many of his Southern colleagues in the United States army chose to stay with the North, among these being one General Meigs, Quarter-Master General of the army.

Meigs was to be the villain of the story, a southerner now consumed by a burning hatred for everything connected with the rebel South. The war at first went badly for the North and the great numbers of dead soldiers swamped the existing burial grounds around Washington. By a ruse, the government confiscated the house and grounds at Arlington and Meigs promptly decided to use the land as a military cemetery. He took particular pleasure in converting Mrs Lee's rose garden into the Tomb of the Unknown, a huge stone vault to hold the remains of over 2,000 unidentified Northern soldiers.

After the war, the Lees returned briefly to Arlington but never lived there permanently again. Their eldest son brought a case on the confiscation to the Supreme Court and, in 1882, it ruled that the seizure had been illegal and awarded damages of $150,000 to the family. The Lees then assigned the property to the government.

Between 1861 and 1865, some 620,000 men from North and South died in the Civil War, but it was not until 1900 that it was possible to have a section of Arlington dedicated to the dead of the South. It took a further fourteen years to get agreement to the erection of a memorial to them. It bears the apt quotation from Isaiah:

> They shall beat their swords into ploughshares and their
> spears into reaping-hooks.

Today, Arlington's 1,100 acres hold the graves of some quarter of a million Americans, almost all former members of her armed forces. Even now about eighteen funerals take place every day and the notes of a bugle sounding 'The Last Post' fall constantly on the ear.

The cemetery has strict controls as to who may be buried there – broadly speaking, any American serviceman/woman who dies on active duty, or who had to retire through disability, or who has been a holder of any of their country's highest military decorations. The deceased spouse or minor child of any of these may also be buried there.

Of course, many distinguished civilians also lie in Arlington, among them Presidents Taft and Kennedy, the boxer Joe Louis and the crew of the Challenger space shuttle.

That Arlington is regarded as a sacred place is reflected in the rules for visitors – no recreational activities are permitted in the grounds. Food and drink may not be consumed, even chewing gum is not allowed. Litter is totally forbidden.

The hushed dignity and reverence accorded to the fallen is caught well in the poignant words of the Civil War song:

> All quiet along the Potomac tonight,
> No sound save the rush of the river;
> While soft falls the dew on the face of the dead –
> The picket's off duty forever.

ZAPRUDER

John O'Donnell

Like many captains of industry, Abraham Zapruder was, in part, made famous by the persistence of his secretary. Zapruder ran a dress-manufacturing business in downtown Dallas, just across from a building called the Texas School Book Depository. He'd planned to go to watch the cavalcade, but believed he'd no chance of actually seeing the President on his visit to Dallas that November morning. But his secretary Lillian Rogers persuaded him to bring his camera, just in case. So he went home to fetch the Bell & Howell 8-mm movie camera. Zapruder had originally bought the camera for making home movies of his grandchildren. Just before lunchtime, however, the little camera would have recorded one of the most significant pieces of live footage of the twentieth century – the assassination of President John F. Kennedy.

In a sense, Abraham Zapruder's film is an A to Z of what happened; what the assassination really meant. In colour and (for its time) surprisingly clear, it shows graphically how a dream can turn into a nightmare. We see the gleaming open-top limousine cruising slowly down the street. The tanned young President is smiling and waving to the crowds, his wife pretty in pink beside him. They shimmer in the midday sunshine as they glide towards us. No matter how much we know now, nothing can prepare us for what happens next. The car emerges from behind a road sign and suddenly Kennedy is clutching at his throat. His wife turns to look at him; something is wrong here, something is terribly wrong. But the car keeps going, bringing them nearer and nearer. A second or two later, Kennedy's head 'explodes like a firecracker', as Zapruder himself put it, before our disbelieving eyes.

Some photographers jumped for safety when they heard the shots, others were too shocked to press the shutter. But Zapruder kept filming.

Shaken, he returned later to his office, locked the film in a safe and called the police. Word soon got out: there was a film of the Kennedy assassination. The FBI made copies. *LIFE* magazine (described by some as the CNN of its day) quickly concluded a deal for the original, in which Zapruder would receive $150,000 over a period of five years. Zapruder gave the initial payment of $25,000 dollars to the Firemen and Policemen's Benefit Fund, with a recommendation that the money be donated to Mrs Tippit, the widow of the policeman Oswald had shot — shortly after the President's assassination — outside the cinema where he was ultimately arrested.

Others were less conscientious. *LIFE* magazine had said they would never sell the broadcasting rights of the film. Inevitably, however, bootleg copies began to appear. Ultimately, the magazine returned the original tape to the Zapruders; the US government then acquired it and finally concluded a multi-million-dollar compensation deal with the Zapruder family in 1999. It is not kept in the National Archives, though copies licensed by the Zapruder family are still commercially available.

And Abraham Zapruder? Well, as you might imagine, life for him was never quite the same. He knew, even as Walter Cronkite was reporting gravely that Kennedy was rumoured to have been seriously injured, that the President was dead.

'They killed him! They killed him!' he shouted as the sirens and engines roared, carrying the fatally wounded forty-six-year-old Boston-Irishman towards Parkland Hospital, away from Dealey Plaza, away from the small green hill and picket fence where Zapruder stood which would afterwards be known as 'the grassy knoll'.

When the Warren Commission investigators came to interview him in 1964, he broke down as he tried to recount what he had seen through the viewfinder. He gave the camera to the FBI, and later on to Bell & Howell — it, too, is not in the Archives. He died in 1970 aged sixty-five. His legacy is a spool of tape that runs, without sound, for less than twenty seconds, a silent witness to a moment in sunny downtown Dallas when the world changed forever.

RAIN IN BOSTON

By John F. Deane

There have been days of rain here in Boston. It comes as a surprise to me who prepared long and hard for snow and frost and ice. I am brought back out of the unfamiliar to days I had thought long faded out of memory and have been smitten again by the vagaries of the mind. Do you remember those long rainy days we would sit inside and watch through half-fogged windows, boredom holding us, tired of the books? Oh yes, you were bustling about, forever busy, a lot of it unnecessary, passing the time, I think, as if time were a threat and not something that would run out for you, as it will for me, sometime, and who knows when? Things here are strange, familiar too. Small hard banks of snow remain and, no, there's no sign yet of spring.

I remember how excited you used to be as the buds appeared, as if suddenly, on the fuchsia hedge. Here the winter holds, it has longer arms, winds stretching down over Canada with thin and chilling finger-tips. I remember that story of the Snow Queen you used to read to me, well over half a century ago, I was stirred by the tale of ice lodged in the eye and heart, throwing a different view of love about the world, where the Snow Queen ruled in her palace of ice, where the Northern Lights, the aurora borealis, was a kind of chill and lovely firework display.

And then there are the birds, or not. During the snowstorm that came through like a vast, rushing express train some weeks ago, all the birds seemed to have disappeared, as if they had caught that train and moved on south. There was an eerie silence in the garden and, among the trees by Boston College, a dreary absence. I heard a chuckling sound one day and saw a congregation of sparrows in under the shelter of a bush where the snow had never reached; they were setting up a rumpus, a debate, no doubt, on weather, but all of them were chattering at once with not a word of sense amongst them. I stopped and watched, feeling, well, here are familiar creatures, behaving as they did when you and I stood out one winter and flung them tiny moistened crumbs of bread. You must remember? How we shooed the eager cat away indoors? And when that bully magpie came, scolding and threatening from the garden wall, how you took pity on it, too.

'Aren't they all God's little creatures?' you said.

Isn't it strange how you may be walking down miles-long Commonwealth Avenue and all that you can think about is the backyard of home, the blue-black apron of your mother speckled with the tiniest of daisies, and the squabbling of house-sparrows, familiar as the old rusty gate you swung on.

Then, today, along with the rain, there came a kind of clearance, that work of sunshine to get through and you can sense a glow in the world, a light that sings already deep in the heart, like the promise of lilac back into the world. And there he was, the cardinal bird, perky red crest and aggressive red beak, there in flesh and feather, a brilliant red with a black bib that takes nothing away from his preening glory. I took his coming as a welcome to this stranger from the west of Ireland, a loud halloo as if to say, 'Now just you wait, all this dull, damp city of Boston will clarify itself and will become a playground filled with sunshine and good cheer.'

And there, right beyond the cardinal, the catbird. Oh yes; I had heard of him, grey and secretive, but with that strange and haunting cry like the mewing of a sorry cat, and he called out, that sharp-shriek mewling sound and all I could think of was your phrase, 'Little boys should be seen and not heard.'

And here I am, talking to you, and you have been gone now a quarter of a century. Something about the heart, and its ongoing will to lift into bright skies of hope and love, something about walking here, in a strange city, growing aware of a love that was offered to me so many years before I grew aware of it, and relished it. Thank you. And God speed.

THE FORM OF INHERITANCE

Anne Le Marquand Hartigan

'Dear little Angie,' was the way my mother always referred to one of her sisters.

I never met Angie, but I know her. She rests there, light and delicate in a sepia photograph of the whole family, formally posed in their childhood. From this photograph, I can see how her fine bone structure has been inherited by my third son. How a few words and stories told to you as child can paint bright pictures of people you will never know.

This Aunt Angie lives with me; her short and young life lies with me in my cupboard where the delicate china she sent home from Shanghai is now kept. I use it with great pleasure, always remembering her life and the poignancy of the fact that things have longer lives than those who owned them.

Angela Josephine Halligan was born on 22 October 1885; my grandfather recorded her birth, in his elegant copperplate writing, in his farm day book, which he started in 1856. All his daughters and one son were well educated and very talented, musically: Angie played the cello, my mother and all her sisters played at least one instrument.

Angela must have trained as a nurse, probably with her sister Frances Clare who trained at the Meath Hospital in Dublin, and who worked there, in the operating theatre with Oliver St John Gogarty, the writer and man who was surgeon during the 1916 Rising.

Angie, however, took the adventurous trail to go nursing in China, to Shanghai, where she worked in a large hospital. I feel she was probably inspired by nuns and her own warm Catholic faith to do this, a form of missionary spirit, the desire to help those in need, the desire to do good. And good she did. She worked there during the First World War and, my mother told me, made good friends with one of the doctors of the hospital and with his wife and family.

The population of Shanghai and, of course, the patients in the hospital, fell prey to the dreadful flu that ravaged the world after the First World War and that killed more than all those who died from the fighting in the war itself. Angie's doctor friend and his family were struck down by the flu and Angie left her work in the hospital and went to nurse the family in their own home. She nursed the whole family back to health, but she herself caught the disease and was not so lucky. She did not recover. Angie, only a young woman herself, far away from all her loving family in Ireland, died.

I have a photo of her tombstone, taken by a sailor from their village at home. He sailed to Shanghai years later and found her grave and took the photo for the family; brought it home to my mother and her sisters. Many years later, in the 1980s, my youngest daughter was travelling the world with her husband. They went to India and Thailand, cycled down Malaysia and on to Australia and New Zealand. They then travelled back to Hong Kong and, from there, took a slow boat to China and came to Shanghai. I was very moved when she told me later that they tried to find Angie's grave. She could not, because no trace of it remains.

She was told that, during the Communist Revolution, all the Western graves were ploughed up and destroyed. So even the memory of her brief life, of giving help to the sick in a foreign country, is destroyed and forgotten.

But I still have the delicate china tea set with its green dragons with blue faces that curl and writhe on the yellow background, china so thin you can see through it. This china itself reflects Angie's own delicate nature that I see in that photo of her as a child. I enjoy this tea set with its cups and plates, the jugs and teapot, that she sent home to her sister, my mother. I use it with delight and celebrate her, sharing tea at family parties, christenings, birthdays, Christmases, and the thin china tea cups carry her delicate life story to us, her family, on and on.

THE SINGER SEWING MACHINE

Vona Groarke

It arrived one year to the day after her death, hauled in by two removal men who set it down as carefully as they could, and asked, a little fearfully, if I wanted it upstairs. I had asked her for it, she had left it to me, and I wanted to have it near. The lid of it makes a tabletop. When I raised it up, the smell – of metal, oil, leather, wood and thread – brought it back.

This was the scent of long ago; afternoons in the family room, spent in failing light; me at my lessons and her, sitting up at the window, at work on the sewing machine. The sound the sheets made when she pulled them open with her hands was sharper than the hum of the treadle and the whirr of the wheel. It would break the quiet rhythms of the room: the fire and its shadows on the brasses; the spruce trees etched in darkness on the glass; the dog, whining gently to come in.

It could be more than twenty years ago, or it could be now, here in the new home I have made. With one push of the treadle, one push of the wheel, the needle rises and drops as it always has; it is another winter afternoon. I sit at the Singer in failing light, and I have laid in yards of cotton to make curtains for the room where my children, not yet born, will one day sleep.

I am no seamstress, though I learned at school; made nylon aprons and a towelling teddy for the missions with the other girls. I could have bought the curtains ready-made, but something of those afternoons, their ceremony and lull, is not lost on me. Perhaps it is the feeling, unacknowledged, that I can make those moments hum again, and somehow that by doing what she did, I'll revive the steady rhythm of her life.

Hers was the last hand to touch this sewing machine. I know she has threaded it for me: gone into the family room, now cold and packed with boxes, past a hollow grate, the chair where I would sit over my books, my knees drawn up. She has gone into this room where she so rarely goes. She has sat at this machine in failing light, and remembered with her hands and a white card held behind, how to wind the thread from reel to bobbin to needle to eye to reel. She knew I would not know how, and the sewing machine would be finally undone. So now, one year after her death, it stands in my house, primed for use, not with the white thread she so often used, but with black she knew would suit most of my clothes.

There is a drawer to the front, shallow and neat. Inside, I found an array of buttons from twenty years of my family's clothes. I could have told her life from them: buttons from best dresses, slacks for everyday, small pearls from my father's shirts, a spare from the winter coat she loved, two peach ones from her dress for my sister's wedding, the summer blouses, the widow's black. I laid them out, the colours and shapes of them so lively, so bereft. These days, my son and daughter play with them: one day, they are medals, the next day, coins. I tell them about her as they spin and barter the bright discs, her life, her stories, the patterns that she stitched in all our lives.

BUNGEE BIRTH

Cyril Kelly

Everyone is familiar with the pernicious 'itises' which can afflict a body from time to time: school-itis, Monday-itis, work-itis, the list is endless. The symptoms, disconcertingly enough, have no outward manifestation, so the sufferer can be cruelly labelled as hypochondriac, malingerer and very often a lot worse. But the shooting pain persists. Most worrying of all, search as you might in sources as traditional as *Pear's Medical Encyclopaedia* or as modern as Ireland's health.com, there is no hope of a diagnosis.

My own peculiar brand of 'itis' happens to be TV-itis. Among my friends and my acquaintances, it is a well-known fact that I cannot sit before a television set for any protracted period of time — like, say, a quarter of an hour. Especially if the television in question happens to be turned on. God forbid that a cross-channel soap or anything with the bray of canned laughter should be transmitted — ten minutes watching such stuff can induce palpitations. One time, three and a half years ago, I stuck with Éamon de Buitléar for twenty-two minutes while he skulked behind a lump of granite on some godforsaken coastline waiting for a hermit crab.

However, I sat in front of a television set for forty minutes the other night and I haven't been the better of it since. It was all my daughter's fault. In common with half the young people of Ireland, she has bunked off on a year's adventure in the Antipodes. I mean, you spend twenty years rearing them and a sizeable percentage of your disposable income trying to educate them and this is what you get.

Just as the tourist in Ireland has to visit certain idyllic sites, the visitor 'down under' has similar innocuous pastimes which are *de rigeur*. For instance, in New Zealand, one must-do is the bungee jump. The daughter's souvenir bungee video arrived the other day, so I was prevailed upon to sit in front of the TV to watch.

I could see it straight away; that peculiar practice of standing upside down, as they do in the southern hemisphere, was not conducive to sanity. While the TV screen was still black, this soundtrack of relentless jungle rhythms began to hammer on hollow mango trunks. There was the distress call of some bird that, like the dodo, sounded as if the poor creature was on the verge of extinction. And, if I wasn't mistaken, that was my daughter's alarmed laugh in the middle of the cacophony. But then this primitive contrivance appeared on the screen. A scaffolding of bamboo cane, forty metres high, swaying in a forest clearing. In quick succession, Maori men wearing skimpy loincloths and tethered to the top by what looked like a *súgán* began to jump from the platform. Arms crossed at the chest as if they were going to meet their maker, they sailed first up, then out and finally down — sublime parabolas of serenity — until they swung, suspended by the ankles, their skulls within a whisker of the jungle floor.

Finally, in close-up on the screen, that face I hadn't seen for over six months. My daughter was smiling nervously. The camera panned away and I could see that she was standing on Kamaru Bridge. This was a box-iron contraption, buttressed by outcrops of volcanic rock 100 metres above Skippers Canyon.

Clinging all the time to the bars on either side, she slides the toe of one petite runner out to the ledge. When she cranes to view the void below, her pendant, a twenty-first birthday gift from myself, dangles from her neck. The laser of reflected sunlight scorches the trillion butterflies clamouring my ribcage in demented vertigo. I'm the arche-typal Kerryman in the joke, watching the video replay, hoping against hope for a better result. I'm screaming silently. Move back! Don't jump! Come home!

Defying death and G-force logic, she leaps. Spread-eagled in the crazy Queenstown air, she's plummeting past the blur of manuka shrubs and rimu trees huddled to the rock face. Till at last, in slow motion, the white umbilical tie line unfurls in her wake; hauls in the headlong plunge; bestows ecstatic liberation. The infant whose birth I witnessed is reborn, supple, swinging — her own unfettered woman.

THE MANY-SPLENDOURED THING

Thomas F. Walsh

It is a cold Saturday afternoon in late December and I have climbed into the attic. I'm supposed to be looking for last year's Christmas decorations, but that's only an excuse. I have really come up here to escape the pre-Christmas bedlam below.

This silent room above a bustling world is, for me, like the still point of a turning wheel. It is a space between past and present, under heaven and above the earth, free from conflict and tension, where I can sit and think.

I don't know about your attic, but mine is a repository of all that is useless and precious in my life. Things I should have thrown out long ago but couldn't, artefacts that have survived as we moved from house to house. In a place barely penetrated by light or sound, they lie like ghostly guardians of the past.

I move apprehensively between the tea chests and cardboard boxes that lurk here in the shadows. Surrounded by old familiar things, I am wary of their power. A tattered schoolbag, a school exercise book whose soft pages once opened on a world of wonder, a tin box containing a white seashell. A smooth stone taken from a windy western beach. Why do we keep things? Why are these the things we keep?

As I look around me the slanted sunbeam from the attic window picks out a blur of white far back beneath the eaves, something half-hidden by an old plastic Christmas tree. I reach in to find a pair of angel's wings, made from two coathangers wrapped in white muslin. And Francis Thompson's poem comes to mind:

The angels keep their ancient places;
Turn but a stone, and start a wing!
'Tis ye, 'tis your estrangéd faces,
That miss the many-splendoured thing.

I am drawn back to a Christmas play and a little girl, at the tender age of six, about to make her acting début as an angel. She has just one sentence to say: 'Do not be afraid, Mary.' She has practised it for weeks, flitting about the house wearing her wings and singing 'Do not be afraid, Mary.'

And now her big moment is approaching. She is bowing down in adoration, her forehead on the boards. There is an uneasy delay and then a slight commotion, as the teacher comes to rescue her. A shepherd has been standing on her hair. Now she trots towards the Virgin Mary and her baby, looking a little flustered.

'Do not be a-scared, Mary,' she says, caught midway between St Luke's Gospel and *The Little House on the Prairie.* She smiles and moves away out of the light.

When she herself left the stage of this world seven Christmases ago, there were people who said 'She's an angel up in Heaven now, you know, you can be sure of that.' I must confess that it didn't mean much to me at that time. But now as I sit here in the gloom and ponder that Christmas past, their words come back to me, and so do hers – 'Do not be a-scared' – and once again a happy memory shelters me from grief

And then I hear a muffled voice calling me from downstairs where angels fear to tread. It is my son, who wants me to give him money so that he can buy me a Christmas present.

Who knows? Maybe he'll buy me something useless that will warm me with laughter in the winter's gloom of some far off future Christmas. It might even make it to the attic and become enshrined with all the other many-splendoured things.

CHATTIE

Sam McAughtry

My mother had ten children; four of them died aged between one and four. Of the survivors, five were boys and one, Charlotte or Chattie, was our sister. She never married and no wonder, for she only had the slimmest of chances to meet boys in the usual way. In the thirties only the Catholic churches ran dances in their church halls, so that was out for us, and Mother believed that ordinary dancehalls were dangerous, morally and physically. Coming out into the cold night air after several hours of dancing, she thought, opened the door to the risk of TB and that was equivalent to a death sentence in those days.

I think that Chattie would have risked death to learn dancing, for, in her job in Gallagher's tobacco factory, the girls around her seemed to talk of little else. An example of the forces that kept her away from dancing and meeting boys was the attitude of our Rector, the Rev. R. Dixon Patterson, to the subject. One evening in our church hall, the Church Lads' Brigade seniors were meeting on the same evening as the Girls' Brigade; someone had brought a portable gramophone, a jazz record was playing, and couples were dancing the quickstep, when in on top of it landed the Rector.

'Stop this ungodly business at once!' he shouted, rushing to lift the needle off the record.

'Don't ever let me see this place desecrated like this again,' he said sternly. When he walked out he left thirty youngsters looking at the floor, burdened with guilt. Chattie was one of them.

We five boys were waited on by Mother and Chattie. They did the housework, washed the clothes and the dishes, and on Sunday morning,

Chattie and Mother made our breakfasts and carried them upstairs to us. Indeed, I had one brother who would stay out so late on a Saturday night that he would have all three meals in bed on a Sunday, reading the Sunday papers in between.

Chattie had a friend called Margaret. Three times a week the two of them would go out to the pictures, arm in arm, and arm in arm walk home again. In this way the years passed.

In the war she had one or two dates with British soldiers; one even called at the house a few times, and tucked away the odd feed, but there was always with soldiers the chance that there was a wife across the water, so nothing came of it.

After the war, a man called Billy came into her life, but it was a funny kind of relationship, for he only visited her at our house, and the two of them would sit in the parlour for hours, until midnight, when he would go off home. I don't know how they met, but Chattie was very fond of him. However, after about five years of this, she broke this one-sided affair off, and it really seemed to wound her, from what we boys could see. Naturally, nobody but Mother and Margaret knew the ins and outs of it. All through the years of his visits, we'd been too shy to ask about Billy's intentions.

The war took one brother away for good; Mother died soon after, and when three of the remaining got married, Chattie looked after the bachelor survivor in the same way she'd cared for us, but in 1965 she was taken to hospital: it was worst kind of news. After some weeks Chattie was sent home to die, and she died as she had lived, quietly, almost shyly, on a roaring, blustering February morning.

In 1995, thirty years later, I was opening the door of my car in Belfast, when I was spoken to by an elderly man. I didn't know him at first, then he introduced himself. It was Billy.

'Poor Chattie,' he said. 'I was very fond of her, you know.'

I didn't ask how they had broken up.

'She'd wanted to see me, when she was ill, but I couldn't.'

'You what?' I said, wide-eyed. 'You couldn't go to see her on her deathbed?'

'Well you see,' he said, 'I didn't want her to see me so well, when she was so bad.'

I left him, standing looking after me. I drove away, and he was still in the mirror, looking. All the time I kept stealing glances at him in the mirror until, in the end, I couldn't see him any more for the tears.

WHEN THE TAR WAS RUNNY

Shane Fagan

When I learned a boyhood friend of long ago had passed away in England, a special sadness pervaded my thoughts. Tommy was the 'second link' in a childhood chain... and now, it was broken.

A few days later, these same thoughts were in my mind as I parked the car near the old bridge that spanned the Boyne.

I'd driven past it a thousand times, never giving it a second glance, but now, on this tranquil evening, I would search for something... something I hoped had endured the decades.

The old bridge had changed little; weather-beaten but unbowed, it stood defiant, a veteran of countless engagements with the elements.

As I walked, my memory began tumbling through the years. Back forty summers to that scorching hot day when, as nine-year-olds, Tommy, Joe and myself set off on our first long walk in the 'country', a walk that would become a wondrous odyssey!

As the town receded behind us, so our excitement grew. It was the first day of the long summer holiday; the liberation put wings on our heels. We frolicked and pranced along the narrow winding road, until rounding a bend, we caught sight of the bridge. Never in our lives had we seen anything like it!

A silvery web of intricate steelwork, it shimmered majestically in the hot afternoon sun. We had come upon a magical vista... an enchanted place. Time stood still that day, as we climbed and swung on the latticed girders.

With an agility akin to a troupe of spider monkeys, we grew ever more daring.

Names, dates, love messages and things we didn't understand were all etched deeply into the steelwork... an earlier generation was showing the world they'd passed this way.

It was decided we also would leave our marks on history. Joe and I had old penknives. We prepared to engrave.

Tommy, the innovative one, was watching from the road. His shrillness pierced the pastoral setting.

'Look boys,' he yelled, 'the tar! The tar is runny! Get sharp sticks, we can write with it.'

So it was. Twigs became our brushes, the tar our paint, the bridge our canvas. The names were painted on an unobtrusive girder.

Then Joe, with a profundity rare in one so young, painted linked circles around the names. These chain-links would never break. We were friends forever.

I'd reached the bridge, my thoughts returned to the present. I began my search.

A few minutes later, I found what I sought, faint but legible, I was gazing upon the tarry masterpiece.

I was recalling how, less than a dozen years later, we were to disperse over the globe. Joe lost his life tragically in America – he didn't see thirty and now, Tommy...

I alone had returned.

To some passing travellers, the old bridge simply spanned a river. To others, it was a keeper of secrets from a simpler time. To me, it was a monument for lost friends, and that long-ago summer... when the tar was runny.

NOBODY'S CHILD

Rita Curran Darby

I watched her play; she was no more than four years old. She shovelled
sand into her bright coloured bucket until it was full, then with both
hands lifted the heavy bucket and turned it upside down. She reached
across for her red spade and with it patted the bucket gently on all sides
while she sang a little rhyme. Then, very carefully, she removed the bucket
to reveal a perfectly formed shape. She squealed with excitement and
clapped her hands while her father scooped her up in his arms and swung
her high. Eventually she wriggled free, eager to repeat her performance.

As she refilled her bucket I watched the golden sand turn dark and
muddy before my eyes. The long colourful beach shrank in size to that
of a small backyard; the only colours were those hanging out to dry in
a triangle from a two per-back window. The smell of fresh sea air
became the stench from an eight-family tenement house.

A child was playing in that back yard. She scraped at the heavy clay
with a piece of glass chaynie, loosening enough earth to fill a shoe-
polish tin. She spat in it, mixed it around with her finger, spat in it again
until it was smooth, then turned it upside-down and waited. She banged
on the tin with her narrow little fist, then sang:

> Pie, pie come out,
> I'll give you a bottle of stout,
> If you don't come out
> I'll give you a kick in the arse.

She lifted the tin slowly and watched her efforts crumble.

'Mummy, Mummy,' cried the little girl on the beach; she twirled around and around, making an umbrella display of her red frilly dress. Her parents watched in rapture.

The child in the back yard found an old wash-pole, she put her big sister's hat on it, stood it straight against the wall and asked,

'Mammy, will you buy me a new dress, a red one like Molly Delaney's?'

'I will, Chrissie,' replied the child to herself in a grown-up voice.

'And,' she added, 'new boots too and… and a pixie to match.'

The child became excited and tried to straighten the tilting wash-pole.

'A pixie!' she repeated, 'and maybe… maybe a pair of hornpipe shoes…' The wash-pole fell, hurling the child back to reality. Slowly she picked up her sister's hat and through her sobs she cried, 'I want a red dress, so I do, and a pixie to match.'

'Lunch!' called the little girl's mother. Her father lifted her onto his shoulders and carried her to the picnic laid out on the rug, they all sat down to eat.

'There'll be goodies if you finish,' coaxed her mother.

The child in the backyard turned to the wash-pole and asked, 'Mammy, can I have a piece of bread and jam?'

'Yes you can, Chrissie,' replied the child out loud.

She smothered a red chaynie with muck, then another one and stuck the two together. She pretended to eat it.

'I love bread and jam,' she told the pole.

The pole didn't answer and the child fell silent. She sat back on her hunkers and stared into the greyness of her surroundings. Her stomach rumbled. The grey wall became blurred and the child ran crying, looking for her big sister Bridie and knew she wasn't fibbing when she said she had a pain.

The little girl gathered her bucket and spade from the sand. Her mother shook the crumbs from the rug before folding it away and tidied the cups and plates neatly into a basket. The little girl yawned, then held up her arms to her Daddy who stooped to pick her up. She curled her arms around his neck and rested her sleepy head on his shoulder. With their bags all packed they walked away, taking with them my bruised memory. I watched until they were but specks on the horizon.

O FOR THE WINGS OF A DOVE

Bryan Gallagher

He was standing behind me at the football match and he was shouting. Shouting those coarse meaningless phrases one sometimes hears at matches.

'Bury him!'

'Get stuck in!'

'Bog him!'

On and on and on.

I turned round to look at him. He had the flushed face and blood-shot eyes of the heavy drinker. His hair was thin and receding, he had the beginnings of a beer belly and he sucked deeply on the cigarette butt he held in his cupped hand.

'How're you doin',' he said. 'You don't know me.'

'No,' I said.

'Well you should,' he said, 'you taught me.'

'Oh,' I said, and turned away.

And then through the cracks in my memory a face looked in, the face of a young fair-haired boy with the voice of an angel singing on the stage in the local feis.

And I remembered how the adjudicator had called me over and asked to speak to him, saying that he should have his voice trained, and the young boy was talking to some girls and said he couldn't be bothered.

I turned back to him.

'It was you, wasn't it,' I said. '"O For The Wings of a Dove".'

'Jaysus, I hated that f-ing song,' he said.

And that, I thought, was that. At half time there was a tug on my sleeve. He signalled me to come with him.

I thought I knew what was coming and wondered would it cost me ten pounds or could I get away with five.

In a quiet part of the stand he stopped and put his mouth close to my ear. I could smell his drink-laden breath and the stale tobacco reek. And in a cracked hoarse voice, my God, he started to sing, 'O for the wings of a dove, Far away, far away I would roam...'

At first I was embarrassed, wondering who was watching us, but then I listened, fascinated. The intonation was perfect, even in the awkward intervals of the second half of the song. The nuances of expression, even the *rallentando* and *diminuendo* at the end, he observed them all, exactly as I had taught him a quarter of a century before.

'Well,' he said when he had finished, 'you never lose it, that's what you always said, you never lose it.'

We got talking. He was home for a few days from England. Yes, he was married, but separated. He had a couple of children, somewhere over there. He was going for a few drinks after the match, did I want to come?

We parted. At the end of the match I watched him leave, an arm carelessly thrown around the shoulders of his drinking companions. He turned to wave at me.

'You never lose it,' he shouted.

'You never lose it,' shouted the golden-haired boy with the voice of an angel.

MY FRIEND THE PRESIDENT

Dan Treston

The first time I saw the President was in O'Connell Street, one evening where he was standing on the steps of a monument, addressing a meeting. Crowds of people stood in the way of the traffic, and tram drivers clanged their bells and shouted, 'Hey, President, get to hell out of the way.'

But the President went on speaking.

'Half a crown in, means half a crown out, and if you amalgamate everything and complicate everything, then everything will be all right with the Harness Markers' Union...'

The traffic was getting impatient, and motor cars' horns screamed out, but the President went on talking, his voice thin and frail as a decayed veil: the shabby trilby hat he wore concealed his thin grey hair, while the silken scarf around his neck hid the absence of a shirt.

He was saying: 'It stands to reason, if we bring back the twelve-shillin' suit and build paper houses like the Japs do have in Tokyo...'

But he was interrupted by the sight of two policemen whose big shoulders rose like boulders above the heads of the mob. The President jumped into the crowd who promptly helped to hide him, moving in escort with him to some other place. The traffic in O'Connell Street moved off again, and I went off on my business, never thinking that I would soon meet the President again.

I saw him next on Burgh Quay, and learned from a man in the crowd that he was called the President because he felt that the biggest insult that

Ireland had offered him was in choosing Douglas Hyde for President, and not himself. Regularly, he spoke on Burgh Quay. Enjoying his talk, I gradually took a hand in helping to conduct the meetings in an orderly fashion. He referred to me as 'my friend' and I referred to him as 'my friend the President'. However, when he spoke of the then President of Ireland, Douglas Hyde, he would say, 'That ould hindquarters of an ass'.

His programme was never quite the same twice. But generally he said, 'To obtain the minimum production from the maximum labour, and to do that I'll have to exile all Irish republicans to Transvaal of South Africa where they'll be compelled to pull a bloody big rope across the South Atlantic Ocean to facilitate Irish shippin'; but at the moment, the only rope that's bein' pulled with any conspicuous measure of success is the one at the back of Leinster House!'

He used all the political clichés, and listening to him made me realise how very little difference there was between his speeches and those I read in the newspapers. If anything, his were easier to see as meaning nothing.

The meetings always ended by the news that police were coming over the bridge. Then the President would take off his hat and pass it to the crowd who would drop whole cigarettes or fag-ends into it, depending on what they could spare. Once he had made his collection he would empty the contents of the hat into his pocket, and say, 'Now, all to attention for the national anthem.' He would lead the singing in a high, gasping whisper, 'Meet me tonight on the old rustic bridge, the old rustic bridge by the mill...'

After this was over, he would mix with the crowd, answering questions, which usually went like this:

'What will you do for the poor, President?'

'They won't be spared any neglect.'

'What about the export of cattle, President?'

'There are more cattle than people; exporting them will balance the population.'

'What's your policy with regard to Russia, President?'

'That Stallion will know when *I* get to Moscow.'

One day I saw him all alone, far from his usual beat, standing outside a big wholesale draper's warehouse, measuring with a piece of string the size of the brass plate outside the door.

I greeted him, 'Well, how's my friend the President?'

He looked around at me. His eyes were very glazed and a tear had left a clean track across his grubby cheek. He spoke in a voice that reminded me of a child's.

'Me mother worked for them people,' and he indicated the brass plate. 'Half a crown a week she got. Wasn't it great for her? God rest her soul. Isn't a brass plate a marvellous thing to make you important?' He paused, then said, 'Me mother hasn't even a wooden cross...'

It was the first time that I'd ever seen him show signs of being unhappy. It made him look much older and weaker than his seventy years. His rosy cheeks were like those of an old broken doll's, where the paint has been scratched away.

Lately his meetings had become less popular, and he asked me not to fail and be at his next one on the coming Sunday. The All-Ireland Football Final would attract some of the crowd, he said, but he expected to have a good audience just the same. I promised, but like many others, I forgot.

Weeks passed without my seeing him. Then months, and finally a whole year. Then, one Sunday, while visiting an old man in the hospital for the old and destitute, I saw him again. He was in a bed at the end of a ward which held sixty old men. All of them lying there, beyond hope, just waiting to die. On his locker was his old, battered felt hat.

That was the good thing about this hospital, they let old men keep some trifle of which they had grown fond. Mostly it was an old hat or a scarf, and you would see them wearing these things as they sat and smoked. The President was lying back on his pillow.

'How's my friend the President?' His eyes brightened at the mention of his title. I held out my hand and he reached for it. His voice was very weak, and only by leaning close to him could I hear what he said. He still had a programme, he would be broadcasting on the Hospital's Requests and would warn all listeners that a gale was approaching our shores. Then his voice failed, and he lay back on the pillow, closed his eyes and said very quietly, 'I'll be meself again soon.'

I waited a while but he was asleep and so I left him. When I reached the end of the ward, I turned around to get a last glimpse of him. But all I saw was a long line of beds, each holding an old man's body under its white counterpane. I didn't know which was his.

GETTING THE BIRD

Dominic Roche

The other day I was asked if I had any more stories of that occupational hazard of an actor's life — getting the bird. In fact, of course, there are enough to fill several books. A strange thing about performers is that, in many cases, their conceit is such that they will attribute violent audience reaction to any cause other than their own failure to please.

An example of this was the very pompous baritone at the Grand Theatre, Stockton-on-Tees. He got through his first number to a restless silence, and ignoring the danger signals, embarked on his second offering, 'Trum-pet-er-what-are-you-sounding-now?' or words to that effect. Half-way through it started: first boos and catcalls, then the missiles. With the courage of an obstinacy shown by most performers in these circumstances, he belted away to the end, and as he hit the last note a very ripe tomato landed full in the middle of his broad, white shirt-front. Walking unhurriedly to the wings, he dabbed at the soppy mess with his handkerchief and calmly remarked to the stage manager, 'They-ah, don't seem to like your conductor 'ere.'

More charged with drama was the occasion when a well-known actor-manager was finding the going very hard in a Shakespearian production at Liverpool. Inevitably a few boos started and the mischief was just gathering momentum when our very experienced gentleman stopped the performance and strolled down to the footlights.

Voice vibrant with anger, he addressed the very full house: 'You dare to hoot at me, you the people of Liverpool, the very stones of whose buildings are cemented with the blood of slaves?'

Record has it that the audience was so stunned that the play was allowed to proceed without further trouble. Was it the guilty truth that struck home? After all, it is not so very many years ago since all the older established Liverpool shipping companies agreed to destroy all books and records of business transactions prior to a certain date.

I would like to tell you the story of Fred Barnes. Fred Barnes was one of the very top music-hall stars of the twenties and early thirties. In physical appearance he could have passed for Ivor Novello, was almost certainly the best-dressed man in the business and would appear in the best bars in London leading a couple of Borzoi hounds. On the bills he would be described as the world-famous, debonair, light comedian. Immaculately tailored, silk-hatted, twirling a cane, he would sweep up and down the stage ogling the middle-aged ladies in the stalls and singing popular sings written and composed specially for him. He packed every hall in the country, was a kindly man and the soul of generosity.

Then suddenly he became involved in an unsavoury incident, and was sentenced to six months' imprisonment. While the morals of the time were nothing to write home about, Fred's offence, regarded with a certain tolerance today, was enough to spell ruin then. On release from prison he could not get a date. The general feeling of the public who had idolised him swung against him. Theatre managers were afraid of hostile demonstrations. At last, some months having elapsed, Moss Empires gave him one week at the theatre in his home town, the Empire, Sunderland.

I heard the story years later from a very old stage hand. The house was packed. The atmosphere was tense, the climate one of silent hostility. The earlier acts went through their routine scarcely noticed. Then Fred Barnes's number went into the frame. Playing with all his old verve he got through his first song to almost dead silence, did a quick change and came back for his second. It was like sitting on a keg of gunpowder – one match struck and the lot goes up. It only needed one boo, one derogatory remark, and that large audience would have erupted into a storm of vilification. Fred Barnes sensed it. He stopped the orchestra and addressed the house in what must be the most poignant personal speech ever made by an actor to his public.

He reminded them that they were his fellow townsfolk, admitted his weakness and his faults and humbly expressed his sorrow that he had let them and Sunderland down. He said he realised that his career was finished, that this was goodbye to all his old friends.

He concluded, 'Before I leave this stage for the last time, may I have your permission to sing one song by way of farewell, one you have always liked, "The Black Sheep of the Family"?'

The whole house dissolved in cheers and tears. 'Black Sheep' was indeed their favourite, a rather sentimental number with a prodigal son theme; so what might have been a riot ended in a triumph.

I wish I could say that the triumph continued, but it was not so. Other theatres were not so responsive to Fred Barnes. He ended his life eking out a living playing the piano in small pubs and was found dead with his head in a gas oven in a shabby little room in Southend.

THE TEARS OF
ALL-IRELAND SUNDAY

Joe Kearney

We must have seemed an odd pairing on that Sunday afternoon. Myself, the fledgling hippy, and the man in the blue suit huddled against a telephone pole in Dollis Hill Park, North London. I had drifted into the tired acres of beaten grass and gaunt shrubbery with a melancholic indifference that can only be provoked by empty pockets. The park was cheating autumn on that September day in 1967 by delivering a display of hot, sunny defiance.

I observed the man in the blue suit, saw him press a small transistor radio against the tall pole and would have sauntered past him had my ears not been arrested by a familiar voice, an unmistakable singsong chant ebbing and flowing from the tinny speaker. The man in the blue suit was using the telephone pole as a conduit to enhance his radio reception. Its own aerial, even fully extended, was as useless at this distance as a hayfork with a broken tine.

The voice on the radio was the voice of my childhood Sundays, from a place I thought I'd lost and a self I thought had vanished forever.

I gestured to the man in the blue suit. Was it OK if I joined him to listen? He shrugged an indifferent 'suit yourself'.

I was aware that he was appraising my appearance; saw him take in the tie-dyed, beaded and long-haired creature that was as contrasted to his white drip-dry nylon-shirted self as could be imagined.

The national anthem followed the county anthems. Emotion within me built in incremental steps. The hair stood on my arms and on the back of my neck. The water level built up behind the fragility of the dam. I defied the overspill with sheer willpower and self-control for as long as I could. That was until Michael O'Hehir extended a welcome to all those listening in Boston, New York, Chicago…London. The Croke Park roar reached us in waves like a phantom sea in a shell held to the ear of memory. It was then that the tears found the line of least resistance and coursed down my embarrassed cheeks.

The man in the blue suit observed all.

'It's times like this that you'd miss the auld place,' he said, offering me a cigarette from the fresh packet of Major.

The softness of his lilt hinted at his origins.

'You're from Cork?' I asked.

His eyes crinkled with mischief. He trotted out his icebreaker, his party piece: 'Cork me hole!' he shouted, 'I'm from Mallow.'

Seeing my reaction, he crumpled under the power of his own wit and was overtaken by a spasm that was part laughter, part cough until the tears that sprung to his own eyes matched mine.

'What county man are you, yourself?' he enquired. I hesitated before replying, for I had grown up in a divided household where the waspish black and amber jostled with the banner of the red- and white-blooded bandage. I could assume either allegiance. However, on this afternoon, county loyalty was unimportant. What was important was the reawakening of memories of previous All-Ireland Sundays and all that they meant – the end of summer and the return to school, pencils in their wooden case, pointed and sharp, school-books that would leak knowledge from the wallpapered protection of their covers. Copybooks with pictures of round towers, also pointed and sharp, as sharp as the attention we promised to pay to our teachers, as sharp as the bittersweet blackberries of the hedgerow. As sharp as the crack of tar bubbles when they burst beneath bicycle tyres in potholed country lanes, as sharp as the memories flowing down the tarred pole and out of the radio.

When finally the 'hip, hips' were counted out, we shook hands and parted. Back home, soda bread was being cut for tea, ash plants were being picked up, wellingtons pulled on and cows gathered for milking.

We left the park and returned not to the small fields of our origins, but to the bedsits of Cricklewood and Kilburn.

I will remember the man in the blue suit today as I do on all other All-Ireland Sundays when I renew my vow. When Micheál Ó Muircheartaigh welcomes those listening in Sydney, New York, Brazil, London, and when the roar goes up, I will not cry; this year I promise I will not cry.

NO FRONTIERS

Michael Timms

Political changes of the last few decades have rendered many frontiers and borders invisible. The barriers are coming down all over Europe. So it's easy to miss the boundaries. Language is about the only border guard left in some places, and most of the time you can slip past him quite easily. Even France, renowned for its haughty disdain of other tongues – particularly English – can surprise. And I am truly thankful, since my attempts at the French language are more comedy than communication. I have enjoyed campsite holidays with my family – spending hot days on the beach and slow nights with good food and plenty of wine – never having to speak a word of French.

It amazes me how far we can travel in a foreign country without speaking at all. I rediscovered this when I arrived in the south of France for the holiday where I was going to 'get away from it all'. I was *en route* to a house in a small hillside village above Carcassonne, just north of the Pyrenees.

Passing through immigration, all I have to do is flash my passport and I'm a part of this different world. I collect my bags and head for the car-hire desk. I present my booking reference, credit card and licence, without needing to understand any of the words said to me. And, *voilà* – that's a word I do know – I have the keys and I'm walking to the car park.

A visit to the supermarket requires no more than another production of the credit card to ensure I am stocked up with the basics to feed myself. I head for the hills and my first evening 'at home' in France – without having had to say a word to anyone.

Maps guide me to the village and then a street plan to the house. These are provided by the landlord, who has also left brief notes on the dining-room table. Guess what – they're in English! So now I know where and when to put my rubbish out. I also learn that the only shop in town is just across the road, an *épicerie* – a sort of corner shop, except it isn't open all hours, just two hours in the morning and three in the evening. And if I want croissants and baguettes for breakfast, I'd better get a move on, because loaves have to be ordered the night before.

I leave the house in high spirits. I'm part of the community now, doing what all the locals do at this time of day. By the time I've crossed the street, the blood has drained to my boots: what else do all the locals do? Speak French.

Inside the shop there's a small queue. I take my place – and as I get closer to the counter I am heartened that no one else has come in behind me. Then, just as I am about to be served, in comes a woman with her young son. Embarrassed by the audience, I nevertheless go through my performance, which is more pantomime than linguistic panache. In so doing, I believe I have secured my breakfast for the next morning. I move to leave, and the young boy stands aside.

'After you, please.'

'Thank you,' I reply.

I don't turn to see it, but I imagine a faint smile of pride on his mother's face. And, as I cross the warm, sunlit street, I realise this boy has just flashed *his* passport. The one that will take him away from this place.

GOING HOME FOR CHRISTMAS, COMING HOME FOR CHRISTMAS

Deirdre Purcell

Going home for Christmas, coming home for Christmas – two of the most evocative phrases in the English language. They encompass a pocket dictionary of others: joy, excitement, hope…filial duty, guilt, paying dues…

I was thirteen when I first came home for Christmas.

A scholarship girl from Dublin, I had spent my first term, a long, *long*, fifteen weeks, in a boarding school by the shores of Lough Conn.

No visits, no outings. Envy of other girls' ease with one another, not to speak of scrumptious Sunday sponge cakes brought in weekly by their mothers.

It's a dismal, foggy weekday morning in late December and we serious travellers – four girls from Dublin and one from Cork – chug away from Ballina railway station. We change trains at Manulla, where the platform is even greyer. Wetter. Colder. We care little. We're going home for Christmas.

The big Dublin train pulls in and we find a compartment to ourselves. We chat quietly as the drowned fields and small towns glide past our window. It is 1958, when people are still conscious of electricity bills, so the outward manifestations of the Christmas spirit are confined to glimpses of paper chains, an occasional Christmas tree or crib, a modest star on a church spire.

We take out the sandwiches the nuns have given us. I can't eat mine. I'm going home for Christmas.

Athlone. People getting on, people getting off. The chat dies away. Just seventy miles to Dublin.

Outside the train window, streaked with grime, darkness falls. Nothing to see now. We chunter through a blind landscape as, like keys on a piano, the swishing telegraph poles count out the miles...

Mullingar. Bustle. Lights. People embracing on the platform. Only fifty miles to Dublin.

At Maynooth, we tidy away our debris like the well-trained convent girls we are. We button coats, check shoelaces, put on our berets.

Butterflies.

We're nearly home for Christmas.

The train squeals slowly into Westland Row. The others pull bags from the overhead nets, stand impatiently in the aisle. I cannot follow.

Because, as we slid along the platform, I caught sight of my family: Mamma, Dadda, my seven-year-old brother in beret and good coat, his hands up, holding theirs.

All three were scanning the windows of the train.

They were looking for me.

I am felled by tears of purest joy.

I bid the others a muffled 'Happy Christmas' from under my seat as I pretend to be searching for something I have dropped; I scuffle and scrabble around the floor until I gain control.

Somehow it had not occurred to me before that my family loves me.

I had not known that I love them.

I am the last to leave that carriage, probably the train – although I don't remember that. I do remember that, as I walk towards my small family, they are as controlled as I am. Delighted to see me but mostly – and jovially – relieved.

'We thought you weren't on it! We were nearly sending out a search party!'

The chat on the way out of the station is about tiredness and train journeys, the Dinky crane my brother wants from Santa and the new house they had moved into while I was away.

But joy, like a brilliant fish in deep water, glistens underneath.

There was a Christmas tree in Westland Row that year, or maybe memory has added it to my picture. There was certainly cloudy breath on cold air, and gloves and scarves and great clatter and chatter.

And on the way home to Ballymun, we made a detour, up one side of O'Connell Street and down the other, to look at the Christmas lights in the trees, in Clery's window, Madame Nora's, and then, at O'Connell Bridge – the *pièce de résistance* – the moving neon Santa, his reindeer and his sleigh on the façade of McBirney's.

My parents are dead now and my brother and I are home at different places for Christmas, but, since that first homecoming to the echoing, clanking, steaming platform at Westland Row, I have known that, no matter what, we four knew what we knew.

A SENSE OF POETRY

NEW YEAR OMENS

Julie O'Callaghan

If the wind is from the West
On New Year's Eve,
Our island will flourish.
And the first foot to enter our dwelling
On New Year's Day
Should be the boot of a black-haired
Man or boy.
Let's not forget the cake theory
And how we all need to throw
Barm brack at our front doors
To banish hunger and famine.
A time of bells, fires,
the banging of pots
and omens for the coming year.

Some say that dropping a plate on the first day
guarantees a special year.
That's why I will be eating the cake – not throwing it –
And dropping the plate
for a cracking good year.

STANDING ON MY HEAD

Chuck Kruger

Hoping that what woke me up would wake my students too, and believing that you don't teach only a subject but who you are yourself, I had no hesitation as a secondary school literature teacher to be passionate about the novels and poems and plays I assigned my students. And I tell stories. Pose riddles. Have anybody late to class tell the biggest lie as to why, the bigger the better. Kids weren't late often and, when they were, we had fun.

All the paper-grading, however, required much of my evening and weekend time, until I discovered a way to shorten my written comments. For each paper, instead of my usual paragraph, I finally learned how to concentrate my evaluations. No matter how weak a paper was, I'd comment on its best quality in one sentence – and, in my only other sentence, I'd constructively comment on the paper's weakest characteristic. And no matter how good a paper was, I'd do the same thing. Two sentences, strength and weakness. At home, I began to have more time to play with my own children.

Realising that I learned more when I had to teach a class than when I simply sat in a class, I'd have each student become responsible for two classes a year. I also encouraged my students to ask questions – and reassured them that sometimes the more silly or even stupid the question might seem to them, that those were the very questions that most often got to the heart of the matter.

One day, having just finished reading aloud a poem by T.S. Eliot or Allen Ginsberg — I can't remember which — a student raised his hand and asked, 'But, Sir, how does your archetypal poet see this world?'

I felt stumped, didn't know what to say, and remained quiet for several minutes, suspense building. Then I did something I'd never done before — and never since. I removed my shoes and crawled onto the large sturdy oval wooden seminar table, right to its middle. Surrounded by twelve utterly quiet students (in that international day school in Switzerland we never allowed more than twenty in any one class), I lowered my head to the table, raised my knees to rest on my elbows, and then slowly, tentatively, lifted my legs toward the ceiling. While standing on my head, and wondering if I would ever more be seen as an utter idiot, forgotten pens, pencils, car keys and loose change falling out of my pockets, I waited for the silence to return, and then, from some upside down somewhere else, said, 'A poet sees exactly the same world you see, but from a different perspective.'

I kept standing on my head for a few more scarily silent minutes, then lowered myself to the table, collected my belongings and crawled back to my chair.

MORNING POEM

Enda Wyley

To wake to this.
If we had known
we would not
have slept so long.
Mist has fought and won
its battle against the sun
and all is murky grey.
The spider's frail line blows
from the sycamore
to the cottage hedge,
while across the lane,
dew looks dense but breaks
like bubbles at a touch.
The fat brown birds
are not afraid of our steps
along the gravelled way,
of our fingers
stamping berries.
Oh purple hunger!
The baby dips
in and out of wonder,
twirling the soft air,
testing the sky

with her sounds.
Geraniums wake bedraggled
in their window beds
and yesterday's paint dries
at last on the red wooden door.
To wake to this.

WALLS, ISLANDS AND WELLS

Joseph Woods

for Mo Irwin

Can this be right? How last Sunday
to walk the Great Wall to a point
where it crumbled, merely a week
passes and this Sunday to be brought

round Omey island, face the Atlantic and out
there a conference of swans, at our back
a hexagon fortress built for a writer.
Here a holy well with an alcove of supplications:

a dolphin's vertebra, a bag of miraculous medals,
smooth stones with girls' or women's names
scribbled upon them, a soother and a single sock,
everything one could wish for.

Then a ruined church of pink-granite
half-sunk in sand whose gable must glow
in the evening sun. But before the tidal
road back what stops me in my tracks

are sand-grains shifting with the speed
of an hourglass, revealing what sand
has been secreting,
the half-concealed imperial yellow shell.

FREE STATE

Gerard Smyth

for John McGahern

Saying Goodbye at the airport
you speak of destinations on that far shore,
of distance that wearies the jet age traveller
and the long journey ahead
through all the beautiful cities.
Cities like stories waiting to be read.

But I am happy
motoring through the Free State,
the Glebe Road where O'Carolan dragged his harp,
the hilly landscape where on some days
the lake is radiant and very still.
On other days it is like a page
of thumbprints, dull and marked
by cloud shadow
and the meadow-dust of Leitrim.

MAYO MANTRA

Gerald Dawe

Lawrence Durrell tells the following story in *Prospero's Cell*, his fascinating little book about Corfu: in the dazzle of the bay (he writes) stands
Mouse Island…this petrified rock is the boat, they say, turned to stone
as a punishment for taking Ulysses home. To which Durrell adds the
poetic 'get-out' clause, 'It might have been here.' Corfu is quite an island
and one can well imagine Ulysses setting sail from any one of its small
bays and inlets before taking the seaward journey home to Ithaca.

   Stuck in the lee of one of our own stunning rivers and bays, the Moy
in County Mayo, there is a time-locked ruin of a concrete boat. I have
looked upon this boat very many times over the past thirty years, staying
with family in Ballina, watching the shoreline, heading up past Belleek
Castle towards Bartra Island and beyond, until the Atlantic opens in all
its splendour and power.

   The concrete boat on the Moy has become a kind of proverbial story
in my mind, an installation from the past. Why it got there, why it is still
there, doesn't really matter. The retelling of a childhood spent on the
river points to a very different way of life to the one I knew, and one that
may have itself remained the same in its essentials for hundreds of years.

   I suppose the following poem, 'Mayo Mantra', tries to bring that
sense of timelessness to the tale of what once was, while keeping in
mind the classical resonance of what might have been as Ulysses took
sail for home and his Penelope.

Many's the time and oft' —
as we skirt the Moy,

at that particular turn in the road,
the river can be low,

the ridge pool sunken, unmoving,
the concrete boat

upright where it was left
unmasted, broken down,

graffiti sprayed on its hulk,
a monument of the sea,

not that far out from the estuary,
the woods and castle,

and, without a second thought,
I think of you

in the arms of your father's boat
the salmon jump so high

it takes your breath away,
crossing the bar,

between land and sea
and the incomparable sky.

SAILING

Mary O'Malley

The last time I sailed from Connemara to Kinvara, it was hot enough to make you want to cool down and – I like the heat. People divided into those who complain at the lack of rain and those who felt a drought was overdue. People sunbathed for hours and lay around the beaches.

Those who had booked their fortnight in Fomentera or along one of the overcrowded costas came home feeling cheated. I don't sunbathe. I get bored on the beach. There are better ways of ways of cooling down.

On Friday, I drove to a pier near Carraroe and was given a place on a boat sailing to Kinvara. Polite exchanges were made and then I sat quietly out of the way and listened to the men talking softly. One smoked a pipe. They ignored me, except for the helmsman, who had known my father. I sat listening to their talk as they moved slowly out the bay, then watched the vast sheets of sail fill out against the sky as they caught the first puffs of wind. They were like the wings of some great rusty butterfly, about to lift us into the sky.

These men hunted the wind on calm days, they were alive to its slightest shift and would use it to their advantage for speed. That day they started a friendly race with two other boats, there was some low calling across the water. Farther out, the wind picked up and the sea began to roll. There was a soft-voiced flurry of consultation and they tacked. One of the men I didn't know watched slyly as the boat swung over. I stood up, climbed the slant of the deck to become ballast and breathed in the green glassy air.

'Here, I am happy,' was my single thought.

The helmsman glanced at me and nodded his approval. He lifted an eyebrow towards the other man. The other man looked put out – there would be no fun out of giving me a fright.

They had a good run, the boat far over, sailing close to the wind.

One of the passengers was afraid. I exulted but only because I trusted the men. I leaned against the great wooden gunwale, laughing as the keel seemed about to clear water. The mast was what they called it in Irish, a vast tree above them.

I love this dance of sail and wind, the defiance of gravity, and I love it because it is the only time I am not afraid, though I measured the angle of the jump needed to clear the swinging boom if it tipped that six inches too far as they cut through the sea, balanced on a knife edge, suspended between two transparent elements. Here, I attained my own critical mass, as if everything that was scattered moved into perfect equilibrium. Here, I was entirely myself.

The wind dropped and the sea stilled as we made the shelter of Kinvara and sailed into the bay a couple of hours before dark. I thanked the men, 'That was lovely,' and walked up the quay. The evening was warm. Voices floated across the water, there was some desultory laughter on the quay. The pubs were full of crews and tourists.

About six boats lay at anchor, beautiful creatures that the men I grew up amongst treasured as they could never treasure women. There in the bay were the only females they understood. They talked about their wiles and their caprices and loved them unconditionally. Who could blame them? These females never answered back and they grew lovelier with age.

I was meeting my family for dinner at a house nearby. A couple we knew were renting it for their holidays. The two families hadn't met since the previous summer.

'So you came from the sea,' the host said. He had a cool voice, slightly mocking.

'Don't be an eejit,' I said, and everyone laughed.

The air was still. We could hear the night birds calling down by the water. Somewhere nearby, a fiddle was playing and, behind that, the low hum of several conversations. The teenagers went into the town.

The air was warm, scented with turf smoke and flowers. A heron flapped onto the darkening shore, '... the heron like a tilted italic/Illuminating the gospel of the absurd.'

I don't know why I said the lines from Montague's beautiful poem that ends with the twin deities, 'and their dual disciplines of tenderness'.

Both couples were still together then, and I am sure I detected nothing prophetic in the rise and fall of Whitman's wonderful lines with which our host responded:

On the beach at night alone...
This vast similitude spans them, and always has spann'd,
And shall forever span them and compactly hold and enclose them.

FOCAL COSANTA

Aifric Mac Aodha

Leagtaí blaoscanna each
Faoi chúinní halla an damhsa tráth,
Go mbainfí macalla as sála bróg,
Go mbeadh na fallaí ramhar le ceol.

Ba choscrach an radharc iad, a chuid:
Lucht ána an ghuairneáin mhóir.
Ní liginn a ndoircheacht lem'ais,
Ach ghuínn go bhfanfá im' chomhair.

IN MY DEFENCE

Horses' skulls used to be placed
Under dance floors long ago:
They coaxed an echo from a heel
And helped the sound ring whole.

Whatever spurs your grand whirl —
I know it for its starkness, dear:
Don't think that I'm not wary,
For all that we're up here.

LANDSCAPES

Denise Blake

We drove past Ailsa Craig, a single molar tooth
standing in the North Channel as we ferried our son
with all his belongings, to Freshers' week in university,
and I thought, 'imagine the pain in having that removed.'

Once it was Ben Bulben, with all its shifting shapes,
embleming our travels to and from his school.
It used to crouch, a snow-coated lion ready to pounce,
or lay down, a brown flecked hound by the hearthside.

On Aidan's last night at home, I heard the sound of him
pouring kettle-boiled water into his sink for shaving.
I asked the pillow, When? And How?
as his growing up speed-reeled through me.

We don't have the Scottish landscape rooted in us
and we can't predict what is around any corner.
In order to come back, he needs to go away —
have we given him all he needs for his journey?

This morning, that final bob of his navy beanie hat
as he was swallowed into the stream of students,

the ripple of his deep-hearted laugh carried back.
And now, as we approach Stranraer,

we are swamped by a muddle-head mist.
Ailsa Craig, in all its certainty, has disappeared,
or has since been extracted. We pass by an empty
horizon, while our son's landscape keeps on reshaping.

AMAZING GRACE

Brian Lynch

Every time I hear the hymn 'Amazing Grace', my pulse quickens. Actually, I hear it so often it's a wonder my heart can put up with the excitement. And why does it cause such a reaction? Well, apart from the catchiness of the tune, there are two reasons: I know the history of the priest who wrote the words, John Newton, and the poet who inspired them, William Cowper.

John Newton lived, by any standard, an extraordinary life. Born in 1725, the son of a London shipwright, he was kidnapped at an early age and press-ganged into becoming a sailor. After some years at sea he was again captured and became a slave on an island off the west coast of Africa. The only book he had there was a ragged copy of Euclid's *Geometry*. And the only free time he had was at night. So on the beach he would trace out the theorems in the sand by the light of the tropical moon.

At last Newton escaped and sailed back to England. But his ship was caught in a storm so violent that some of the crew were washed overboard and drowned. Newton, who was at this time a blaspheming atheist, prayed to God for deliverance. The ship was saved and Newton was converted. But he continued to sail the oceans and – oddly for a born-again Christian – to make his living out of trading in slaves. Like most people then, he had nothing against slavery in principle, though, as he said, he did sometimes wonder whether the chains, the whips, the tongue-wedges used to keep the slaves quiet were quite compatible with Christian kindness.

Eventually he left the sea, became a sort of ranting street-preacher in Liverpool and at last, with great difficulty, was ordained a priest of the Church of England, which was then experiencing the revolution of Methodism. The difficulty was caused by the fact that Newton fought with everyone, including John Wesley.

It was at this stage that he met William Cowper, the poet who is the hero of my novel *The Winner of Sorrow*. Cowper was as odd as Newton, but in exactly opposite ways. He was born in 1731 into an aristocratic family – one of his ancestors was the great poet John Donne, and one of his grandfathers had been Lord Lieutenant of Ireland. Cowper was offered a soft job in Parliament, Clerk of the Journals, but he was pathologically shy and the thought of appearing for interview before the House of Lords drove him to attempt suicide – and very nearly to succeed.

After a long period in a mental hospital, the quaintly named College for the Insane, he experienced a religious conversion and moved to the town of Olney in Buckinghamshire, where Newton was the parish priest.

Church-going was a serious business in those days: it was quite common for Newton's sermons to last as long as six hours. He also tried the patience of his parishioners in other ways: when he denounced them for celebrating Christmas as if it was a pagan festival, with lighted candles and, worst of all, with kissing under the mistletoe, they rose up in drunken rebellion, attacked the vicarage with stones and empty bottles and would have burned it to the ground were it not that Newton's wife sent him out in his nightshirt to buy them off with money for more drink.

But that was enough for Newton: he packed his bags, departed to London and threw himself into the less troublesome battle for the abolition of slavery.

The relationship between Newton and Cowper was a curious one: the cockney ex-slave trader who could still swear like a sailor, and the trembling aristocrat, afraid of meeting someone who might use the Holy Name in vain.

Newton's method of dealing with his friend's shyness was what we would now call aversion therapy: he bullied him into being a preacher, with disastrous consequences – Cowper soon went mad again. But Newton also cajoled Cowper into helping him to write the once-famous Olney Hymns, one of which is 'Amazing Grace'. It helped, of course, that Cowper was already a great poet in the making. He was to go on to produce some of the best poems in the English language, poems so familiar we have now forgotten who wrote them.

In a marvellous lecture given last year in St Patrick's College, Drumcondra, Seamus Heaney showed how much Patrick Kavanagh had been influenced by the poems he had learned off by heart in Iniskeen National School. For example, when Kavanagh describes himself as 'king of banks and stones and every blooming thing', he is echoing these lines by Cowper:

I am monarch of all I survey,
My right there is none to dispute
From the centre all round to the sea,
I am lord of the fowl and the brute.
Oh solitude! Where are the charms
That sages have seen in thy face?
Better dwell in the midst of alarms,
Than reign in this horrible place.

There are other poems which are, or used to be, familiar to generations of schoolchildren. For instance, this beautiful lament for lost times, 'The Poplar Field':

The poplars are felled; farewell to the shade,
And the whispering sound of the cool colonnade...
Twelve years have elapsed since I first took a view
Of my favourite field, and the bank where they grew;
And now in the grass behold they are laid,
And the tree is my seat that once lent me shade...
My fugitive years are all hasting away,
And I must ere long lie as lowly as they,
With a turf on my breast, and a stone at my head,
Ere another such grove shall rise in its stead.

And of course there are lines, torn out of context, which have become proverbial or clichéd: 'variety is the spice of life', 'the cup that cheers but not inebriates', and this still startling image:

God moves in a mysterious way
His wonders to perform.

He plants his footsteps in the sea
And rides upon the storm.

'Amazing Grace', too, was written by Cowper – but only the title. As far as we know, Newton wrote the rest of it. And now both of them, the fanatical sea-captain and the suicidal poet, are pretty much neglected, their names remembered, if at all, only by Methodist historians, professors of eighteenth-century literature and novelists with an eye for a good story.

But 'Amazing Grace' lives on. As recently as 1971 it was a Top Twenty hit for Judy Collins. One rather bizarre website, the Hollywood Jesus News, claims that it is the most recorded song of all time. There are certainly more than 2,000 recordings, by artists as diverse as Elvis Presley, George Gershwin, Jimi Hendrix, the Von Trapp Family, and last but not least, our own Frank Patterson.

But all the musicians who have done it justice have one thing in common – they've got soul. And if I'm forced to choose the one with the most soul, it's perhaps not surprising that the choice comes down to someone with roots in Gospel music, a black woman, descended from slaves. I mean Mahalia Jackson and, thanks to the amazing grace of radio, we can hear her again.

THE POET

Francis Harvey

Picture, if you can, a boy, who at that time wanted, more than anything else in the world, to be a poet. A boy sitting at an upstairs window overlooking green fields, a wide river full of salmon, an ancient town and bridge, a gapped greystone eel-weir, and, in the distance, mountains and the sea.

Picture as well, in bed in that room, a man time had beached among the blankets and pillows like a dying seal beached by the tide. A very old man who keeps telling that boy, over and over again, about how when *he* was a boy he once saw, and only once, a now long-dead poet walking through the fields by the winding banks of the river that flowed past outside and of how the poet had stopped to have a word with him and to give him a hard sweet to suck.

And in that room, after all these years, the boy, who is now a man, can still smell the compounded smells of sickness and new-mown grass. In that room with its big brass bedstead whose shining convex knobs reflected the distorted images of both of them, the boy, who is now a man, can still hear the old man repeating the story of his childhood encounter with the poet, as he sits there looking out at the fields where the poet had walked, sacred ground to him, as were the river and the waterfalls and the bridge and the eel-weir and the town.

And he would imagine he could see the figure of the dead poet clambering maybe over a low limestone wall or stopping to look at one of the waterfalls between whose white cascades stood the house in which all this was happening so many years ago. And he would begin to whisper the names of the places the poet had hallowed with his presence: Tullan, Camlin, The Commons, Bulliebawns, Coolmore, Kildoney, Portnason, The Knather, and The Mall, while the old man, in a voice that had begun to quaver with weakness and age and yet was still audible, not hearing him but seeing his lips move, would ask him what he was saying. And when he'd tell him, he'd begin to recite a stanza from the work of the poet he had once encountered on the riverbank and whose poetry he knew by heart, and the boy would join in a voice as low as the voice of the waterfalls in summer, both of them unaware that it might be the last time they would ever do this together.

Both would recite a single stanza for this was all the old man was capable of now, from William Allingham's 'Adieu to Belashanny':

Farewell to every white cascade from the Harbour to Belleek;
And every pool where fins may rest, and ivy-shaded creek;
The sloping fields, the lofty rocks, where ash and holly grow,
The one split yew-tree gazing on the curving flood below.

KAVANAGH'S HOLY DOOR

Una Agnew

During the year that is coming to a close, we have celebrated the life and works of Patrick Kavanagh in honour of his hundredth birthday. The longed-for holy door of acceptance and recognition has, in Ireland at least, been finally opened for him. One could say that his poetic life evolved in a space between two holy doors — his initial doorway to life on a farm in Inniskeen, and the ultimate holy door he dreamed of when he would at last claim his inheritance as a poet.

Love's doorway to life first opened for him on his small farm at Shancoduff in Monaghan when he fell in love with a field:

> They laughed at one I loved —
> The triangular field that hung
> Under the Big Forth.

The Rocksavage fields were his patrimony — an eldest son's inheritance — economically speaking, a poor investment. Instead, they became his poetic territory, a landscape of the soul, a platform from which to experience the rhythms and moods of life as they pulsated for him through each month and season.

His life of love evolved, with the unhurried pace of a ploughman, from Mucker in Inniskeen, to the Merrion Nursing Home in Dublin where he breathed his last in November 1967. His poetry moved in harmony with an attendant liturgy, attuned to the moods and farming activities of each calendar month. He learned from Melville at the outset of *Moby Dick* that Ishmael, the narrator, was experiencing 'a damp and drizzly November in his soul'; so, too, did he discover that each month was not only a unit of time, but a state of mind, a season of the soul.

Christmas was his Eden time, a time which summoned up 'the luxury of a child's soul', culminating in 'a prayer like a white rose pinned on the Virgin Mary's blouse'. Each month in turn drew on the contents of his rag and bone shop of the heart, comprised of bits and pieces from school books, the *Messenger, Ireland's Own* and T.S. Eliot. The months provide him with metaphors for the various moods and vagaries of his poetic soul.

In January, the intrepid coltsfoot breaks a hole in 'winter's wall' to announce its presence to the earth. This budding metaphor, later in his writing, becomes the mystical revelatory moment when 'Christ comes with a January flower'. As apprentice-poet he moved symbolically out of winter, through the harrow pins of non-acceptance into a Genesis of poetry and earth.

Meanwhile, in 'March':

> The trees were in suspense
> Listening with an intense
> Anxiety for the Word
> That in the Beginning stirred.

The poet is on his way. Soon March is a silversmith, advancing with glistening wand, brightening the poet's outlook and surroundings. Mystery broods over the harrowed fields, where:

> ...in the green meadows
> the maiden of Spring is with child
> by the Holy Ghost.

Then ecstasy erupts when April dances in a wild celebration of life:

> O give faith
> That I may be alive
> When April's ecstasy
> Dances in every whitethorn tree.

Although 'clouds over fields of May' remind the poet, sadly, of unrequited love, May can still fill him with a frisson of enchantment and romance:

There will be bluebells growing under the big trees
And you'll be there and I'll be there in May...

And so Kavanagh moves in and out of hope and disillusionment, claiming as his own the mixed moods of his soul as he pursues his illusive ideal of love across the months and seasons:

I followed you...
Through April, May and June into September
Now I woo the footprints that you make across November

His 'Great Hunger' forlornly chides each passing month for its missed opportunities, lost dreams and wasted life. Time passes, and on New Year's Eve 1954, he bitterly remonstrates with a whole year that had almost cost him his lamp of contemplation – a lost lawsuit, a failed venture, the end of romance and worst of all, lung cancer.

O Nineteen Fifty-Four, you leave and will not listen,
And do not care whether I curse or weep.

Then, almost miraculously, and 'at the end of a tortuous road', the poet is healed in soul and body, on Dublin's Grand Canal, in the tremendous silence of mid-July. This mid-July moment is a time to let go of grief and regret and contemplate the healing sacramentality of earth. A new springtime of life awaits! Though now in the late summer of his life, a new April ecstasy pours over him its colourful catharsis.

Green, blue, yellow and red –
God is down in the swamps and marshes,
Sensational as April and almost incred–
ible the flowering of our catharsis.

This late summer, with its outburst of gratitude, released onto the world his Canal-bank poems, which speak of heightened sense-awareness and are retuned to the cadence of flowing water, warm sunshine and the heady joy of being alive. It is fitting that his poem 'October' hints at the completion of a life perennially dedicated to sowing, reaping and eventually bringing home his harvest.

O leafy yellowness you create for me
A world that was and now is poised above time,
I do not need to puzzle out Eternity
As I walk this arboreal street on the edge of a town.
The breeze, too, even the temperature
And pattern of movement, is precisely the same
As broke my heart for youth passing. Now I am sure
Of something. Something will be mine wherever I am.
I want to throw myself on the public street without caring
For anything but the prayering that the earth offers.
It is October over all my life...

And so, Patrick Kavanagh, you've experienced all the seasons and months of your star-crossed life. And this year, 2004, we have lived them with you all over again, and, at least posthumously, have whole-heartedly endorsed the opening of your holy door. It is truly October over all your life — you're 100 years old and your harvest is home. We rejoice as we listen once more to your prophetic words as you say 'Thank you! Thank you!' for the acceptance of a 'holy hearing audience'. You might speak these words now, perhaps with more conviction, than when you first uttered them to an audience of students at University College Dublin almost fifty years ago:

... how glad
I am to have lived to feel the radiance
Of a holy hearing audience
And delivered God's commands
Into those caressing hands,
... I thank you and I say how proud
That I have been by fate allowed
To stand here having the joyful chance
To claim my inheritance,
For most have died the day before
The opening of that holy door.

POETRY MAKES NOTHING HAPPEN

Stephen Matterson

'Poetry makes nothing happen.' That phrase is one of W.H. Auden's most widely quoted, and yet it is, on its own, a rather misleading sentiment for understanding Auden.

'Poetry makes nothing happen' appears in his elegy for W.B. Yeats, a poem that Auden wrote in February 1939, a month or so after Yeats' death, and only a few weeks after Auden's arrival in the United States. For many of Auden's readers, 'poetry makes nothing happen' must have seemed like a statement reflecting a shift in his own poetry, a move away from the public commitments that his renowned work of the 1930s had so clearly and so brilliantly embraced. Auden's moving to the United States seemed like a flight from that earlier self and its commitments, an act of turning his back upon both England and on the 1930s, the period that he was soon to label a 'low, dishonest decade'.

While there is some truth in this perception, it is very far from being the whole story. The phrase 'poetry makes nothing happen' is quoted far more often than the whole, long sentence in which it appears, where those four words are nuanced and developed towards a searching examination of what poetry is and does:

> For poetry makes nothing happen: it survives
> In the valley of its making where executives

Would never want to tamper, flows on south
From ranches of isolation and the busy griefs,
Raw towns that we believe and die in; it survives,
A way of happening, a mouth.

Poetry is a 'way of happening'. It's a mouth; we turn to it for the expression of things we find difficult to say, for things that touch us, move us, delight us. Rather than locating the importance of poetry in its immediate historical and public effect, Auden sees it in a larger, historical perspective, which is the difference between making something happen, and a 'happening'. He refers to the astonishing range of poetry and the themes and ideas that it can accommodate; like a river, it will flow through valleys, ranches and towns, bringing life and meaning, reaching and touching lives. Lives that include my own, as I realised when I first read Auden's long poem 'New Year Letter', in which he wrote, as he often did, of the landscape in which I was growing up: 'those limestone moors that stretch from Brough/To Hexham and the Roman wall' where the river Eden 'leisures through its sandstone valley'; 'Always my boy of wish returns/To those peat-stained deserted burns/That feed the Wear and Tyne and Tees.' Poems don't just speak to us, they speak for us.

Auden's poem in memory of Yeats ends with a kind of rhapsody. As so often happens, one poet's elegy for someone else turns out really to be about the poet, and about what poetry means. In this darkening world of 1939, Europe is clearly heading towards another catastrophic war:

In the nightmare of the dark
All the dogs of Europe bark,
And the living nations wait,
Each sequestered in its hate;

Rather than being silenced by this terror, this dread, there is more need than ever before for the voice of the poet, a voice that can connect us to each other, to the world, and to history; this is what 'survives', raises us above ourselves, above the immediate, and above our failures. Auden, born 100 years ago in 1907, ends his elegy for Yeats with a vision of the work of the poet in the public world, and Auden concludes his poem with the two lines that appear as his own epitaph on his memorial plaque in Westminster Abbey:

Follow, poet, follow right
To the bottom of the night,
With your unconstraining voice
Still persuade us to rejoice.

With the farming of a verse
Make a vineyard of the curse,
Sing of human unsuccess
In a rapture of distress.

In the deserts of the heart
Let the healing fountains start,
In the prison of his days
Teach the free man how to praise.

IN NOMAD'S LAND:
LOUIS MACNEICE (1907–1963)

Liam Harte

'Speaking as an Irishman of southern blood and northern upbringing, whose father was a Protestant bishop and also a fervent Home Ruler...' – Louis MacNeice's circuitous self-introduction in a 1953 review article is that of a writer whose identity was an amalgam of diverse and competing influences, which rendered him continually uncertain about where he belonged.

Displacement, indeed, was MacNeice's birthright, since home, for him, was always elsewhere. Born in Belfast on 12 September 1907, he grew up in the Church of Ireland rectory in Carrickfergus, where his father ministered. But birthplace and home were not coeval, not least because the claustrophobic rectory and its environs were full of Gothic terrors. Wherever young Louis turned within this 'cramped acre', as he called it, he felt besieged by sinister, static forces: a daunting cemetery on one side; a dour granite obelisk on another; a forbidding Norman castle behind; and everywhere the sound of church bells, factory klaxons and shipyard hammers reverberating in a cacophonic tumult.

Within the rectory walls, MacNeice's kindly but austere father was given to nocturnal praying that sounded to his son like a frightening 'conspiracy with God', as he described it in his posthumously published autobiography, The Strings are False (1965). Add to this a pious children's nurse who indulged in sadistic threats and warnings, and a gentle but infirm mother who died when Louis was just seven, and one begins to see why the poet would always associate the North with tyranny.

MacNeice's sense of inner exile was deepened by his discovery that his parents were themselves displaced people from the west of Ireland. His mother's homesickness for Connemara bred in him such a profound yearning for an imaginary homeland of windswept mountains and welcoming cottagers that the pastoral west became, in the words of his sister Elizabeth, 'a kind of lost Atlantis where we thought that by rights we should be living ... We were in our minds a West of Ireland family exiled from our homeland.' And so Connemara became a 'dream world' for MacNeice, a mystical, unseen realm where a fresh identity might be forged.

'Born here, I should have proved a different self,' he conjectures in 'The Once-in-Passing', and in 'Day of Renewal' he reflects:

Where I was born,
Heckled by hooters and trams, lay black to the west
And I disowned it, played a ticklish game
Claiming a different birthplace, a wild nest
Further, more truly, west, on a bare height
Where nothing need be useful and the breakers
Came and came but never made any progress
And children were reborn each night.

Such hankering after an illusory elsewhere is one of the hallmarks of MacNeice's life and work. Elsewheres play a vital role in his imaginative geography since they hold open the possibility of defying the deterministic imperatives of history and subjectivity. In 'Valediction', a love/hate letter to Ireland written in 1934, he acknowledges:

I cannot be
Anyone else than what this land engendered me ...
I can say Ireland is hooey, Ireland is
A gallery of fake tapestries,
But I cannot deny my past to which my self is wed,
The woven figure cannot undo its thread.

Yet the desire for self-unravelment remained, being the corollary of a physical and metaphysical restiveness. MacNeice is a poet caught in a perpetual vagrancy, forever poised at some threshold of travel, chasing an illusive authenticity here, courting self-dispersal there. His description of himself in his autobiography as 'a mere nomad who has lost his tent' suggests that homelessness was, for him, a mode of being in the world. Repeatedly, we find him in transit in his poems, from the early 'Ode', in which he resolves to become a 'migrating bird following felt routes', to the late 'Solitary Travel', where he admits 'the futility of moving on/To what, though not a conclusion, stays foregone'. All of which makes MacNeice the supreme poet of unsettled exile, whose 'glad sad poetry of departure' speaks to the unrooted Irish everywhere.

And so if, having read his verse, we feel we still don't fully know him, then perhaps that is as it should be, for part of MacNeice remains permanently unhoused, tantalisingly eluding full and final definition. His epitaph for his friend and fellow poet Dylan Thomas could also be his own:

> What we remember is not a literary figure to be classified in the text-book but something quite unclassifiable, a wind that bloweth where it listeth, a wind with a chuckle in its voice and news from the end of the world.

MARKED PRESENT

Seamus   Heaney

The photograph shows two little boys with two guitars slung round their necks, their left hands on the frets, their right hands flung high in the air, as if the photographer had snapped them in the final triumphant moment of a performance. They are up on a pretend stage, a picnic table in a woodland picnic area, and they look as if they might be the children of hippies living in some nearby commune: their hair is just that bit longer than you'd expect and there's something about the amount of denim they're wearing that suggests an alternative lifestyle, late 1960s Calfornia, perhaps.

But the photograph was taken in County Wicklow in the early 1970s, although the young brothers had, in fact, spent the academic year 1970–71 in the San Francisco Bay area. One of their most memorable experiences was attending an open-air concert given by the folksinger and storyteller Pete Seeger. 'If I Had a Hammer', 'Where Have All the Flowers Gone', 'Casey Jones', 'Abiyoyo', 'John Henry': they listened that sunlit morning to the thrilling, beguiling songs of those glamorous radical times and, during the coming months, they would listen to them over and over again on a big long-playing record until Seeger's voice and music began to represent the music of what happened in the course of that liberating year.

But now the year of liberty was at an end. I took the photograph of those boys in the Devil's Glen Wood, the evening before they started school in Ashford and I remember well the sadness I felt as their father, the bittersweetness of that moment which is both the end of a child's brief freedom as a creature of family and the beginning of his or her life as a citizen, the exit from Eden, as it were, before the entry into the roll book.

And yet it may be that the photograph affects me because it marks an unforgettable moment of beginning and ending in my own life. The next morning, which would introduce the children to their first taste of the discipline of the classroom, would give me my first morning of escape from it. A few months before, I had given notice to the English Department at Queen's University that I would resign in the summer, and now it was early September, and my wife and I had made the move from the semi-detached security of a house and a job in Belfast to the chancier life of a full-time writer in the adventure playground of Wicklow. So the toy guitars held aloft, the dramatic gesture on the picnic table, the call of the wild green woods in the background have come to represent that moment of change.

I remember very clearly coming back from enrolling the boys with Master Whelan and going upstairs to inaugurate my own new freelance life in front of the blank page. Sitting there, under the low tongue-and-groove ceiling of the gate lodge we had rented, I was very conscious of the silence in the house and the absence of the children. But I was also conscious that, for the foreseeable future, our livelihood would depend not on the monthly salary cheque but on the muse's favour, on my pen and ink, and my own writerly confidence and stamina. So it was a happy coincidence that the work I started on that morning was my first go at translating the story of Suibhne Gealt, the legendary king who deserted his former responsibilities to become a man of the woods. Just as there had been something marvellously fortifying about a thing that happened earlier down at the school, when Master Whelan was filling in the children's particulars on the roll book. When he came to the column where the father's occupation had to be registered, he asked me no question but wrote down in his firm clear hand, *as Gaeilge*, '*file*'. And I knew that, from then on, I was going to be a poet in earnest.

WHERE DID YOU SAY SLOVENIA WAS?

Theo Dorgan

One of the more absurd consequences of the Cold War, an American
rhetorical invention, was the shrinking of old Europe to more or less the
Atlantic fringe countries and Germany. Everything east of the Iron
Curtain vanished into the steel grey penumbra of communist Eastern
Europe, a kind of virtual unreality where great cities, whole cultures,
entire literatures dropped off the map. National boundaries became
notional things, as if they signified no more than administrative divisions in the Soviet Empire. We imagined, many of us, if we thought
about it at all, that life in Prague could be little different from life in
Budapest, or Ljubliana, or Warsaw. As if distinction could be so easily
erased. As if we could so easily escape from ourselves.

It was Tom McCarthy's idea that as part of Cork 2005, a team of
Cork poets should translate a poet each from the new accession countries. Between the time Tom conceived of this translation series and Pat
Cotter, the inspired manager of the project, handed out assignments, I
was out of the country. By the time I got home there was only Slovenia
left. What I knew of Slovenia then – its culture, its history and its literature – could have been written on the back of an average-sized rejec-
tion slip. Still, I was intrigued. It was the only one of the former
Yugoslav Federation countries that had avoided the murderous civil wars
that followed the break-up of the Federation. Trieste, I knew from the

life of James Joyce, was a Slovenian city that had somehow ended up annexed by Italy.

With the help of the newly appointed ambassador, I armed myself with anthologies and journals containing recent poetry in translation. I made 'Slovenia plus poetry' the default search term in Google on my laptop. I was looking, as one should, for a kindred spirit, someone who had a quality to her poetry that I responded to on an intuitive level. I was looking for poems so different from those I write myself that I could write them out in another kind of English, in another voice. I found Barbara Korun, and how I found her tells a certain kind of story all by itself.

I was sitting at my desk, late at night, reading a poem called 'Wolf', in a fairly clumsy translation to be sure, but nevertheless one that disclosed the hypnotic power of the original.

'Ah,' I was thinking, 'this is the one.' Just then, my companion knocked and came in, a magazine in her hand.

'Here,' she said, 'I think this is the one you'll go for.' The page folded over so that the lamplight fell on 'Wolf'.

I neither read nor speak Slovene. I would become deeply indebted, therefore, to Ana Jelnikar, who supplied me with line-by-line literal versions of the poems and with minutely detailed, illuminating scholarly notes – I was able to cross over into the territory of Barbara Korun's poems by means of a strong, well-engineered bridge. The poems in their final English versions would come out of these bridge translations, and even more out of the extraordinary email conversations that flowed through the long nights between Barbara Korun and myself. Barbara's English is good. Not enough for her to be her own translator, but good enough for her to spot where I was going wrong, missing an emphasis, creating the wrong kind of atmosphere.

In the end, as she said herself, she got a master class in English, I got a fool's pardon for my temerity and errors and we both learned a great deal about poetry.

In the central square of Ljubliana I was shown a monument of a ragged vagabond, a burly, bearded fellow in a great cloak. Even the erudite Ms Korun cannot explain how he fetched up there in the long ago, this wandering Irish Druid. Not a monk, mind you, a Druid. I've been think-ing of him all this time, of his long journey on foot to the heart of old Europe. A long time he's been waiting for us to come find him.

IN FLANDERS FIELDS

Val Mulkerns

When I was in Belgium recently I remembered something I thought I'd forgotten. It happened on a dark November evening when my brother Jim and I were taken to Dorset Street for the first fitting of new winter coats. My mother always preferred to walk, if there was time, instead of taking a bus or a tram, so when we emerged from the tailor's into some sort of confusion on the street, we were surprised when she told us to be quick and we might catch the approaching tram. She could run faster than either of us, and so we were dragged on board and in a position to look down from a safe height at the angry crowds who were jostling and shouting at two or three women shaking collection boxes.

'Stupid, stupid people,' my mother muttered. 'They can't see that other people have a perfect right to buy and wear poppies in memory of those poor slaughtered young men – many of them Irish anyway.'

It was grown-up talk, and it didn't particularly interest me then, but the words came back vividly as we stood on the bleak cold day in Flanders Fields. In the grey gloom, the thousands of small white crosses seemed to stretch for miles in every direction. On the horizon, just beyond the cemetery, a tall trio of soldiers stood among the trees as though on guard. They turned out not to be real, but a very fine and moving piece of sculpture.

When we drove on to Ypres we found under the Menin Gate, and covering every inch of the town walls beyond it, many thousands of names similar to those under the entrance to St Stephen's Green at home, names like Murphy and Fitzgerald and Kelly and Mangan and O'Neill and O'Connell. They mingled with the thousands of Welsh and English and French and Belgian names of men who had fought and fallen too and it was extraordinary to learn, by looking at the archive photographs in the Cloth Hall, Market Square, that this small town which we were exploring had been completely gutted by shells and cannon fire, and meticulously rebuilt exactly as it had been before the First World War. Nobody looking at the tall fourteenth-century cathedral could believe that it too had been gutted. But the people of Ypres have done more that just rebuild. Every morning and every evening to this day they sound the 'Reveille', in memory of those innocent dead, and townspeople gather in the square to stand in silence for the duration of the ceremony in winter and summer alike.

It seemed fitting, somehow, to be exploring, in sleety cold, places like the awful death trenches, and the grave of Francis Ledwidge who was blown away by a shell not far from there. That grave, unlike those of Wilfred Owen and Siegfried Sassoon, was not actually part of our itinerary, but when we mentioned Ledwidge to the knowledgeable gentleman from Bruges who was our guide, he at once decided to include it. And so we discovered, eighty years after his death, that somebody had left fresh spring flowers on the grave of the young Irishman, and nearby was his memorial sculpture. When he died, he was only twenty-nine years old, so maybe Seamus Heaney is right in the closing paragraph of his introduction to Ledwidge's Collected Poems:

> Ledwidge solved nothing. As a poet his sense of purpose
> and his own gifts were only beginning to come into mature
> focus. As a political phenomenon he represents conflicting
> elements in the Irish inheritance which continue to be
> repressed or unresolved.

Indeed, since that disgraceful scene on Drumcondra Road, all those years ago, not much has changed. One sees a tiny minority of people in Ireland wearing a poppy on Remembrance Day, as I do myself, despite an acknowledged republican background. But it takes a long search to find a poppy seller.

For all that, the First World War and its Irish connections have continued to provide inspiration to writers as far apart as Neil Jordan and Sebastian Barry, or Frank McGuinness and James Plunkett. It's there still as a tantalising contradiction, and it seems it won't go away.

In you, our dead enigma, all the strains
Crisscross in useless equilibrium
And as the wind tunes through this vigilant bronze
I hear again the sure confusing drum

You followed from Boyne water to the Balkans
But miss the twilit note your flute should sound.
You were not keyed or pitched like these true blue ones
Though all of you consort now underground.

from 'In Memoriam Francis Ledwidge' by Seamus Heaney

CLIMBING CROAGH PATRICK

Iggy McGovern

We have things to talk about
man to man, that's why
I'm scrabbling up this stony slope
under a doubtful sky.

Weaned within sound of the bell
of the Protestant church, St Patrick's!
I grew up believing you were
naturally, one, as well:
I had you banishing the snakes
with the same bleak certainty
that pitched the monks in the river
and planted the best of the County.

A rest at the First Station.
For seven-fold penance recall
my seven years' re-education
that you were Catholic, after all.

We'd a great day out on Slemish
for our Patrician Ceremonies,
fifteen hapless centuries
of your Mission to The Irish.

Of which I remember only
the Union Jacks all along the route
(reminders that they held you yet)
and sweet, scalding tea.

Hugging the chapel-gable
coveting the tourists'
sandwiches and flasks:
A rain-swept Tower of Babel

Fast-fainting, I now summon
from the vaults of the Old School,
swaddled in cotton-wool,
your One, True Jawbone
that, once, under cover of cleaning,
I closely questioned, slapping
your toothless, brown half-grin:
Whose side were ye really on?

It was all a waste of time.
We saints are trained to say nothing:
Except that on a better day
you must have a great view of Clew Bay.

CUIMHNE AN UISCE

Nuala Ní Dhomhnaill

Uaireanta nuair a bhíonn a hiníon
sa seomra folctha ag glanadh a fiacla le slaod tiubh
is le sód bácála,
tuigtear di go líonann an seomra suas
le huisce

Tosnaíonn sé ag a cosa is a rúitíní
is bíonn sé ag slibeáráil suas is suas arís
thar a másaí is a cromáin is a básta.
Ní fada
go mbíonn sé suas go dtí na hioscaidí uirthi.
Cromann sí síos ann go minic ag piocadh suas
rudaí mar thuáillí láimhe nó ceirteacha
atá ar maos ann.
Tá cuma na feamnaí orthu –
na scothóga fada ceilpe úd a dtugaidís
'gruaig mhaighdean mhara' nó 'eireaball mhadraí rua' orthu.
Ansan go hobann téann an t-uisce i ndísc
is ní fada
go mbíonn an seomra iomlán tirim arís

Tá strus uafásach
ag roinnt leis na mothúcháin seo go léir.

Tar éis an tsaoil, níl rud ar bith aici
chun comparáid a dhéanamh leis.

Is níl na focail chearta ar eolas aici ar chor ar bith.
Ag a seisiún síciteiripeach seachtainiúil
bíonn a dóthain dua aici
ag iarraidh an scéal aisteach seo a mhíniú
is é a chur in iúl i gceart don mheabhairdhochtúir.

Níl aon téarmaíocht aici,
ná téarmaí tagartha
ná focal ar bith a thabharfadh an tuairim is lú do cad é 'uisce'.
'Lacht trédhearcach, 'a deir sí, ag déanamh a cruinndíchill.
'Sea,' a deireann an teiripí, 'coinnibh ort!'
Bíonn sé á moladh is á gríosadh chun gnímh teangan.
Deineann sí iarracht eile.
'Slaod tanaí,' a thugann sí air,
í ag tóraíocht go cúramach i measc na bhfocal.
'Brat gléineach, ábhar silteach, rud fliuch.'

A RECOVERED MEMORY
OF WATER

Paul Muldoon

from the Irish of Nuala Ní Dhomhnaill

Sometimes when the mermaid's daughter
is in the bathroom
cleaning her teeth with a thick brush
and baking soda
she has the sense the room is filling
with water.

It starts at her feet and ankles
and slides further and further up
over her thighs and hips and waist.
In no time
it's up to her oxters.
She bends down to pick up
Hand towels and washcloths and all such things
as are sodden with it.
They all look like seaweed –
like those long strands of kelp that used to be called
'mermaid-hair' or 'foxtail'.
Just as suddenly the water recedes

and in no time
the room's completely dry again.

A terrible sense of stress
is part and parcel of these emotions.
At the end of the day she has nothing else
to compare it to.
She doesn't have the vocabulary for any of it.
At her weekly therapy session
she has more than enough to be going on with
just to describe this strange phenomenon
and to express it properly
to the psychiatrist.

She doesn't have the terminology
or any of the points of reference
or any word at all that would give the slightest suggestion
as to what water might be.
'A transparent liquid,' she says, doing as best she can.
'Right,' says the therapist, 'keep going.'
He coaxes and cajoles her towards word-making.
She has another run at it.
'A thin flow,' she calls it,
casting about gingerly in the midst if words.
'A shiny film. Dripping stuff. Something wet.'

A SENSE OF THE PAST

THE FLIGHT OF THE EARLS

Eamonn Ó hUallacháin

One of my favourite places in Rome is San Pietro in Montorio on the Janiculum Hill, not too far from the other St Peter's. It is here, in front of the main altar, that the Earls of Tír Eoghain and Tír Chonaill, the Great Hugh O'Neill and Ruairí O'Donnell, lie buried. This is where their epic journey, known forever in Irish history as the 'Flight of the Earls', finally ended. A simple stone marks the grave of O'Neill and states, in Latin, that 'Here lie the bones of the Leader Hugh O'Neill'.

The journey began in Slane, a little under 400 years ago, in 1607. While he was in Slane, word came to O'Neill from a Drogheda businessman named John Bath that a Breton ship had arrived into Lough Swilly and would soon sail for the continent. Hugh travelled quickly northwards on horseback, covering up to fifty miles a day. On Wednesday he passed Tullyhogue, where twelve years previously the crowds had proclaimed him 'The O'Neill' and leader of Tyrone. But no crowds greeted him this time, and even the stone on which the O'Neills were enthroned for centuries, the Leac na Rí, lay broken, smashed into pieces by Lord Mountjoy. On the Friday, at dawn, he arrived in Rathmullan on Lough Swilly, where the ship lay at anchor. O'Donnell and his people were already there, loading the sixty tons of provisions which they were taking with them. At midday the party of ninety-nine set sail for A Coruña in the north of Spain. The group consisted of O'Neill, his wife, Catherine McGuinness, some of their children, Ruairí

O'Donnell, his brother, Cafarr, their wives and children, and others from the leading Ulster families.

They sailed down the west coast of Ireland and stayed further from the land than they would have liked, fearing the English ships. The weather conditions on the twenty-one day voyage were sometimes awful. At one stage, they trailed a gold cross in the sea, which contained a relic of the true cross, in an attempt to calm the sea. Eventually they decided that it was too dangerous to make for Spain and landed instead in France, not far from Le Havre. As a gesture of goodwill to the local governor, they presented him with two falcons that had landed on their ship during the storms. King Philip of Spain asked them not to go to Spain, but to remain in Spanish Flanders instead. They stayed in Louvain, which had strong Irish connections, and were well treated there. One of those they met was O'Neill's son, Enrí, a colonel in the Spanish Army at nineteen, who he hadn't seen for seven years.

At the end of February they were advised to go to Rome, and thirty-six of the group set off on horseback; six of the women went in a carriage. It was an amazing trek at that time of the year. They crossed the Vosges Mountains and the Alps in frost and snow. On St Patrick's Day, their first day in the Alps, while crossing a raging river over a small bridge, known to the locals as 'the Devil's Bridge', one of the horses slipped in the icy conditions and fell into the torrent below. It was the horse that carried their money, about £50,000 in today's values. Though they searched for days, the money was never found. They went through the St Gotthard Pass, 7,000 feet above sea level, and stopped in the old traveller's hospice there, which is still in use.

Finally, 235 days after leaving Slane, they arrived in Rome. They went along the Tiber, into St Peter's Square, unyoked the horses, tied them there and went into the Basilica. The Pope received them with great respect at his palace on the Quirinale, where the President of Italy resides today.

Events soon began to turn against them, however. In July, due to the oppressive heat in the city, some of the younger members of the group went to Ostia, on the sea, fifteen miles from Rome. They stayed two days and lay out overnight in the moonlight. Almost immediately they were struck by a fever, probably malaria, which was common there until Mussolini drained the Pontine marshes. Despite being attended by the Pope's physician, O'Donnell died on 28 July and was buried in St Pietro in Montorio. He was just thirty-three years old. One by one, the Ostia group died in rapid succession. When Hugh's son, the heir to Tyrone, died aged twenty-four, it was a mortal blow to the whole group's morale.

O'Neill continued with his efforts to get help from the Pope and Spain, but to no avail. He grew increasingly disheartened and died in July 1616, aged sixty-six, a very broken and dispirited man. He too was buried in St Peter's on the Golden Mountain.

Some years ago I was amazed to see Romans still putting flowers on Julius Caesar's final resting place in the Forum, after more than 2,000 years. Last year, a couple of us from O'Neill's own territory of the Fews in South Armagh took some fuchsia from there to Rome, and put them on the Irish chieftain's grave, so that it might be known that our Caesar too has not been forgotten, among his own people, even after hundreds of years.

JOHN MILTON: CROMWELL'S SPIN DOCTOR

Mary Russell

When the King of England, Charles I, was beheaded way back in 1649, it sent a shiver of fear throughout all the other crowned heads of Europe. What if the same thing happened to them? What if they were called upon to be accountable to the people? What if their soldiers were allowed to question their officers? In England, this is exactly what happened, for the world was turned upside down by the trial and execution of Charles I.

Then, in order to counteract the anti-republican propaganda that followed, Cromwell, the leader of the Parliamentarians, decided it was important to put forward the pro-republican point of view to explain to the rest of Europe what had been done and why. But who would be the best person to take on this important task? Whoever it was would have to have a good working knowledge of Latin which was the lingua franca of the day. He – it goes without saying it would be a man – would have to have a commitment to the ideals of republicanism, to accountability and to the rights of the common man.

Thus it was that John Milton was chosen, charged with the task of writing about the evils of the monarchical system and of the benefits of a republican one, which he did persuasively, eloquently and in Latin, of course, leaving no stone unturned in his effort to make sure that the Parliamentarian point of view was understood.

He was, therefore – to use present day parlance – Cromwell's spin doctor, appointed to the Council of State with the title of Secretary for Foreign Tongues.

As a schoolchild, I had been forced to learn off by heart large tracts of *Paradise Lost* and *Samson Agonistes*. The poem 'Lycidas' I could relate to because it was Milton's lament for a young friend who had drowned but, by and large, I found him a difficult poet whose writings were dense and hard to understand. He was also a bit puritanical and we all knew that puritans were never any fun. But beyond that, I knew nothing about the man.

And then, one day, I visited the house he retreated to in Buckinghamshire during the Great Plague. He came to this house a couple of years before the monarchy was restored, bringing with him his third wife and his daughter Deborah who helped him once his blindness made it impossible for him to read.

It's a lovely old timbered house with an inglenook fireplace and a ladder leading to an upstairs bedroom which Milton, then seventy-three, was unable to climb. Instead, he used a room to the right of the front door which served both as a bedroom and as a study.

Here, in the pre-dawn stillness – he got up regularly at 4 a.m. – he completed *Paradise Lost*, which deals with the restitution of the monarchy, and then he started and finished *Paradise Regained*. In fact, on the wall is a framed receipt for £5 – a lot in those days – which was the first half of the payment for *Paradise Lost*.

Milton had always been a political animal who would have made common cause with many political activists of today. In the run up to the Civil War, he had published numerous pamphlets dealing with issues such as divorce, which he favoured. This last was written when his first wife, Mary Powell, left the family home and returned to live with her mother. They had married when she was seventeen and he was thirty-four. The Powell family didn't at all like his views on divorce but, far worse for Milton, was that the Powells came down on the Royalist side so that, politically, husband and wife were seriously divided. This treatise on divorce caused mayhem and was finally banned. This led to further trouble when Milton wrote *Areopagitica* which denounced any attempt by the powers that be to silence a writer or to ban a book and which showed him to be a passionate champion of freedom of the press.

'As good Almost to kill a man as kill a good book,' he wrote.

Two weeks after the execution of Charles I, he published a pamphlet called *The Tenure of Kings and Magistrates* which sets republican principles against those of an arbitrary, and therefore undemocratic, government and which has led him to be called England's greatest republican.

CROMWELL, CALLAN AND COCA-COLA

Gerry Moran

Strange as it may seem but Oliver Cromwell is partially responsible for the success of one of the world's most famous and popular soft drinks: Coca-Cola. We associate Oliver Cromwell with many things – not least cruelty and tyranny – but now we – well I, certainly – can add at least one pleasant ingredient to the list: Coca-Cola.

This story begins not a stone's throw from where I live – in the small town of Callan in County Kilkenny, a town that has, for its size, produced more than its fair share of famous people, among them Edmund Ignatius Rice, the founder of the Christian Brothers; the architect James Hoban, who designed the White House in Washington, a design he based on our own Leinster House; and most recently the renowned artist Tony O'Malley.

As for Callan and Cromwell and the Coca-Cola connection – it all began with an army officer by the name of William Candler who came to Ireland in 1649 with Oliver Cromwell. As a reward for his military successes, Willliam Candler received large tracts of land in counties Wexford, Offaly and Kilkenny, and finally settled in Offaly.

William's second son, Thomas, also an army officer, moved to Callan where he married, settled down and lived in Callan Castle. Thomas and his wife raised a family of six children and it was his fourth son, Daniel, who set the Coca-Cola connection in motion, thanks, of course, to

Oliver Cromwell but also to 'that old devil called love'. Daniel fell madly in love with a local Catholic girl, which caused quite a scandal at the time due to their different religions and social standing. Much to his father's annoyance, Daniel refused to give her up and his father duly disowned him. He did, however, give Daniel enough money to emigrate to America where he and his wife, Hanna, who lived to a remarkable age of 105 years, became Quakers. We know this because one of Daniel's sons, William, became an officer in George Washington's army during the American War of Independence and made such an impression that he had a biography written about him.

It was this William Candler's grandson, Asa Candler, a pharmacist by profession, who went on to found the Coca-Cola Company in Atlanta, Georgia, in 1892. Coca-Cola was created by another pharmacist Dr John S. Pemberton in 1885 as a tonic for minor ailments. It was Pemberton's book-keeper, however, a man called Frank Robinson, who suggested the name Coca-Cola and penned the now famous trademark in his unique script.

Doctor Pemberton died in 1888 and, over the next two years, Coca-Cola was gradually acquired by the ambitious and dynamic Asa Candler. Three years later, in 1891, he became the sole proprietor of Coca-Cola.

Asa Candler was a brilliant marketing man and, under his guidance, Coca-Cola became one of the world's most famous and most recognised brands. It also made Asa Candler a multimillionaire. In 1916, he retired as president of Coca-Cola and later became Mayor of Atlanta. In 1919, Asa Candler, the pharmacist who had come to Atlanta with $1.50 in his pocket, sold the business for a whopping $25,000,000 – a phenomenal fortune at the time. He died in 1921 and his son, Charles, succeeded him as chairman of the Coca-Cola Company.

Asa and Charles Candler never forgot their Irish roots. As a tribute to their Kilkenny ancestors, they both built mansions in Atlanta – one called Callan Castle and the other Callan Wolde.

Coca-Cola is still one of the most famous and most recognised brands in the world, all thanks to several generations of the Candler family, that old devil called love, the small town of Callan in County Kilkenny and, of course, one Oliver Cromwell.

PICTURE

Mae Leonard

It's the kind of picture you'd love to step into and be part of the scene. A bunch of women stand in the shallows of a river – half of them, skirts hitched up, busily flaying cloth with some kind of paddle whilst the others, back a bit from the water, are wringing out lengths of dark cloth. A few more are captured walking away with buckets of water on their heads whilst a huge dark cloud up above is moving away, allowing rays of sunshine to spotlight teetering three-storey houses of old Limerick. Central to all the activity is a stone bridge with four rickety arches. And would you believe it? There is a row of houses built on the bridge itself and if you look a bit closer, in a gap between the buildings there are masts of sailing ships anchored in the harbour.

I'm looking at a W. H. Bartlett print from an engraving by E. J. Roberts entitled 'Old Baal's Bridge, Limerick'. I know it, that bridge. Well, at least I know the newer version – that little humpbacked bridge you meet as you come into Limerick City on the Dublin Road – it's where you cross the river to avoid the town if your destination is in a westerly direction.

Maps of ancient Limerick show the walled Irish and English Town linked together by this bridge which was identified, way back then, as Droichead Maol Luimneach – the Bald Bridge of Limerick – bald, some say, because it didn't have parapets.

I look at the picture and put myself in amongst the washerwomen of Limerick. I sniff the wet smell of water mingled with wood smoke coming from several tall chimneys. And fish: Moll Darby's Market is just above the river wall. It's early nineteenth century and the women are talking about a recent trial in the courthouse up the road where Daniel O'Connell defended John Scanlan, one of the landed gentry. Despite the efforts of 'the Liberator', Scanlan was found guilty and sentenced to death for the murder of sixteen-year-old Ellen Hanley, better known to us as the Colleen Bawn. The condemned man was taken from the old gaol to be executed at Gallows Green.

But was Scanlan really guilty? What do the women in my picture say? That fateful morning, they strained to get a look at the prisoner as the sound of horses' hooves clattered up Gaol Lane then came towards Baal's Bridge. Three times an attempt was made to drive the horse-drawn carriage across the bridge. Each time the horses refused. The women saw it all. There was consternation. It was a sign that he was innocent.

Above the clamour one of these women shouted, 'It's the hand of God – he's innocent.'

I hear her telling me now, 'You should have seen him, such a handsome lad, I cried when I saw him jump from the carriage, his hands tied behind him, and he walked with his head held high across that bridge there. We followed him to Gallows Green.'

John Scanlan died on 16 March 1820 at Gallows Green, Limerick, on the end of a rope, protesting his complete innocence of the murder of Ellen Hanley, the Colleen Bawn.

The women in the picture carry on their day's work, hands raw from wringing heavy cloth. The Abbey River flows onward to join the Shannon. A strong westerly wind blows the chimney smoke off towards Tipperary and the sun forces its way out from the big black cloud. A good day for washing and a great day for drying. Soon life will change forever for these Limerick women when the old Baal's bridge is taken down and a new one is erected in its stead. That's the little humpbacked you meet now coming into Limerick City on the Dublin Road.

LACEY'S CROSSING

Jacqueline Morrissey

At a crossroads in county Waterford stands a small pub. A long, low, cottage-style building, it sits discreetly into the side of a hill. Its roof is of corrugated iron, but it must once have been thatch. Although small, it does a busy trade, snagging customers as they converge from the various branches of the crossroads to travel the Waterford City road. One hundred and fifty years ago it was attracting travellers on the same journey, when it served as inn and stagecoach station, and was known locally as Lacey's Crossing.

It was here in the black years of the 1840s that two of my ancestors met, in a soup kitchen set up at the Inn to feed the hungry victims of the potato famine. During the grim summer of 1847, John Tobin arrived to help with the relief effort. The son of a hedge school master from the Comeragh Mountains, he too held classes in the kitchen of the cottage he shared with his elderly father. Many of the local Irish-speaking population acquired their basic education at his turf fire. By day, however, he worked on the estate of one Captain O'Shea, a local Catholic landowner. It was in this capacity that he arrived to help the relief effort.

Waterford was not as badly hit by the Great Hunger as were many other areas. Parts of the county escaped almost unscathed, but to the west, and up in the small villages that dotted the Comeragh Mountains, starvation, disease and death were common.

There is a road, high in the mountains above Kilrossanty, which leads nowhere. In the harsh creed of the mid-nineteenth century, it was never acceptable to feed people merely because they were starving. Work had to be created to justify famine relief. The lonely mountain road was the result. Many of the people who built it died along the way, weakened by hunger and exhausted by the labour. For them, death was the only relief from famine. The population which might have used the road was soon dead too, or in exile. Some made their way down from the mountains and in towards the east of the county, seeking the institutional aid of the city poorhouse or the temporary relief offered by makeshift soup kitchens.

Lacey's Inn was one such place of relief. Here, at the age of thirty, John Tobin met Catherine de Lacey, the landlord's seventeen-year-old daughter. Working together in the midst of such catastrophe must have created a considerable bond. In the midst of the squalor and starvation of the time, a romance developed. The oddly matched pair went on to marry. Amongst the children born in the years that followed was my great-grandmother, Cáit.

Greek mythology had it that three sinister women were responsible for spinning the threads of human destiny. One carried a scissors with which she would snip an occasional thread, thus ending a life. Her shears were certainly busy in those grim famine years, slicing through the fabric of rural Irish society, leaving ragged edges of death and destruction in their wake. Amongst those broken threads and ended loves, it is hard to imagine that a new link could have been formed. To me it seems almost more surprising that now I can still trace that fragile connection, through family reminiscences and oral tradition, back into the dim, frayed, tapestry of time.

WHAT IT SAID IN
THE FREEMAN'S JOURNAL

Vivien Igoe

Thursday 16 June 1904 was an ordinary summer's day in the Irish capital. *The Freeman's Journal* reported in the 'Dublin Money Market' column that there was a rise in the price of government funds. Breweries were flat, however, with Guinness stock moving to lower values. Railways fared better, with the Great Southern and Western recording a rise of 1¼, but the Tramway shares tended to fall. Bank of Ireland stock did not attract buyers.

Kellet's of South Great George's Street, and Todd, Burns and Co Ltd both had great summer sales with bargains in every department.

The report on 'fairs' on that auspicious day showed that there was little demand for store cattle, as most large cattle farmers already had full supplies. Unfavourable weather conditions during the spring and early summer months had cattle in a backward condition.

The 'Shipping News' reported a number of arrivals and departures the previous day. Many of the ships to Dublin were carrying cargoes of coal. *Breeze* from Preston with coal; *SS Captain McClure* from Cardiff with coal; and the wind-driven, masted *Rosevean* from Bridgewater with bricks.

In the Proteus episode in *Ulysses*, Stephen Dedalus sees the *Rosevean* from Sandymount Strand.

It was a weekday and a working day for most people. As the day wore on, the Dublin pubs began to fill with groups of people discussing everything from the weather to the horses running at the various meetings. The official starting prices at Ascot were quoted. There was an abundance of runners that day in the seven races. There were twelve runners in the Gold Cup run at 3 p.m. over 2½ miles. Among the runners were Mr M. J. de Bremond's Maximum the Second, and Mr F. Alexander's Throwaway.

Around the city there were five theatres, with plenty of entertainment to cater for all tastes. Eugene Stratton, the world-renowned comedian, was performing at the Theatre Royal – in a series of recitals from his celebrated repertoire. The Theatre Royal was good value that night, as Mr Russell Wallett and Mr W. Smith & Co were also performing in the new musical comedy version of *Fun at the Bristol*.

The Elster-Grime Grand Opera Company was engaged at the Queen's Royal Theatre with their tremendous success, the three-act opera *The Lily of Killarney*, whilst the Gaeity Theatre staged *Leah*, with Mrs Bandman-Palmer, supported by her specially selected London Company. Leopold Bloom considers going to it.

Piggotts and Co advertised *Famous Irish Songs*, which costs one and sixpence each, post-free. Included in the collection was 'The Croppy Boy', which James Joyce sang at the Antient Concert Rooms, when he shared the platform with John McCormack and J. C. Doyle at a concert held on the last night of the Horse Show Week on 27 August 1904. In *Ulysses*, it was the favourite song of Ben Dollard, Simon Dedalus and Tom Kernan.

The American disaster of the steamer *General Slocum* near Hell Gate in New York Harbour, which Tom Kernan in *Ulysses* reflects on, is covered extensively. Appalling American Disaster – Excursion Steamer on Fire – 500 Lives Lost – Wild Scenes of Panic – Children Thrown Overboard – Women Trampled to Death.

The weather forecast reported southerly fresh or strong winds, later veering westerly and moderating; unsettled with rain generally, some fair intervals. It turned out to be a fresh sort of evening for a walk.

A young man accompanied by a striking auburn-haired girl walked to Ringsend on 16 June, on what was their first date. The man was James Joyce and his companion the Galway-born Nora Barnacle, whom he had met a few days previously walking down Nassau Street. She was employed in nearby Finn's Hotel in Leinster Street.

Joyce subsequently immortalised the day and the enigmatic, earthy girl in his novel *Ulysses*. He chose the 16 June 1904 for the action of his novel. This was the first Bloomsday.

REFLECTIONS ON A PHOTOGRAPH

Elaine Sisson

There is a famous photograph taken at 2.30 on the afternoon of Easter Saturday, 1916 which shows Patrick Pearse in his official role as Commandant-General of the Army of the Irish Republic surrendering to Brigadier-General Lowe of the British Army. The photograph was taken at the junction of Parnell Street and Moore Street and shows Pearse in a long military coat wearing a slouch hat tied under his chin. Even though he was over six feet tall, Pearse seems small. His hands are clasped behind his back and he looks straight ahead, his familiar side-profile distinguished under the unbecoming hat. In his hands General Lowe holds a sword-stick and a pistol in a holster, both of which belong to Pearse. They were given over in addition to Pearse's pouch of ammunition and his canteen, containing two large onions, as part of the ceremony of surrender. General Lowe is smartly dressed with a peaked military cap, knee-high leather boots and displays the impressive paraphernalia of rank. Records tell us that he was mannerly towards Pearse, treating him as a military peer, a courtesy Pearse appreciated.

While the focus of the picture is on Pearse and Lowe, there are, however, two other people in the photograph. One of them is hardly there at all. If you look closely at the bottom of Pearse's trench coat, you can see four legs: Pearse's boots, and beside him two small feet in sturdy shoes disappearing into a light-coloured skirt. This anatomical mystery is easily explained. The legs belong to nurse Elizabeth O'Farrell, who had walked with Pearse to the top of Moore Street as part of the conditions of surrender. It was Elizabeth O'Farrell, dressed in her nurse's uniform, who carried the white flag. You'd have thought that her role in history deserved to be remembered in a photograph. But, for whatever reasons, Elizabeth O'Farrell was hastily airbrushed out of the photograph, which appeared in numerous newspapers the next day. It was obviously a quick editorial decision as her neatly shod feet and the hem of her uniform remain, visible yet unseen, like the trace of a ghost. Maybe it was considered unseemly to surrender in the presence of a woman; maybe it was considered unseemly for a woman to be involved in military combat. It's impossible to know. In recent years the recovery of women's role in our history has been underway and perhaps one day it might be possible to restore Nurse O'Farrell's torso, arms and head to her proper place beside Pearse.

There is also a fourth person in that photograph. He is a young British soldier; handsome, dark, tall and slender in boots and light-coloured breeches. He's looking at Pearse's letter of surrender, which he holds in his hands. His stance is casual, even nonchalant. His name is John Muir Lowe and he's the Brigadier-General's son – it's possible he's only holding the letter so that his father can take charge of Pearse's belongings.

John Lowe was a seasoned soldier; he was a Second Lieutenant with the 15th Hussars and had served at Gallipoli during the 1915–16 campaign there. Sometime after this photograph was taken, he must have ended up back in combat in France, as he spent time as a German prisoner of war. Yet after the First World War ended he stayed in Germany to run a pickle factory. It was probably during this time that he changed his name from John Muir Lowe to John Loder, possibly because it sounded more Germanic. But his real love was acting and he appeared in a number of German films, some by the director Alex Korda, during the 1920s.

Leaving pickles behind forever, he moved to America and appeared in the first talkie for the Paramount Studio in a 1929 film called *The Doctor's Secret*. That year alone he appeared in ten films and his career seemed to be on the rise. However, he returned to England in the early 1930s and featured in over forty films over the next eight years, including *Lorna Doone* in 1934, Hitchcock's *Sabotage* in 1936 and *King Solomon's Mines* in 1937. For the most part, however, he played secondary or even tertiary characters; occasional roles with little importance.

When war broke out in 1939 he left England promptly and returned to America. He had probably had enough of war and at forty-two he was still young enough to serve. During the 1940s he found work in B movies under the name John Loder, playing stiff-upper-lip types. His six-foot-three frame and ageing, debonair looks made him perfect for playing decaying aristocrats. His profile increased, however, and he appeared in some major hits of the day, including *Now, Voyager* with Bette Davis in 1942. It was probably by moving in these circles that he met the Viennese-born film star Hedy Lemarr. Lemarr, one of Hollywood's most beautiful and glamorous leading ladies, married John Loder in 1943. Lemarr was his third wife, he was her fourth husband. By the end of their lives, between them they chalked up eleven spouses. They had three children together, but they divorced in 1947. Loder later married an Argentinean heiress called Alba Larden and semi-retired to her ranch. He wrote a book called *Hollywood Hussars* in 1977 and died in 1988, aged ninety.

If you happen to spot that picture of Patrick Pearse, Elizabeth O'Farrell, Brigadier General Lowe and John Loder on the corner of Moore Street and Parnell Street, then look carefully. Look for a nurse's small tidy feet sheltering underneath Pearse's coat and a debonair, slightly bored twenty-year-old who was dreaming of Hollywood at a pivotal moment in our history.

ORANGE SONGS

Kevin Casey

I am holding a book that is, at first sight, unremarkable. It has a ring mark on its faded blue cover, because someone must have once placed a damp glass there. It's called *A Collection of Orange and Protestant Songs*, compiled and arranged by William Peake, and was published under the authority of the Grand Orange Lodge of Ireland and the Grand Black Chapter of Ireland in 1907.

The quality of the songs in the book varies – some are fine ballads and some are not – but most have two things in common. They suspect or dislike or loathe all things 'Popish' or 'Papist' or 'Roman' and they celebrate the glorious achievements of King William.

Here are just two typical verses from a typical song:

In time of tribulation
God raised a warrior bold;
'Twas William Prince of Orange
Whose memory dear we hold.
He fought the foe with courage
The Popish hosts o'erthrew,
He is the joy and pattern
Of all good men and true.

He stood before all nations
Truth's champion to be.

'Twas he who saved our country
From Priest and Popery.
The blessings that he left us
Our Church and Liberty,
From Rome and Ritualism
For ever we'll keep free.

This gives a flavour of the tone of these songs. All of them are well worth reading, if only for the insight that they provide into popular Orange culture of the time – just as nationalist and republican song-books provide equivalent insights.

I have said that, in itself, this book is unremarkable, but perhaps there is an aspect to it that provides considerable added interest. This is the record of some – or perhaps all – of its previous owners. One of these was the Reverend W. Harper of Dalkey House, Dalkey, who has inscribed his name and address in pencil just inside the back cover. Another, whose signature I simply cannot decipher, wrote on the flyleaf: 'Was Ireland worth losing to the Empire for this?' That's an interesting question, although almost certainly too simplistic.

Most interesting of all is the inscription just inside the front cover, which reads: 'J. C. Bowen-Colthurst, Capt, 2/RI Rifles, Downpatrick.' That's a name that I expect many of you will recognise as infamous.

In 1916, in Portobello Barracks, on the day after he had murdered an unarmed seventeen-year-old boy who was simply returning from church, an out-of-control Bowen-Colthurst ordered, without the benefit of any charge or any trial, the summary execution of three Irish jour-nalists he had arrested the previous day. They were Patrick McIntyre, the editor of a paper called *Searchlight*; Thomas Dickson, the editor of a magazine called *Eye-Opener*; and the celebrated journalist and pacifist, Francis Sheehy-Skeffington, who was out and about only because he was attempting to prevent the widespread looting of goods from shops.

On Bowen-Colthurst's orders, they were forced to stand against a wall in Portobello Barracks and were shot so quickly that it has been suggested that they would not even have known what was about to happen.

And so the name of Bowen-Colthurst, a previous owner of this book, entered into Irish history.

How can I be certain that the signature is genuine? That's the final surprise of this book. A handwritten letter has been somewhat crudely gummed inside its back cover. It was written by Frederick W. Shaw – a first cousin of George Bernard – and the paper is headed by the printed address of his residence: Bushy Park, Terenure. It is dated '22.3.09' and reads as follows:

> Dear Colthurst,
> I got that book of Songs and did not know who had sent it, certainly it is a most – [here there is a word that I cannot decipher] production and whoever compiled it ought to be set-upon but gently. Remember I told you that there are many extremists in the Orange Society whose style and views I never did approve of but it is the same in all secret societies. Please do not imagine that the tone of those songs with their willing to swagger reflect the views of the Orangemen in general. I am glad that you called my attention to it as I may be able to do something to check such effusion.
> Frederick W. Shaw

This remarkable letter, so moderate in its tone, suggests something about Bowen-Colthurst that may not have been generally known. In 1909, when he was stationed in Downpatrick and acquired this book, he was obviously concerned by the extremism of the songs that it contained. Yet, a mere seven years later, when he was stationed very close to Shaw's house in Bushy Park – where he may or may not have been a visitor – he was responsible for acts infinitely more barbaric then anything even hinted at in the most extreme of these songs.

I wonder why.

A CHILD'S WAR

Joan McCabe

Despite the fact that I was only five years old, I did realise that the wail of the siren was not to be ignored. When it sounded over Belfast, the grown-ups had only one thing to say: 'The Gerries are coming!' This was followed by a flurry of activity. Those words struck terror into my heart and a fear that this time they would definitely get me. I wasn't too sure just how this would happen, but my main scenario seemed to picture hundreds of stark black figures slowly dropping from the inky sky, white silk parachutes drifting above them. Their faces would be hidden behind black goggles, unseen and intent on murdering us all in our beds. Hadn't I seen them myself in the newsreels in the Saturday morning show in the Curzon Cinema?

I knew the flat roof over our coal shed would be an ideal landing place for them, since the big house across the entry from us had been taken over by Yanks and the Gerries would be able to fight them from our roof. I could see the Yanks in the yard opposite, peeling their way through big sacks of spuds and vegetables, yet ready for action, should the Germans strike. I could hear them talking and singing in their Roy Rogers voices in the weak May sunshine. Sometimes they drank a dark liquid from funny shaped bottles, which I later learned to be a drink called 'Cola'.

Now and again the Yanks would see me peeking and would wave in a friendly, easy way. I would jump back, mortified at being caught out, but was drawn back again and again to spy on them. Then I began to wonder what would happen if the Gerries found out I was friendly with the Yanks. I decided to keep away from the return room and to mind my own business in future.

The warning siren usually went off at night, and it was the signal for our family to leave warm beds and head fearfully for the space under the stairs. Sometimes called 'The Glory Hole', it was the choice of shelter for most Belfast families during the air raids. It also served as a safe place for the family treasures. During a raid I loved to pass the time inspecting the old musty boxes, with their treasure trove of china, silver and ornaments, all carefully wrapped in pages from *Ireland's Saturday Night*.

One particular night I was wakened by the dreaded siren blaring loudly. In great fear we all tumbled into our hidey-hole to await the German planes. From the wee door I watched my father preparing to join the men of our street in the nightly watch. I followed his large comforting shadow in the dim candlelight, dreading the moment he would disappear into the unknown, not sure if he would ever come back to us.

At these times my greatest comfort was our large and extremely fat black cat, Felix. During the raids it was the custom to open all windows and doors in the hope of lessening the effect of any blast from a falling bomb. Satisfied that all was in order, my mother would join us at last. Ignoring the distant whine of the enemy places, we curled up with the *Dandy* and the *Beano*. Felix lay between my knees, purring and dozing. Suddenly he rose and headed for the open door and the freedom of the night. I was too young to understand the workings of the feline mind, or what drove that cat to his nocturnal wanderings. All I felt was terror for his safety, and he sailed nonchalantly into the hell that was Belfast that particular night.

I could hear the Gerry planes droning over the city and I could see the flash of arc lights searching out the enemy. I clapped my hands over my ears as the drone grew louder, and a insane fear for my beloved Felix gripped me. I opened my mouth and screamed. No one could pacify me, I wanted that cat and nothing else would do. Where were the Yanks when you needed them?

Finally my mother gave in and crawled out to a cold and draughty kitchen. Wishing all cats to hell and back, she felt her way into the pitch-black yard, calling softly to the missing Felix. After what seemed an eternity, his black shape danced up the yard wall, down on to the mangle and in through the door. Purposefully he ran between my legs, tail stiff as a ramrod, and straight into my waiting arms.

Ecstatically I buried my face in his cold musky fur, feeling the damp black weight of him on my lap. He had escaped the Germans and their bombs! A deep resonant purr filtered from his soft body to mine as his claw rhythmically kneaded the arm of my blue woolly jumper. In the soft flicker of the candle I watched his green eyes narrow and close. In the distance I heard the fading drone of the departing German planes. We would live to fight another day!

PADDY THE PIGEON

Gail Seekamp

When news broke of the D-Day landings – sixty years ago – an elderly gentleman in Country Antrim was surely listening to his radio with particular interest. He was Mr Andrew Hughes of Carnlough: a World War I veteran and a well-travelled and educated man. But he was also a pigeon breeder of some repute.

A quarter of a million carrier pigeons served with British and US forces on World War II. Of these, just a few hundred took part in the Normandy campaign that began on D-Day – 6 June 1944. They included a pigeon called Paddy, bred by Mr Hughes.

Paddy was a black-and-white dappled pigeon, described as 'highly intelligent' by his RAF handlers. But when he was hatched in Spring 1943, he looked as unpromising as all pigeon chicks do – blind and helpless with damp scraggy feathers. When Paddy was a week old, Mr Hughes slipped a ring on his leg. It bore Paddy's National Pigeon Service number: NPS 43-9451.

That May, Paddy left Mr Hughes' loft for his first posting. It was at RAF Ballykelly, a Royal Air Force base near Derry. Paddy began training and was assigned to Air/Sea rescue missions.

At that time, RAF planes and supply boats were still at risk from marauding German U-boats and stray bombers. Even lack of fuel or bad weather could bring down a plane, so the RAF equipped crews with metal pigeon carriers. Each held two birds, placed beak to tail. The containers floated. If a plane ditched into the sea, a crewman would try to scribble its co-ordinates on wafer-thin paper. With luck, he might stuff the message into a cigarette-sized tube strapped to the pigeon's leg. Once released, the bird would 'home' to its RAF loft, bearing the vital SOS.

In this way, RAF pigeons saved hundreds of lives, braving storms, injury and exhaustion to deliver their messages. Perhaps Paddy rescued such a crew. For in March 1944 he was sent to an RAF base near Portsmouth. By then, preparations for the Allied invasion of France were at fever pitch. Men and materials were being secreted into camps all over Britain's south coast. Soon, they would cross the English Channel and strike at Hitler's forces.

Early on 6 June, almost 5,000 vessels of all shapes and sizes surged through a chilly grey sea towards Normandy. There, thousands of soldiers would meet their destiny on five beaches, code-named Sword, Juno, Gold, Omaha and Utah.

It seems Paddy came ashore on Omaha on 9 June, a beach which had seen the bloodiest combat of D-Day. Even now, the sector was still in turmoil. Tanks from crack German divisions were pouring into Normandy, clashing with Allied Troops in countryside that was ribbed with ancient hedgerows. It was ideal defensive terrain. Somewhere, against this chaotic backdrop, Paddy was released.

We do not know what his mission was. Nor his message. But we do know he was liberated on 12 June, at 8.14 a.m. He flew from Normandy back to his RAF base near Portsmouth in four hours fifty minutes. It was the fastest crossing by a carrier pigeon in the Normandy landings.

For this achievement, Paddy was awarded a Dickin Medal for bravery on 1 September 1944. This is the animal equivalent of the Victoria Cross. Paddy was the only Irish animal to be thus honoured for his service in World War II.

Imagine the feelings of Mr Hughes as he hunched over his wireless on 6 June and in the heady days that followed. And how he felt, a few months later, to learn that Paddy would return to Carnlough a hero. Perhaps glad. Bemused. And proud. Mr Hughes' own days of military service were long over. It was left to his pigeon, winging furiously across the Channel in June 1944, to play a part – however small – in those momentous Normandy landings and earn them *both* a place in history.

THE PIGEON FANCIER

Larry Brassill

Jack was every city boy's dream of the ideal adult. I could not wait to meet him again. He worked on my aunt's farm in County Limerick and knew everything about nature, as well as the idiosyncrasies of such wild unknown creatures as otters, badgers and foxes.

And so, within days of the closure of our school in that summer of 1943, I was already on my way to the country. Wonderfully, little had changed since the previous year, but when I met Jack I found that he had developed a new and fascinating hobby – racing pigeons. He had built a loft for them in an old disused outhouse. Soon I knew all about them, how there were only two eggs in each clutch, with both cock and hen sharing equally in the hatching and rearing of fledglings. To complete this picture of wedded bliss, each bird took only one lifetime mate.

Jack explained that pigeons had been trained to carry messages as far back as Our Lord's time and could race for distances up to 500 miles at speeds of 60 mph. Races took place all over Europe. Extraordinary though it seems, this practice continued throughout the war. But how could the pigeons find their way home from so far away? Jack said that no one knew the answer to this, but they seemed to have compasses in their brains and could navigate by the sun.

Bud was Jack's pride and joy, a super racer. He had nearly died in January as he pined after his mate, who had been killed by a local hawk. Now he was about to have his first race since then, from Dover in three days' time. Jack expected that Bud would fly home in about 12 hours, after his release on Saturday.

We were up at dawn on Sunday, anxiously scanning the sky, but no joy all day. Even cheerful Jack grew glum, as night descended. Had the hawk got Bud too? But we could not believe our eyes on the following morning. There was Bud in the loft, not on his own, but with a beautiful lady friend too. He had been romancing instead of racing! How had they met up? When we examined her leg we found that she did not carry the countermark of a racing pigeon but, instead, a small cylinder containing a hand-written note in a strange language. Jack gave them both to me as a souvenir and on my return home I placed them in a box of treasured possessions, there to remain undisturbed for a further thirty-five years.

Twenty years ago our daughter shared in a student exchange with a French girl, Yvette, who was accompanied on her journey from France by her Grandad, Pierre. His hobby, surprisingly, was racing pigeons. I told him of my own past experience and resurrected my tiny cylinder from 1943. When he opened it his face grew ashen. Slowly he translated the message to us.

'Rocket launchers moving North towards Normandy. Suspect under observation by Gestapo. Hold further messages.'

He had instantly recognised that handwriting – his sister's final message from the French Resistance to British Intelligence in Dover, before she had been arrested by the Germans at midnight on 5th July 1943, never again to be seen by her family.

THE CHRISTMAS PANTOMIME

John Ryan

Nothing revives so many good memories of childhood as the word 'pantomime'. Nothing evokes so well the magic of long ago, the spirit of Christmas past.

Time passes and it becomes harder to recall what a child really feels about the season (as against what we think it should feel), just as it becomes increasingly more difficult to see properly through the layers of irrelevancies and gift wrappings that mask what should be at the heart of Christmas.

Pantomime for some reason has retained the authentic flavour of the time. Perhaps it is because the people who give us this yearly confection are wise enough not to tamper with the cooking of it too much and offer it to us as the traditional fare that it is.

Dublin could once boast of about a half-dozen of these entertainments every year, with the major productions at the Gaeity and Olympia theatres. True, the mammoth Theatre Royal also attempted to give us something in the same vein, but pantomime, however well presented, fell flat on its face in that vast neo-Aztec jazz-modern mausoleum of the varieties.

The Gaeity held the slight edge over the Olympia as far as elegance was concerned, catering as it did for the Rathmines and Rathgar and Foxrock carriage trade. I can still hear the Minervas and Delages purring alongside its canopied vestibule and see invaluable cargoes of silk- and satin-bedecked pigtailed moppets being discharged. These argosies were later to be observed consuming vast quantities of chocolates, framed in the red plush and gilt of the dress-circle boxes like bevies of diminutive Czarinas.

But the Olympia had its own special attractions too. It was more spicy and less cloying and it was raffish by nature. It was the temple of vaudeville and Edwardian beyond words. The patrons expected and got a heady measure of uninhibited jokes and business as well as splendidly high-kicking 'gals'. It was only when men who balanced billiard cues on their noses took to the stage that a considerable number of the audience took to the bars. But to us, concerned only with the story of Little Red Riding Hood or Puss In Boots, as it was being tenuously unwound, all these happenings were grossly superfluous.

There was a carpeted hush and a lingering aroma of coffee about the Gaeity that not so much screamed as whispered wealth, so that the discreet bar there played but a minor role in the larger Palm Court setting. On the other hand the Olympia's was a superb rococo saloon that echoed the full-blooded ribaldry both during the intervals and, as we have noted, those periods during the show which the customers deemed to be *longeurs*.

The lord of these revels for more than thirty years was Jimmy O'Dea. He must have been one of the greatest Dames in the long history of pantomime. He was often partnered by that most gifted of comediennes, Maureen Potter, who in time became his most worthy successor at the Gaiety. No memory of the art will be even partly complete without him.

Let us bring back the scene: at long last the house lights dim and the compulsive chatter ceases, to be replaced by the frou-frou of tafetta and the rustle of sweet-wrappers. The footlights suffuse the velvet curtains in amber and gold and the orchestra attacks the overture with vigour. At last the tab goes up to reveal a village square all ablaze with light as the limes and travelling spots find their targets. It is somewhere in Ruritania. The lads and lassies of this place are chirping animatedly each to each, having been assembled here for some reason of which we will learn more anon.

They are in fact *all* girls, as is, indeed, the principal boy who now trips onstage to the cheers of the villagers, in shiny tights and high-heeled shoes. I once found myself trying to explain this and the fact that the Dame was a man but the Good Fairy a woman to a friend but he mumbled something about it seeming to be 'incredibly bent', so I thought better of it and dropped the subject. The conversation took place in Hoboken, New Jersey where they have never heard of pantomime.

Then, the principal girl and the Baron and his shady assistants come forward and introduce themselves with all the formal ritual of oriental drama. Indeed pantomime may be the nearest thing we have to Japanese *Noh* drama. All this is but a build-up for the great moment when the conductor, responding to some unseen cue (or was it that little red light that went on for a moment?), suddenly rushes the orchestra through the last bars of 'Biddy Mulligan The Pride Of The Coombe' whereupon our hero bursts on to the stage either on a bike, in a car, astride a donkey, by balloon or the simple and even more popular expedient of sliding through on his derrière.

And from that moment on, we were Jimmy O'Dea's children and Christmas had been, once more, marvellously accomplished.

THE GIRLS

Aodhan Madden

They came every Monday night for supper. Mother called them 'the girls' but Alice and her sister May were well past their prime when they used to sit by our fireside on winter nights, nibbling roast beef sandwiches and revelling in the gossip of the parish.

On the surface they were the epitome of maidenish rectitude. We all had to be on our very best behaviour when 'the girls' arrived with the customary bag of assorted sweets. They came after the Monday evening devotions in the parish church. They seemed to exude a certain odour of sanctity and their visits always began with a recitation of what we came to call their 'sorrowful mysteries' – all the aches and pains and disappointments which had beset them since the week before.

There was only one man in their lives – and he was the great comedian Jimmy O'Dea. The very mention of his name and their sad faces would suddenly light up with illicit pleasure. Mother always knew precisely when to introduce the subject of Jimmy O'Dea into the proceedings. Just on the point when Alice or May was getting carried away by some painful bunion or a lingering cold, she would strike, cutting the self-pity like a knife through blancmange. I can still hear their laughter pealing through the house as they described the latest sketch that their hero had adorned. The more risqué the sketch, the more hysterical was their laughter.

Alice and May followed Jimmy O'Dea's shows everywhere in Ireland and Britain. They planned their holidays to take in shows in places like Scunthorpe or Newcastle or Birkenhead and every new sketch was reported back to our fireside with a breathless delight that seemed like madness.

The highlight of their year, of course, was the Gaiety pantomime. Every St Stephen's night they set off in their taxi dressed up to the nines like two opera dowagers. They always brought with them a huge box of chocolates which they munched in the parterre while they waited like two overgrown and overexcited schoolgirls for the orchestra to strike up and their hero to appear.

They brought me along with them one year. I was about eight and had never been inside a theatre before. I remember the huge excitement as the great red curtain slowly rose to reveal a world of Arcadian magic. The pantomime was *Babes in the Wood* and the stage was a riot of colour as dancers tumbled out fairytale windows and a girl dressed like Robin Hood sang 'Younger Than Springtime' from *South Pacific.*

Then suddenly, the whole theatre rocked with laughter. May almost leapt out of her seat with excitement.

'Look at him. *Look* at him!' she squealed.

Jimmy O'Dea appeared at the top of an illuminated staircase. He was wearing the most outrageous dress I'd ever seen and on top of his head was a gigantic contraption that looked like a wedding cake. He moved down a step and the theatre roared again as little candles flickered on the cake. Alice and May were now clutching each other and screaming with delight.

But what fascinated me was the strange garden gnome face beneath the wedding cake and those great dark octopal eyes which slowly moved across everyone in the theatre and then homed in on me. Jimmy O'Dea then winked a black feathery wink and a mischievous smile crept up his face. He passed some remark to the audience which sent Alice and May into further convulsions. Then the orchestra struck up again and O'Dea continued on down the staircase.

So this was their hero, this little man in a ridiculous frock! I was a little bemused that the two grown women had given their hearts so completely to such strangeness. And yet, as the pantomime continued, I found myself drawn increasingly to this man, to the huge black eyes, to the comic outrage in his voice, to something unsettling yet funny in the way he moved about the stage as a woman, in the way he communed with each one of us personally.

In the taxi going home Alice and May sat back in silent pleasure. Then May whispered one word out the window to the passing night.

'Magic,' she said.

PICTURING THE PAST

Barbara McKeon

The photograph was taken in the summer of 1956. It shows children in a suburban garden holding hands, encircling a girl whose birthday it was, all pretty party frocks, beaming up at the camera.

Over forty years later I have a copy of that picture. And I'm still friends with the birthday girl.

That picture captures for me the essence of my growing up in Dublin in the fifties. For so many, that time meant poverty and despair, repression and ignorance. But my photograph reflects a different image; we were part of a new prosperous Ireland, offspring of professional and commercial people who owned their own mortgaged houses, drove cars and sent their children to nice schools.

But more importantly, the photograph is significant because it encapsulates another aspect of the Ireland I grew up in. Of the ten little girls in the picture, three were Jewish, two were Protestant and the other five Catholics. We went to different schools and churches and learned the ethos of our separate religious identities, but we came home and played in each other's gardens. While we were conscious of our differences they rarely impinged on our friendships, having no more bearing than being on opposing teams for a game of tag.

Except for one potentially combustible occasion. On a summer's day, shortly before her birthday, Beverly was taking me and another friend, Maura, to the Macabi Club, a Jewish sports and social club near the Kimmage Crossroads. I had been to the club before but it was Maura's first visit and she felt a little apprehensive about entering a Jewish enclave. For some reason she chose that moment to tell Beverly that the Jews had murdered Jesus.

Beverly hotly retorted that Jesus himself was a Jew, and besides he wasn't the Messiah, just a prophet and holy man. This piece of blasphemy staggered Maura, especially as we were passing the Holy Ghost Fathers at the time.

'Jews are doomed to eternal damnation in the fires of hell for not believing in Our Lord,' Maura solemnly warned.

Then, looking at me, added in equally regretful tones, 'So are Protestants for not believing in Our Lady.'

That led to a good old, stand up, ecclesiastical knockabout that involved a bit of hair pulling and a kick on someone's shin. An adult cycling by ordered us to behave ourselves and the holy war ceased abruptly.

In festering silence we crossed the Kimmage Road and were about to enter the club grounds when Beverly pulled off a theological masterstroke.

'Catholics aren't allowed to be in here,' she announced, as Maura's jaw dropped open, 'but Protestants are,' she added triumphantly, grabbing my arm and hauling me off towards the clubhouse.

Maura's eyes were brimming with tears as we left her standing outside the gate, thirsting after the promised lemonade.

There was no intentional sectarianism, just words and attitudes that had filtered down from the grown-up world. A world we would one day inherit ourselves.

It took a week and a packet of Matzoth biscuits to patch up that row, but we were pals again in time for the birthday party that was to be captured in a photograph for all time.

THE STRAP

Pat Boran

Like a Christian Brother of old, my father kept a leather strap, and was known to use it. It was not enough simply to use a leather strap: in the confines and privacy of one's home, it was necessary to be known to use it, the power being as much in the threat as in the application. More of a belt than the apparently custom-made straps the Irish Christian Brothers liked to carry, wide and undulating as the tongue of a cow, my father's strap was, I recall, about nine inches long and made of a flat leather band, folded over onto itself lengthwise, then sewn along the length so that there was a slight but distinct seam down the middle.

Seam side up or seam side down, however, my father's strap, when it bore down on your fingers, left your hand on fire, your eyes on fire and terrible confusion in your heart. For it was clear, from early on, that my father loved us, even us three boys for whom the leather strap was all too often taken down from the shelf where it rested between the scissors and combs, to be removed from its double-strength elastic band and allowed to unfurl itself like, I always thought in a fearful, distracted way, the serpent in the Garden of Eden.

To be fair to him, my father had grown up in a different time, a time in which such forms of discipline were not uncommon and where, if you were not receiving corporal punishment at home, you were almost certainly receiving it at school. My father's generation had a war in common, and childhoods of scarcity and hardship in which men disciplined their sons the way a farmer might a beast who had strayed off the path. There were crude and sometimes cruel solutions to problems that ought to have been solved in other ways.

And yet, incredibly as it now seems to me, for a long number of years, my father's strap was wielded in our house, and many evenings I sat there in the front room, or the breakfast room as it had once been called, squeezing a still-burning hand and gazing out through the lace curtains at Main Street, Portlaoise, like a prisoner gazing out between steel bars.

And there must have been shame in the beatings too, for my father and for us, because I remember how dark a thing it felt to tell it to a friend one day in school (would we have been eight or nine?), who confessed to me that his father did it too, but preferring a stick or his open hand and, once in a while, his fist...

Still sucking on gobstoppers in the bicycle shed, it suddenly became clear to us that we were very likely a whole school, a whole generation of young lads, being routinely beaten, and beaten down, for no real reason and with no real purpose, and little chance of it coming to an end. The strange thing was that it was nearly always the beatings, the straps and the sticks themselves, which were the enemy. Only when a schoolfriend swore revenge on his father, and looked as if he meant it, did it dawn on us that the solution to such a widespread problem lay in individual, particularised action.

So it happened that, one day, long enough after such a beating to be calm and clear about how to proceed, my younger brother and I decided to destroy my father's strap. We simply made up our minds that this particular chapter of our lives had come to an end. The details are sketchy, but I do recall that *Sesame Street* was playing on the television upstairs as we made our way down to the kitchen, hearing the fifth-last and the third-last stairboard creak as they had since we were born. By chance, my father was away somewhere, gone to a nearby town on business, and, despite the ominous warning that 'He'll miss it', from our mother, who had always been horrified by its sight, I stood on a chair and took it from its resting place.

My brother, as I recall it, opened the front door of the range, and, holding the strap in the tongs from the open fireplace upstairs, I lifted it inside, this black coil of darkness, this leather, hand-held weapon of domestic terror. And we stood and watched it for a minute or two, twitch and straighten, spark and twitch, rise and snap and spark again, until the flames at last took hold of it and, bathed in the sheer heat of the moment, we shut the door of hell on it and moved well back.

All lives, simple or complicated, are full of mysteries. One from my own is how did my father react when he found his leather strap had vanished? For apart from looking for it, and threatening now and then to get another — which he never did — he never asked us directly if we'd taken it or what had become of it.

As if he knew. As if maybe he'd needed to have the decision made for him. As if it had long been clear, even to him, that the strap's time, if ever it had one, was long since gone. Soon his sons would be young men; his daughters, young women. He and his wife would be a late-middle-aged couple, growing old in patterns they had built for themselves.

And, in the midst of all this change, at its mercy one might say, sometimes letting go turns out to be a kind of blessing: for without his leather strap, my father's own beautiful hands, even while ours visibly toughened, slowly softened again.

LONG AGO AND FAR AWAY

Hilary Boyle

Well over half a century ago I lived in Port Royal, Jamaica; a spit of land separated from the mainland by eight miles of mangrove swamp plentifully supplied with enormous crocodiles. We were served by a ship that came three times a day from Kingston bringing over our ice which would be delivered to the house by a little boy carrying it in an enormous pair of tongs with claws. The ice came in the winter by the *Canadian Fisher* or the *Canadian Forester*, cut from the St Lawrence River when she was frozen over. Our mail came on these ships too, and at one time of the year they brought huge red, mealy, tasteless apples, much prized by the English whom they reminded of home. I despised them, preferring the mangoes, pawpaws and watermelons grown locally.

We swam in a bath of the sea netted in against sharks, and sea and sand comprised most of our lives. My husband and I bought a ten-foot dinghy, the good ship, *Shillelagh*, upon whom we put far too much sail, so that she was only too apt to overturn when one swung the boom. I toted sackfuls of soil from the mainland and made a garden of sorts, and rather revolting – if any living thing can be revolting, but they did stink – land crabs came out of holes beneath the coconut trees and leered at us.

Our house was at an angle and sloped since the '07 earthquake, and all the furniture slid towards the windows. We fished, swam and sailed while the English played bridge and tennis and thought me a bit mad; the more especially as my daughter was the first European baby to be born in Port Royal since it had been a city in the days of Captain

Morgan before most of it went under the sea in the earlier earthquake of the seventeenth century. The natives used to say one could hear the church bells ringing and even see the buildings on a clear day.

One day at dawn there appeared on the horizon the last seven-masted schooner in the world, the *Robin Hood*. As she slowly and majestically came in to port and tied up at the coal wharf, I fell in love irrevocably. Was I not the daughter of a sailor who had trained under sail? Later I learned she was dirty, needed much paint and her captain, aged about fifty, was an old drunken reprobate; but my love was unabated and I bought him drinks and hung on his every word, for was not the *Robin Hood* going to the Bahamas when she left Port Royal? I yearned to go with her. The captain yielded to my importunities so far as to say I might go with them as far as St Lucia.

In vain I pleaded I could not get back from there, while a fishing smack sailed nearly every day from Nassau. He was adamant: St Lucia or nowhere; and there came the day when my love deserted me and sailed, taking my heart with her. I accompanied her as far as I was able in the *Shillelagh* until all her sails unfurled and she gathered speed and vanished into the hazy distance. I turned me about and rowed home – for every breath of wind had gone – wearily and heartbroken through the heat of the day.

In due course we learned of her safe arrival and then of her departure from St Lucia.

A short distance off Nassau she went afire. All the crew, even the parrot, took to the boats and were rescued safe and sound, but the *Robin Hood* went down and there she lies until the sea gives up its dead. She was insured for an astronomical sum and the company payed up without a murmur. Only to this day I wonder if my love was murdered for money. I have held my peace for over half a century but I have never ceased to doubt the origin of that fire, nor to grieve for my lovely ship, sloven as hateful men had allowed her to become. In full sail one saw only the incredible beauty that had once been hers.

CONTRIBUTOR BIOGRAPHIES

UNA AGNEW: Born in Courtbane, Co. Louth. A St Louis Sister, educated at St Louis Convent, Carrickmacross, Co. Monaghan. Read English and Irish at UCD. Head of the Spirituality Department at Milltown Institute, Dublin.

GREGORY ALLEN: Former member of An Garda Siochána. Sometime curator of the Garda Museum. Author of *An Garda Síochana 1922–92*. He died in 2001.

PAUL ANDREWS: A Jesuit priest from Omagh. Teacher, psychologist, therapist and online editor in the Jesuit Communication Centre. Formerly Rector of Manresa Retreat House, Dollymount.

DENISE BLAKE: Born in Ohio, USA, in 1958, her family moved back to Ireland in 1969 where she grew up in Letterkenny, Co. Donegal. Her first collection of poetry, *Take a Deep Breath*, was published by Summer Palace Press.

JOHN BOLAND: A literary and television critic for the *Irish Independent* and an arts broadcaster. His first collection of poems, *Brow Head*, was published in 1999.

PAT BORAN: Born in Portlaoise in 1963, his *New and Selected Poems* was published by Dedalus Press in 2007. He received the 2008 O'Shaughnessy Poetry Award and is a member of Aosdána.

HILARY BOYLE: Born in Jamaica, she spent most of her childhood in Ireland. She left Ireland as a young married woman but returned in 1934. She was active with the Dublin Housing Action Committee and championed a variety of causes, including peace issues. She died in 1986.

LARRY BRASSILL: Retired Borough Engineer of Dún Laoghaire, and sport fanatic. Part-time consultant. Nine grandchildren keep him fully occupied.

TONY BREHONY: Short story writer, historian, novelist. First radio story accepted by Francis MacManus in 1949. Regular contributor to *Sunday Miscellany* since 1977.

FIONNUALA BRENNAN: Lived on the island of Paros, Greece, with her young family in the late 1970s and has written a book about that experience, *On a Greek Island*. She teaches creative writing and tutors on an adult education course at University College Dublin.

CATHERINE BROPHY: Born, reared and educated in Dublin, she has written novels, short stories and screenplays and facilitates writing workshops.

MATTHEW BYRNE: Priest, broadcaster, writer. Formerly producer, presenter with BBC and RTÉ. Books include *Heaven Looked Upwards*.

KEVIN CASEY: Kevin Casey was born in Kells, Co Meath in 1940. His novels are *The Sinner's Bell* (London, Faber 1968); *A Sense of Survival* (Faber, 1974); and *Dreams of Revenge* (Faber, 1977). He lives in Dublin.

MAUREEN CHARLTON: Contributor to various RTÉ radio programmes. Has written drama for the stage and radio. Published work includes *Selected Fables of La Fontaine* (Irish nomination for a European Translators' Prize). She died in 2007.

CLAUDE COCKBURN: The son of a diplomat, he was born in China in 1904. After obtaining a degree from Oxford University he became a journalist with *The Times* until 1933, when he started his own journal, *The Week*. In 1947 he moved to Ireland and wrote a weekly column for *The Irish Times*. He died in December 1981.

JAMES COTTER: A film scriptwriter, RTÉ television producer and director, his writing for adults and children has featured on RTÉ.

MAURICE CRAIG: Born in Belfast in 1919, he has written on subjects as diverse as Irish bookbindings, biography, poetry and topography, but it is for his books on architectural subjects that he is best known. His seminal *Dublin 1660–1860* appeared in 1952.

RICHARD CRAIG: Born in Glasgow. A graduate of London, Leeds and Strathclyde Universities. Now lives permanently in West Cork.

ANTHONY CRONIN: A poet, novelist and critic, his many works include *No Laughing Matter: The Life and Times of Flann O'Brien* and *The Last Modernist*, his acclaimed biography of Samuel Beckett. He was a founding member of Aosdána, of which he was made a Saoi in 2003.

ERIC CROSS: Born in 1905 in Newry, Co. Down, he was raised and educated in England. His book, *The Tailor and Ansty*, was banned for a number of years and was the subject of a Seanad Éireann debate. He died near Westport, Co. Mayo, in 1980.

LEO CULLEN: Author of *Clocking 90 on the Road to Cloughjordan* and *Let's Twist Again*. A frequent broadcaster on RTÉ Radio I, RTÉ lyric fm and the BBC. He hails from Co. Tipperary and now lives in Monkstown, Co. Dublin.

RITA CURRAN DARBY: Born and educated in Dublin. Writes regularly for radio. Currently writing a novel. Rita has been shortlisted for the RTÉ P.J. O'Connor Radio Drama Awards on three occasions and was first runner-up in Gay Byrne's *A Day in the Life*.

GERALD DAWE: Born in Belfast, he lectures in English at Trinity College Dublin, where he is director of The Oscar Wilde Centre for Irish Writing and and co-director of the Graduate Creative Writing Programme. He has published numerous books of essays and poetry and his most recent poetry collection is *Points West*. He is a member of Aosdána and lives in Dún Laoghaire.

JOHN F. DEANE: Born on Achill Island, Co. Mayo, he writes poetry full time and is a founder member of Poetry Ireland and a member of Aosdána. In 2007, the French government honoured him by making him Chevalier dans l'Ordre des Arts et des Lettres. His latest poetry collection, *A Little Book of Hours*, was published in 2008.

PAT DONLAN: Director of the National Library of Ireland from 1989–1998. Member of the Royal Irish Academy and the Heritage

Council. She is the current director of the Tyrone Guthrie Centre, Annaghmakerrig.

FRANCES DONOGHUE: Dublin-based. Worked as a teacher, guidance counsellor, social researcher and part-time writer. Regular contributor to various radio programmes.

THEO DORGAN: Born in Cork, he is the author of the poetry collections *The Ordinary House of Love, Rosa Mundi* and *Sappho's Daughter*. A former Director of Poetry Ireland and member of Aosdána. Appointed to The Arts Council in 2003. A broadcaster with RTÉ.

NORRIE EGAN: Taught for several years in the North. Has had stories and plays broadcast.

ANNE ENRIGHT: Her writing includes short-story collections, non-fiction work and four novels including *The Gathering*, which won the 2007 Man Booker Prize and Listowel Writers Week Kerry Award for Literature 2008. She lives with her family in Bray, Co. Wicklow. Her recent publications are *Taking Pictures* (2008) and *Yesterday's Weather* (2009).

SHANE FAGAN: Retired maintenance supervisor. Writer of prose and short stories, he is a regular contributor to *Ireland's Own* magazine and LMFM Radio.

BERNARD FARRELL: An award-winning playwright who, since *I Do Not Like Thee Doctor Fell* in 1979, has had his subsequent twenty-one plays, which have been seen extensively abroad, premiered mainly at the Abbey Theatre and Gate Theatre.

MICHAEL FEWER: Born in Co. Waterford, he is the author of numerous books relating to nature, landscape and the environment, most recently *The Wicklow Military Road*.

JOHN FLEETWOOD: Author of several books, including *The History of Medicine in Ireland*, and of five pantomimes. Regular contributor to various radio programmes.

NORMAN FREEMAN: A retired radio officer and author of *Seaspray and Whiskey: Classic Hurling Matches 1976–1991*. 'The Phantom Whistle Blower' and 'The Squinting Eye' are among the essays he has contributed to An Fear Rua.

BRYAN GALLAGHER: A former headmaster, took early retirement in 1997. Author of *There'll Not Be a Crowd Till the Crowd Gathers* and *Barefoot in Mullyneeny*. Lives in Enniskillen.

MADELEINE GOING: Took up writing after living all over the world and raising a family. She was a teacher in Africa and published a collection of short stories called *Going Places*. Madeleine died in 2007.

TED GOODMAN: Born in Co. Louth in 1932 and grew up in Newry, Co. Down. Worked as an Inspector of Taxes with the Irish Revenue from 1955 to 1995.

VONA GROARKE: Born in Edgeworthstown, Co. Longford, she is an award-winning poet and a member of Aosdána. Her many poetry collections include *Lament for Art O'Leary*. She currently divides her teaching time between the Centre for New Writing at the University of Manchester and Wake Forest University in North Carolina.

HUGO HAMILTON: Living in Dublin, he is the author of the bestselling German-Irish memoir *The Speckled People*. His second memoir is entitled *The Sailor in the Wardrobe* and his latest novel, *Disguise*, was published in 2008. He participated in *Sunday Miscellany Live from Listowel* in 2008.

MICHAEL HARDING: Novelist, poet, playwright and director. He has written several novels, including *Bird in the Snow* (2008). A member of Aosdána, he lives in Mullingar and writes a weekly column in *The Irish Times*.

LIAM HARTE: He lectures in Irish and Modern Literature at the University of Manchester and his books include *Modern Irish Autobiography: Self, Nation and Society* and *The Literature of the Irish in Britain: Autobiography and Memoir*.

ANNE LE MARQUAND HARTIGAN: Born in England and living in Ireland for many years, she is a poet, playwright and painter. Her sixth collection of poetry, *To Keep the Light Burning*, was published in 2008. She has a family of six children and likes a bit of craic.

FRANCIS HARVEY: Born in Enniskillen but has lived in Donegal for most of his life. Poet and playwright. *Collected Poems* was published with Dedalus Press in 2007.

SEAMUS HEANEY: Born in Co. Derry, he now lives in Dublin. Since his first collection of poetry, *Death of a Naturalist*, he has published numerous collections of poetry and prose. He is the recipient of many awards and honours including the Nobel Prize for Literature (1995).

PHYL HERBERT: She has a background in teaching and theatre and, in 2008, completed an M. Phil in Creative Writing in Trinity College Dublin. She is published in the anthology *Sixteen after Ten*.

JOHN HEUSTON: John Heuston is a Dublin-based public servant with a strong interest in Irish social history and genealogy.

VIVIEN IGOE: Curator of the James Joyce Museum. Her previous books include *James Joyce's Dublin Houses*, *Nora Barnacle's Galway*, *City of Dublin*, *A Literary Guide to Dublin* and *Dublin Burial Grounds and Graveyards*.

PETER JANKOWSKY: Born in Berlin in 1939, he has lived in Dublin since 1971, where he has been teaching, acting and writing. His memoir, *Myself Passing By*, was published in 2000.

JOHN JORDAN: Born in Dublin in 1930, he was a poet, short story writer, celebrated poetry and theatre critic, editor, academic and broadcaster. A member of Aosdána, he died suddenly in Wales in 1988.

MICHAEL JUDGE: Born in Dublin, where he still lives, he has written extensively for stage, radio, TV, screen drama and multimedia shows. He has published two novels, *Vintage Red* and *From the Left Hand*.

MAUREEN KEANE: Lives in Sutton, Dublin. Has written two biographies, *Mrs S. C. Hall*, and *Ishbel, Lady Aberdeen* and holds a PhD in Anglo-Irish Literature.

JOE KEARNEY: Born in Kilkenny in 1951. He is a full-time writer, and has been involved in making documentaries for RTÉ Radio 1. He teaches creative writing and is currently working on a PhD in Creative Writing at UCD. His latest collection, *The Bend of the Road*, will be published later this year.

CYRIL KELLY: From Listowel, Co. Kerry. Was a primary school teacher in Dublin for many years and a regular contributor to RTÉ Radio.

BENEDICT KIELY: Born in 1919, near Dromore, Co. Tyrone, Kiely is the author of numerous short story collections, novels, works of non-fiction and an autobiography, *Drink to the Bird: An Omagh Boyhood*. A member of Aosdána, he lived for many years in Dublin. He died in 2007.

CHUCK KRUGER: A regular contributor to RTÉ Radio's *Sunday Miscellany*, *Quiet Quarter* and *Seascapes* and NPR's *Weather Notebook*, Kruger grew up in New York's Finger Lakes. In protest against the Vietnam War, he moved to Switzerland. He has lived on Cape Clear Island for many years.

GERALD V. KUSS: Writer. Born in Tampere, Finland in 1920. Died in 1969.

MELOSINA LENOX-CONYNGHAM: Born in Sri Lanka on a tea estate, she spent her youth in Co. Louth and now lives in a cottage in Kilkenny. She is the editor of an anthology, *Diaries of Ireland*.

MAE LEONARD: Originally from Limerick, she now lives in Kildare. A broadcaster, award-winning writer and poet, her publications include *My Home is There*, *This is Tarzan Clancy* and *Six for Gold*. Amongst the many honours received for her writing are the Scottish International, Francis McManus, Belmont and Cecil Day Lewis Awards.

NICOLA LINDSAY: Published works include a children's book and a collection of poetry. She is the author of five novels. Her work has been broadcast and anthologised in Ireland and Britain.

BRIAN LYNCH: Award-winning poet, playwright, screenwriter, art critic and novelist. His book, *The Winner of Sorrow*, about the poet William Cowper (1731–1800), was published in 2005. He is a member of Aosdána and lives in Dublin.

AIFRIC MAC AODHA: Born and still living in Dublin, her poems have been published in several magazines, including *Poetry Ireland, Innti* and *Bliainiris*. She has won many prizes for her poetry and was recently awarded an Arts Council endowment. Her début collection of poetry is soon to be published.

JOHN MACCONVILLE: Doctor and regular contributor to early *Sunday Miscellany* Programme.

MARGUERITE MACCURTAIN: Born in Co. Galway, Marguerite travels extensively. She is a former model and is married to Frank Flannery of the Fine Gael Party.

DES MACHALE: Full-time associate professor of Mathematics at University College Cork, he is a prolific author, most notably on humorous subjects. He has written 14 books of lateral thinking problems with Paul Sloane.

TOM MAC INTYRE: Widely published as a playwright, poet and author of fiction and non-fiction, he won the Stewart Parker Prize in 1999 and the *Irish Times*/ESB Irish Theatre Best New Play Award in 2002. He is a member of Aosdána and lives in Cavan.

MARIE MACSWEENEY: A Kerrywoman born in Dublin and living in Co. Meath. As well as *Sunday Miscellany* pieces, she writes radio plays, short stories, articles and poetry. Winner of the Francis McManus Short Story Competition in 2001.

AODHAN MADDEN: Award-winning playwright, fiction writer and journalist. Several of his plays have been staged by The Abbey and broadcast on RTÉ and BBC. His screenplay, *Night Train*, won Best Actor for John Hurt at the Verona Film Festival, and was nominated as Best European Feature at the Brussels Film Festival. A member of Aosdána, he lives in Dublin.

STEPHEN MATTERSON: He has published widely on many aspects of American literature. His major research interests include the work of Herman Melville and the history of exceptionalism. His publications include *A Glossary of American Literature*. He was Head of the School of English at Trinity College Dublin from 2006–2009.

SAM MCAUGHTRY: Born and lives in Belfast. Published author of nine books, broadcaster, journalist and trade unionist. Columnist of the Year with *The Irish Times* in 1986, a member of Seanad Éireann from 1996–99. Received an Honorary Doctorate from NUI Maynooth in 1998.

JOAN MCCABE: Teacher. Born in Northern Ireland.

SINÉAD MCCOOLE: A historian and author of a number of books, including *Hazel: A Life of Lady Lavery* and *No Ordinary Women*. Keeper/curator of the Jackie Clarke Library, Ballina, Co. Mayo. Currently Sinéad is working on the third part of her trilogy on Irish revolutionary women, *Easter Widows*, the untold story of the wives of the executed leaders of the 1916 Rising.

KEVIN MCDERMOTT: Born in Dublin, where he now lives with his family. He is a teacher and writer.

VINCENT MCDONNELL: An award-winning author of books for adults and young readers. Currently Writer in Residence for Co. Cork, he has also served two terms for Co. Limerick. He now lives in Co. Cork with his wife and son.

PADRAIG MCGINN: A retired school principal, living in Carrick-on-Shannon, Co. Leitrim. His stories have been published in *The Leitrim Guardian* and *First Cut*. He has been shortlisted in a number of Irish writing competitions, including The Bard of Armagh and the Strokestown Poetry Award.

IGGY MCGOVERN: Born in Coleraine and now living in Dublin, he is an Associate Professor of Physics at Trinity College Dublin. He is also the recipient of the McCrae Literary Award and the Hennessy Literary Award for Poetry. His collection, *The King of Suburbia*, received the inaugural Glen Dimplex New Writers Award for Poetry.

LEO MCGOWAN: A Dubliner who teaches Management at NUI, Galway. In addition to creative writing, his hobbies include swimming, acting, and dog-walking.

BARBARA MCKEON: Born in Dublin, has published and broadcast numerous short stories and many radio and TV dramas. Associated with *The Irish Press* for years, she now lives and writes in Galway.

JUDITH MOK: Born in The Netherlands, she now lives in Dublin. An internationally renowned soprano, she has also published many works of poetry and fiction. Her most recent novel, *Gael*, is published by Telegram.

GERRY MORAN: From Kilkenny, he is a former primary school principal whose writing has featured in various publications. He is the author of *Kilkenny City and Co.*

JACQUELINE MORRISSEY: Lives in Dún Laoghaire. She works as an Associate Lecturer for the Open University. She was the winner of the Co. Waterford Arts Office Molly Keane Memorial Award in 2004.

PAUL MULDOON: Born in Co. Armagh, he has, since 1987, lived in the United States, where he is now Howard G.B. Clark '21 Professor at Princeton University and Chair of the Peter B. Lewis Center for the Arts. He is the author of numerous collections of poetry including *Moy Sand and Gravel* (2002), for which he won the 2003 Pulitzer Prize. In 2007 he was appointed Poetry Editor of *The New Yorker.*

VAL MULKERNS: Born in Dublin in 1925, she moved to London after working in the civil service. She returned to Ireland in 1952 as the associate editor of *The Bell*. A novelist and short story writer, she jointly won the AIB Prize for Literature. She is a member of Aosdána.

ÁINE MULVEY: A professional singer and choral conductor. She is a member of the National Chamber Choir of Ireland, and musical director of the AIB Choral Society and choirs of Mount Argus, Dublin. She lives in Firhouse, Dublin, where she also manages a busy teaching practice.

ORLA MURPHY: Born in Cork and the daughter of sculptor Seamus Murphy. Her writing has been shortlisted for Hennessy Awards and the Fish Short Story Competition, and has appeared in *New Irish Writing* and *The Phoenix Short Stories Anthology* (1999). Her work has been broadcast on BBC Radio 4 and RTÉ Radio I.

NUALA NÍ CHONCHÚIR: Born in Dublin in 1970, she won the inaugural Cúirt New Writing Prize (2004), RTÉ's Francis Mac Manus Award (2002), the Cecil Day Lewis Award (2003), and has twice been nominated for a Hennessy Award (2001 & 2005), all for fiction. She lives in Galway. Her third short fiction collection, *Nude*, was published in 2009.

NUALA NÍ DHOMHNAILL: A distinguished Irish-language poet and mother of four children. Born in Lancashire in 1952 of Irish parents, she was brought up in the Dingle Gaeltacht and in Nenagh, Co. Tipperary. She is a member of Aosdána and lives in Co. Dublin.

FACHTNA Ó DRISCEOIL: Brought up in an Irish-speaking family in Dún Laoghaire, he works as a television reporter and radio producer for RTÉ.

TADHG Ó DÚSHLÁINE: A senior lecturer in Modern Irish at NUI Maynooth, he is director of the Frank O'Connor Project, the writer in residence with Cork Corporation and was the writer in residence with the Munster Literature Centre from 1999–2000. He has published poetry collections and books of criticism.

SEÁN Ó FAOLÁIN: Born in Cork in 1900. He edited the literary journal *The Bell* from 1940 to 1946. As well as novels and the short stories for which he is most famous, he wrote biography, criticism and travel books. He was a member of Aosdána, and was elected Saoi in 1986. He died in 1991.

EOGHAN Ó HANLUAIN: A Senior Lecturer Emeritus in Modern Irish at University College Dublin.

ÉAMONN Ó HUALLACHÁIN: Living on the border between north Louth and south Armagh, he has long had an enthusiastic love of the culture, language and history of his native place. He often takes groups around this scenic and historically interesting area.

CONOR O'CALLAGHAN: He has published three collection of poetry, including *Fiction* (2005). His comic prose memoir, *Red Mist*, has since been adapted into a television documentary. He currently lectures part-time at Sheffield Hallam University in the UK and at Wake Forest University in North Carolina. He was awarded the 2007 Bess Hokin prize by *Poetry* magazine.

JULIE O'CALLAGHAN: Born in the US. Writes poetry for adults and children. Her most recent book is *The Book of Whispers*. She received the Michael Hartnett Award for Poetry in 2001 and is a member of Aosdána.

JOSEPH O'CONNOR: A Dublin-born, award-winning novelist, his most recent books are *Star of The Sea* and *Redemption Falls*, both of which have been translated into many languages. He has written non-fiction articles and books, as well as film scripts. He participated in *Sunday Miscellany Live from Listowel Writers Week* in 2007.

JOHN O'DONNELL: His work has been published and broadcast widely and his awards include the Irish National Poetry Prize, the Ireland Funds Prize and the Hennessy/*Sunday Tribune* Poetry Award. A barrister, he lives in Dublin.

MARY O'DONNELL: A poet and novelist, she is a regular broadcaster and a member of Aosdána. Her short story collection, *Storm over Belfast*, was published in 2008.

MICHAEL O'LOUGHLIN: A poet, screenwriter and translator, he is currently writer in residence with Galway City.

MARY O'MALLEY: Born and reared in Connemara, she now lives in the Moycullen Gaeltacht. She broadcasts, travels and lectures widely and is a member of Aosdána. She has written six collections of poetry and is currently writer in residence at NUI Galway, where she teaches on the MA in Writing and in Arts Administration.

THADDEUS O'REGAN: Born in Roscarbery, West Cork in 1951, he studied English and Geography at University College Cork. He works as a secondary teacher and lives near Carrigaline, Cork.

ARTHUR O'REILLY: Retired occupational psychologist. Interests include human rights, grandchildren, talking, tennis. Regards humour as underestimated pathway to learning.

PATRICIA O'REILLY: Writer, lecturer, researcher. Author of several non-fiction books, including *Writing for the Market* and *Working Mothers*. Her first novel *Once Upon A Summer* was published in 2000. Her latest novel was *Time and Destiny* and her latest non-fiction publication was *Writing for Success* (2006). She lives in Dublin.

JOE O'TOOLE: Born in Dingle, Co. Kerry. An independent member of Seanad Éireann since 1987. Former General Secretary of the Irish National Teachers' Organisation (INTO) and former President of the Irish Congress of Trade Unions (ICTU). Published his autobiography, *Looking Under Stones*, in 2003.

DEIRDRE PURCELL: Born in Dublin in 1945. A former Abbey actress, her novels include *Falling for a Dancer* and *Tell Me Your Secret*. Her non-fiction includes *Be Delighted: A Tribute to Maureen Potter* (2004) and her memoir, *Diamonds and Holes in my Shoes* (2006). A former TV and press journalist, she has been awarded The Benson & Hedges and Cross awards for journalism.

ARTHUR REYNOLDS: Staff journalist with *The Irish Times* for 34 years. Was director of BIM and edited the fishing industry magazine *Skipper* for 27 years. He lives in Dublin.

DOMINIC ROCHE: Writer and actor. His adaptation of Farquhar's *The Mullingar Recruits* was produced in the 1969 Dublin Theatre Festival.

MARY RUSSELL: A journalist and writer with a particular interest in travel. Born in Dublin, her books include *The Blessings of a Good Thick Shirt*, *Please Don't Call it Soviet Georgia* and *Journeys of a Lifetime*. She lives in Oxford and Dublin.

JOHN RYAN: Born in Dublin in 1925, John Ryan edited the literary journal *Envoy* and *The Dublin Magazine*. A long-time contributor to *Sunday Miscellany*, his book, *Remembering How we Stood*, featured stories of the many

Dublin characters who patronised his famous pub, The Bailey in Duke Street. He died in 1992.

STEPHEN RYNNE: A well-known journalist and RTÉ broadcaster, he is the author of three books: *Green Fields, All Ireland*, and *The Vision of Father Hayes*. He died in 1980.

DENIS SAMPSON: Living between Ireland and Canada, his most recent book is *Brian Moore: The Chameleon Novelist*.

TOMMY SANDS: A singer, songwriter and social activist from Co. Down. As part of the acclaimed Sands Family, one of the most important traditional groups in the early years of Ireland's folk revival, Tommy has worked to add beauty to the world and to point out where it still needs improvement.

GAIL SEEKAMP: Lives in Dublin with her family. Enjoys travelling, writing and rearing her children.

ELAINE SISSON: She is an IADT Research Fellow at the Graduate School of Creative Arts in Dublin.

HELEN SKRINE: Née Boxwell, comes from a long-established, post-Cromwellian family in south-east Wexford. She returned to live at Butlerstown Castle, where she grew up, after living in Malaysia with her husband for many years. She is a farmer and writer of short stories.

AILBHE SMYTH: Has been a feminist activist since the 1970s, and is head of the Women's Education, Research and Resource Centre (WERRC) at UCD.

GERARD SMYTH: Has published poetry widely in Ireland and abroad since the late 1960s. His most recent collections are *A New Tenancy* (2004) and *The Mirror Tent* (2007), both published by Dedalus, and he is also a journalist with *The Irish Times*.

SHEILA SMYTH: Taught for thirty years in London. Retired to Co. Waterford. A regular contributor to *SQ* magazine and *Ireland's Own*. 'A Touching of Spirits', one of her short stories, was broadcast by RTÉ.

MICHAEL TIMMS: Director of Centre of Disability Studies at UCD. He has written for radio and had a winning entry in the P.J. O'Connor Radio Drama Awards.

DAN TRESTON: Writer and radio drama producer, his play *Piano in the River* won the 1964 Prix Italia for RTÉ Radio. He died in 1995.

MERVYN WALL: Born in Dublin in 1908, he was a novelist, short story writer and playwright, as well as the author of a local history volume. He was secretary of The Irish Arts Council/An Chomhairle Ealaíon from 1957–75. A member of Aosdána, he lived in Dublin, where he died in 1997.

THOMAS F WALSH: Compiler of the series *Favourite Poems We Learned in School*. He was formerly a primary school headmaster and is a regular contributor to *Sunday Miscellany*.

JOSEPH WOODS: He is a poet and has been Director of Poetry Ireland. A winner of the Patrick Kavanagh Award, his two poetry collections, *Sailing to Hokkaido* (2001) and *Bearings* (2005), are both published by The Worple Press (UK).

PADDY WOODWORTH: An author and journalist, born in 1951 in Bray, Co. Wicklow, he has written extensively for *The Irish Times*. He is best known for his work on Spain. His books include *Dirty War, Clean Hands* and *The Basque Country*.

ENDA WYLEY: Born and still living in Dublin, she has published four collections of poetry: *Eating Baby Jesus, Socrates in the Garden, Poems for Breakfast* and *To Wake to This*.